ROMANTICISM
AND
WILD PLACES

ROMANTICISM
AND
WILD PLACES

—ESSAYS IN MEMORY OF PAUL EDWARDS—

Edited by

Paul Hullah

©   The Authors 1998

First Published by Quadriga, 1998

Printed and bound in Great Britain
by Antony Rowe Ltd, Chippenham, Wiltshire

Distributed by The Centre for the History of Ideas in Scotland,
University of Edinburgh
22a Buccleuch Place, Edinburgh EH8

For information regarding international distribution
email pwh@cc.okayama-u.ac.jp

Cover design by Frankie Murphy

ISBN   1   85933   008   8

ACKNOWLEDGEMENTS

Some things take longer than others, so I would like to thank all the contributors for patience beyond the call of duty, for believing and bearing with me smilingly as a project we all wanted to run crept slowly to fruition. I owe sincere gratitude to Colin Nicholson for his significant assistance in the initial stages of organisation and to Cairns Craig and Quadriga for providing the book with a home a scant four years later. Warm thanks go to Kazuya Okada for his advice on Romantic images and, at other times, word processing, and to my wife Hitomi who diligently typed a mountain of material for me. Marie Campbell looked after things well in Edinburgh on the formatting front and Jon Curt has been a friend indeed throughout this and all the rest.

Paul Hullah

CONTENTS

Editor's Introduction

Anyone fortunate enough to have spent five minutes in Paul Edwards' genial, convivial company would, painlessly and literally, have learned many things. Firstly, that he was the kindest, wittiest, most affable, erudite and unpretentious dispenser of genuine wisdom that one could ever hope to meet. Secondly, that the range of his knowledge and his reading was staggeringly wide and vast. He was an 'expert' (though he would have objected to the term and certainly never used it himself) in so many fields; a colleague at Edinburgh used rightly to say, 'You don't read Paul Edwards' C.V. – you weigh it.' Romantic poetry, Icelandic literature, Caribbean and West African slave narrative, and home brewing are the disciplines in which he is remembered as having excelled, though there were many more strings to his bow. And in all these aspects (even, perhaps, in home-brewing) his central reference point was Romanticism. He liked to explore the margins of that unclearly defined movement's jurisdiction and relate seemingly unconnected topics back to the fundamental (albeit controversial) tenets of Romantic thought, always (like a magician pulling a rabbit from a hat; it was that enjoyable to witness) illustrating new connections, new relevance, putting the pieces together into a wonderful new whole. I hope that the essays collected in this book reflect Paul's ability to connect and cross-relate topics 'marginal' to Romanticism, the wild places, though I fear that the reflection must only be a pale one.

This is a necessarily eclectic volume then, as the approach to life and art of the man to whose memory it is dedicated was eclectic. Only two essays in this collection bear Paul Edwards' name at their head, but he played a part in creating every line of every page of this book. None of the authors herein included would deny that fact: only Paul himself would have protested. For all the breadth of his academic achievement, he was a modest man. He had done so many great things but he was never snobbish, boastful or proud. When I was billed to introduce him as speaker at a stuffy academic function, the only piece of information he insisted that I include in my hastily scribbled resumé of his colourful career was the fact of his having played in goal at the age of fifteen for a Birmingham Schoolboys soccer side. He never lost touch with the real issues. He lived in a tower, the David Hume Tower at Edinburgh University, but it was not fashioned of ivory. Everyone was as welcome to share in his learning as they were free to sample his wine.

For, above all else, Paul Edwards was the greatest, most enthusiastic communicator of knowledge that I have ever met. Without hectoring, in a seemingly effortless manner he could instill in people the desire to learn, and he never pre-judged. I remember visiting the Pear Tree hostelry with him one June lunchtime (where are those summer days now?). We had been seated with our drinks a scant two minutes when Paul was suddenly approached by an alarmingly belligerent-looking youth resplendent with pink mohican, tattoos and a rusty stud through his nose. 'You're in my seat, pal,' he snorted. 'Fine,' said Paul, cheerfully. 'There's plenty of room at the table. Why don't you join us? We're just discussing Shakespeare's history plays. Ever read any of them?' The next time I met the pink-topped one he had enrolled in a course in English Language and Literature at an Edinburgh College, a course which he would pass a year later. Though he never admitted it, I think Paul had written the youth a reference. That is a true story. As I have said, Paul simply made people want to learn. If to be learned was to be like Paul Edwards, well, that seemed like a pretty good target for which to aim.

He was a generous man. In teaching and in everyday conversation (with him, the two were usually inseparable) Paul Edwards gave so much, so wisely. I learned more in his office on Friday afternoons over a bottle or two of raisin wine than I ever did in a lecture theatre. So did many others, not least those who have freely contributed to this volume. He told me a story once about being on a day-long train journey across northern Europe, confined for the duration to a small carriage in the sole company of a beautiful young woman. 'Twenty-four hours. Just the two of us,' he said, 'I felt like the luckiest man on earth!' I remember thinking the contrary; that she had been the lucky one. What I wouldn't give for a day with him now.

We miss his company so. He will always be missed. These essays are a small drop in the ocean of his legacy, a way of saying thank you, sincerely though too late. His spirit lives on in so many different places; that this book might be one such fortunate region is our greatest, humblest hope.

Paul Hullah
Okayama, Japan

Thomas Campbell's
Gertrude of Wyoming

Angus Calder

'The Poet Campbell', as Jeeves would have called him is a curious case
in the history of literary canonisation. Jeeves probably does thus refer
to him somewhere in the Wooster cycle, since Campbell was a copious
source of such familiar quotations, imbibed from anthologies used in
schools, as his giant fish-fed brain constantly produces for the instruction of young Bertie. 'Tis distance lends enchantment to the view', the
seventh line of *Pleasures of Hope* (1799), is, like 'coming events cast
their shadows before' from 'Lonchiel's Warning' (1801), clearly a gem
of poetry, though few remember that Campbell cut it. It is less obvious that the stock phrase 'few and far between' is another gem from
Pleasures of Hope.[1] *The Pleasures of Hope*, published in April 1799
by Mundell of Edinburgh inflicted on its author the blight of runaway
success, accompanied by fatuously high expectations, when he was
still only 21. Three editions appeared before the end of the year. Its
significance in literary history was enormous. As A. D. Harvey claims,
it was:

> ... the first commercially successful long poem written in a 'ro-
> mantic' style; it showed the reading public what they wanted
> from poetry, and it showed other men of letters what the public
> wanted... If during the 1790s there was a year of revolution
> in poetry – a supposition not to be readily admitted – it was
> 1799, the year of Campbell, not 1798, the year of *Lyrical
> Ballads.*[2]

Campbell was quite soon eclipsed in terms of sheer number of poems,
editions and sales by Scott and Byron. But for the whole of the nineteenth century, or almost all of it, he was regarded by most people as
a major, even a great poet. Through the half century after his death in
1844, new editions of collected Campbell appeared, at a rate of at least
one every two years. When Gall and Inglis of London and Edinburgh
produced in 1857 a volume combining *The Poetical Works of Thomas
Campbell and Samuel Taylor Coleridge* (not all the 'works', in fact, of
either, by a long chalk), Campbell's name appeared on the title page

in much larger type than Coleridge's. After all, his burial in Poet's Corner of Westminster Abbey in 1844 had been a great state occasion. The pall bearers had included Sir Robert Peel, the prime minister, with nine peers of the realm, including the 4th Earl of Aberdeen, later to be prime minister himself. And Benjamin Disraeli also attended.[3]

Campbell himself had anticipated as early as 1809 that he would 'go to sleep in Westminster Abbey'.[4] In 1803, aged 25, he had found that his recently published 'Hohenlinden' was in use in Liverpool in a course of lectures on elocution.[5] His long-time colleague in journalism, Cyrus Redding, remarked in his *Reminiscences and Memoirs* of a man whom he had loved well this side of idolatry, that Campbell, for years before his death, 'had the pleasure of hearing his verses quoted oftener than any other contemporary writer, in the senate, on public occasions, and in the social circle, wherever a patriotic appeal, a philosophical truth, or a tender sentiment, required illustration'.[6] There were, from the earliest stages of his career, a few who thought Campbell a flimsy poet. As a Whig and devout admirer of Pope, he had reasons to be at odds with the Lake Poets. Coleridge in 1811 told John Payne Collier that Campbell was 'incomprehensible'. Wordsworth's view, as recorded in 1829 by H. N. Coleridge, was that 'No man ever attained to such eminence with so little merit as Campbell', going on to object that he was 'a thorough Anti-xtian' (sic).[7]

However, the chorus of acclaim in Campbell's favour contained a surprising range of strong voices. Scott, admittedly a pretty close friend from his early twenties, praised Campbell's early verse vastly to Washington Irving – later, his chief complaint (echoed by many) was that Campbell was writing too little poetry and too much unimportant prose.[8] Byron also liked Campbell personally, rating his poetry below Scott's but above the Lakers'.[9] Madame de Stael told Campbell in 1813 that she had read a certain episode in *Pleasures of Hope* twenty times with undiminished admiration and Goethe was reported as saying that he thought Campbell 'far above any modern English poet whose works have fallen in my way'.[10] More impressively still, Hopkins called Campbell 'a perfect master of style'. He was struck by a form of spring rhythm used in Campbell's 'Battle of the Baltic' and was moved to set that poem to music.[11]

However, by the days of Hopkins, born in the year of Campbell's death, certain reservations about both man and poet were becoming commonplace. The man, according to Redding and others, had been idle and on occasions much the worse for alcohol – this explained, or seemed to, the lack of productivity which Scott regretted. (In fact both traits can be related to serious depressions and perhaps to the long term effects of syphilis contracted on a youthful visit to Germany[12] – this illness was not disclosed by his doctor, executor and biographer, Beattie, but had it been common knowledge would hardly have mitigated the verdict that Campbell lacked that industrious uprightness so much prized by Victorians.) Some of the distinguished pens which contributed introductions to the popular editions of Campbell's works did not trouble to disguise irritation with him. W. M. Rossetti, prefacing Moxon's popular edition began: 'A mild and moonlike lustre surrounds the name of Campbell', but went on to make it clear that he thought this 'lustre' had attached itself to work mostly overrated: the ironic tone of his piece prefigures Lytton Strachey.[13] William Allingham in the Aldine Edition of 1891 pointed out that had Campbell died at 32 'his fame would stand no hair-breadth lower than it does, nor were English poetry the poorer . . . '.[14] When the estimable J. Logie Robertson edited Campbell for Oxford University Press in 1907 – this is by far the best collection – he expressed 'mingled surprise and indignation that he is at present so much neglected'. But he unwittingly put his finger on the reason why Campbell would be relegated, in our own century, to minor status. Listing thirteen of Campbell's shorter works, Robertson claimed that 'These and other such poems will never be forgotten so long as the national heart responds to manly sentiment'.[15] Quite so. Campbell features in current Oxford anthologies (including Jon Stallworthy's book of War Poetry and those of English verse by Gardner and Wain) as the author of just such short, ardently phrased, 'manly' pieces about violent action.[16] George Saintsbury wrote, in the *Cambridge History of English Literature*, of one of these poems, 'Hohenlinden', 'except in two or three passages of Homer and Aeschylus there is nothing anywhere that surpasses the last and culminating stanza in poignant simplicity'.[17] If we may judge for ourselves:

> Few, few, shall part where many meet!
> The snow shall be their winding-sheet,
> And every turf beneath their feet
> Shall be a soldier's sepulchre.

Saintsbury's view, as it happened, was published in 1915, when a Great War was stimulating a very different kind of 'war poetry'. Campbell stood at that 'romantic' distance which, as he put it, lends enchantment to the view' – quite literally, he was in the vicinity of the battle of Hohenlinden in 1800, but did not witness it, though he did see the after-effects of the battle of Ratisbon earlier in the same year. Wilfred Owen, writing with equal hyperbole of men marching 'sore on the alleys cobbled with their brothers' experienced war from the common soldier's hateful standpoint. The views of Logie Robertson and Saintsbury represent an imperialist self satisfaction with the results of 'manly' slaughter, still conceived as potentially 'Homeric', which was discredited in 1914–18.

Since then, critics have paid Campbell very little attention – less than a handful of articles, one short monograph, few mentions in works discussing the British Romantics generally, effectively none at all in the most recent histories of Scottish literature.[18]

The purpose of this lengthy preamble has been to establish clearly two facts. Firstly that Campbell was a 'major poet' – and a Scottish one – in the nineteenth century when his statue went up in George Square in his native town of Glasgow and a biography appeared in the 'Famous Scots' series.[19] Secondly, that his reputation has slipped, over the last century, to that of the 'English' author of a few short 'battle pieces'. What follows will seek to suggest answers to certain questions about his reputation. How was it that Hazlitt in 1825 could be moved to ecstasies over *Gertrude of Wyoming*, published by Campbell sixteen years earlier? ('There are passages... of so rare and ripe a beauty, that they challenge, as they exceed, all praise... a light startling as the red-bird's wing; a perfume like that murmuring of pathless woods or of the everlasting ocean.')[20] Why was it that a narrative admitted to be incompetent, as narrative, even by Hazlitt, and blatantly deficient both in historical truth and in topographical and zoological accuracy, was so much admired by the strict critic Jeffrey and the normally sensible critic Walter Scott? (Private utterances confirm the sincerity of the praise bestowed by both in published reviews.) What are we to make of Campbell's handling in *Gertrude* of savage Indians (Native Americans) and frontier scenery? Can it be related to his complex relationship with his own Highland genealogy, and to constructions of the Highlands erected by Ossian Macpherson, Walter Scott and others? A quotation from *Pleasures of Hope* may usefully preface this enquiry:

> Come, bright Improvement! on the car of Time,
> And rule the spacious world from clime to clime;
> Thy handmaid arts shall every wild explore,
> Trace every wave, and culture every shore,
> On Eries' banks, where tigers steal along,
> And the dread Indian chants a dismal song,
> Where human fiends on midnight errands walk,
> And bathe in brains the murderous tomahawk;
> There shall the flocks on thymy pastures stray,
> And shepherds dance at summer's opening day;
> Each wandering genius of the lonely glen
> Shall start to view the glittering haunts of men,
> And silence watch, on woodland heights around,
> The village curfew as it tolls profound.[21]

If Campbell's indifference to zoological fact is obvious, so is the opposition he facilely sets up between the 'glen' representing both savagery and Scotland and the 'village curfew' of Thomas Gray's England, a country seen by implication as the fountainhead of Improvement. The conflation of Improvement with pastoral is extremely piquant, published at a time when 'flocks' were indeed moving into Scottish glens, not without resistance from some of the people they displaced. The mindset which the young Campbell displays here combines sentimental reverence for English poetic tradition with the cult of Improvement characteristic of the Scottish Enlightenment which, in the persons of Adam Smith and Reid, Millar and Dugald Stewart, had poured its treasures on him from infancy (his father, a friend of Smith, named him 'Thomas' after Reid, another friend) through his days at Glasgow University, and as a questing literary novice in Edinburgh. The couplets evoke Pope, but the thoughts are expressed with a pleasing, relaxed enthusiasm suited to a post-Augustan audience. Somewhere among the dialectics of 'feeling' and 'reason', 'nature' and 'improvement', 'classicism' and 'romanticism', the significance of Campbell's *Gertrude* for his contemporaries can be reconstituted. At the centre of this reconstruction will be Francis Jeffrey's criticism of Campbell (and others) in *Edinburgh Review*.

2

Gertrude of Wyoming, published in April 1809, exactly ten years after *Pleasures of Hope*, was Campbell's second major success. It was also his last. His lengthy narrative poem, *Theodric* (1824) was loyally praised in *Edinburgh Review* but the public was not deceived into enthusiasm for a remarkably fatuous production. *The Pilgrim of Glencoe* (1842) fell even flatter, though arguably its rather Crabbe-like handling, in couplets, of a plain story of ordinary people makes it less ineffectual than *Theodric*. When D. M. Moir gave a series of lectures in 1850–51 to the Edinburgh Philosophical Institution, later gathered into a volume of *Sketches of the Poetical Literature of the Past Half-Century* which still sits with an air of authoritative reference on the open access shelves of the National Library of Scotland, he remarked it was a 'pity' that Campbell's later narratives 'ever saw the light', but enthused over *Gertrude* as 'The greatest effort of Campbell's genius'.[22]

Gertrude is a poem of 87 Spenserian stanzas divided into three parts. In the first, Gertrude is a child of 9, in the second, aged 24, she is blessed with true love. In the third, set three months later, she and her husband die.

> On Susquehana's side, fair Wyoming!
> Although the wild-flower on thy ruined wall
> And roofless homes, a sad remembrance bring

Of what thy gentle people did befall;
Yet thou wert once the loveliest land of all
That see the Atlantic wave their morn restore.
Sweet land! May I thy lost delights recall,
And paint thy Gertrude in her bowers of yore,
Whose beauty was the love of Pennsylvania's shore![23]

'Distance lends enchantment...'. The first stanza of *Gertrude* presupposes a reader indifferent to geographical veracity (the Wyoming valley is many miles, in banal fact, from 'Pennsylvania's shore') but attuned to the pathos of distance and ruin.

Wyoming was a modern Arcadia, the result, as recommended in *Pleasures of Hope*, of Improvement brought to a wild frontier. Here 'happy shepherd swains' do nothing but 'feed their flocks' or 'skim the lake...with light canoe' until, in the evening, the 'timbrel' struck up and 'lovely maidens would the dance renew':

And aye those sunny mountains half-way down
Would echo flagelet from some romantic town.
(Part 1, St. 2)

As Coleridge objected, one cannot find prose sense in such lines. The only conceivable defence in our own day of such characteristic Campbell verses is that he unconsciously anticipated *symbolisme*.

In Wyoming immigrants, 'exiles' from all over Europe gathered: the German 'changed his sword to pruning hook', the Andalusian played his saraband:

But who is he that yet a dearer land
Remembers, over hills and far away?
Green Albyn! What though he no more survey
Thy ships at anchor on the quiet shore,
Thy pellochs rolling from the mountain bay,
Thy lone sepulchral cairn upon the moor
And distant isles that hear the loud Corbrechtan roar!
Alas! poor Caledonia's mountaineer.
That want's stern edict e'er, and feudal grief,
Had forced him from a home he loved so dear!
Yet found he here a home, and glad relief,
And plied the beverage from his own fair sheaf
That fired his Highland blood with mickle glee:
And England sent her men, of men the chief,
Who taught those Sires of Empire yet to be,
To plant the tree of life – to plant fair Freedom's tree!
(Pt. 1, Sts. 5–6)

Like Scott and Byron, Campbell supplies his texts with numerous, and often voluminous, notes. 'Pelloch' is glossed as 'The Gaelic appellation for the porpoise'. A substantial end-note explains that the 'Corbrechtan' is a whirlpool near Jura:

> On the shores of Argyleshire, I have often listened with great delight to the sound of this vortex, at the distance of many leagues. When the weather is calm... its sound, which is like the sound of innumerable chariots, creates a magnificent effect.

The 'chariots', of course, would be those of Ossianic heroes: Campbell's note transports his readers to precisely those fictive Isles evoked in Mendelssohn's 'Fingal's Cave'. His poem, however, hints not at the extinction, mourned throughout Macpherson's texts, of a race of ancient heroes, but the poverty of the Highlands and the 'feudalism' abolished there after Culloden. Gaelic 'Albyn' equates with barbarous beauty:

> 'England', from which men are 'sent', not 'forced', is the home of 'Freedom'. The one, passive, provides tears for the eyes, the other actively, rationally, extends 'Empire'. And also, naturally, provides the sole 'judge' needed in the Wyoming Arcadia.

This is the 'serenely aged' Albert, who had sought 'a Briton's independence' here. His motherless 'only child' is the poem's eponymous heroine. Their domestic situation is evoked with a reassuring lack of frontier particularities. By stanza 13, when the story begins, we have nothing more than an idyllically generalised father-daughter relationship in a pastoral landscape enhanced not by 'mock-birds' but by 'flamingoes'; Sicily, Sydenham or Stoke Poges with piquantly exotic embellishments.

Anyway, one fine evening during Gertrude's 'ninth blue summer', an Indian of 'buskin'd limb', Outalissi, rows up and approaches the 'bower' of Albert, leading a boy of 'Christian vesture, like morning brought by night'. He comes in peace:

> This little nursling, take him to thy love,
> And shield the bird unfledged, since gone
> The parent dove. (Pt. 1, St. 14)

He is an Oneida, from a tribe allied to the settlers. Their Huon rivals attacked and destroyed a Christian fort, then the Oneida fell on them, and Outalissi found the widow of the slaughtered 'Captain of the British band' dying with this boy beside her. With her last breath, she begged him to convey her young Waldegrave to their old friend Albert.

Quite why the latter wanted to emigrate becomes obscure in stanza
21, as he apostrophises the lad:

> Whose grandsire was my earliest life's compeer,
> A happiest home of England's happy clime! (Pt. 1, St. 21)

Campbell now sets up another opposition. While Albert grieves over
days of yore, Outalissi stands by, 'A stoic of the woods – a man without a tear'. 'England' at this point produces the sentimentalism of
Mackenzie, the savage Oneida with look unchanged as 'monumental
bronze' represents the neo-classical rigidity found not only in the Indian posed by Benjamin West in his famous painting of 'The Death
of General Wolfe' but in the Roman paintings of David. This balanc-
ing of 'Romantic' and 'Classical' was, as we shall see, important for
Campbell's admiring readers.

Outalissi, however, and this is stressed, is really a nice chap and
before he goes he sings an 'uncouth' lullaby 'true to nature's fervid
feelings' over the sleeping Waldegrave Junior, reporting how in future
in 'lonely wilderness' he will:

> . . .greet
> Thy little footprints – or by traces know
> The fountain, where at noon I thought it sweet
> To feed thee with the quarry of my bow. (Pt. 1, St. 25)

Come back, 'my own adopted one', sings Outalissi:

> And I will graft thee on a noble stock,
> The crocodile, the condor of the rock,
> Shall be the pastime of thy sylvan wars;
> And I will teach thee, in the battle's shock
> To pay with Huron blood thy father's sears. (Pt. 1, St. 26)

Uncouth, indeed, ('the crocodile, the condor of the rock,' is pure
Wodehouse) but Campbell has already informed his readers in a
footnote that 'The Indians are distinguished, both personally and by
tribes by the names of particular animals' : perhaps we are to assume
that the Oneida had heard from roaming Jesuits, or whatever, about
crocodiles and condors and had decided they sounded like fine creatures. Leaving zoology aside, Outalissi is functioning here as a fairly
complex version of the Noble Savage: the assimilation of this concept
with the heroism of Ancient Greeks, Ancient Romans and Ossianic
warriors was, by 1809, far from unusual. Within one such figure,
'Romantic' and 'Classical' interests could be satisfied.

Lullaby sung, Outalissi launches his pirogue and disappears back
into the wilderness for fifteen years. During these years many
unexplained things happen, but one development is fully explained:

as Rousseau (and perhaps even Wordsworth) had taught Campbell, 'sweet influence' from the natural world around her inspires in Gertrude a physical and moral beauty to match the 'hills with high magnolia overgrown' and their 'groves' to which she hies, 'romantic and alone' (Pt. 2, St. 5).

On her sunrise path she thinks of 'loved England' – 'Land of my father's love' – where she might embrace her kindred and see in their faces features like her dead mother's. But she does not sigh 'for foreign joy' : though she cannot have her cake and eat it, Campbell's English readers can enjoy the comfortable sensation that home's best after all, along with the mildly exotic charm of the devoted daughter in her 'deep untrodden grot' on the frontier among the magnolia, panthers and flamingoes. Her preferred 'lonely spot' might, Campbell suggests, be a site sacred to the Indian tribes, so it is surrogate for some moorland spot 'neath which Ossianic lovers lie in eternal embrace, or for some Old World ruin:

> rocks sublime
> To human cot a sportive semblance bore,
> And yellow lichens colour'd all the clime,
> Like moonlight battlements, and towers decay'd by time.
> (Pt. 2, St. 9)

And when the wind moves through the grove, the sound is like 'the first note of organ heard within/Cathedral aisles...'. Sitting here, reading Shakespeare, Gertrude is suddenly surprised by 'a youth, the stranger of a distant land'.

Quite what the youth has been doing and why, is not really clarified. It seems he has passed the equator and encountered 'Californian gales', but the date of the narrative, as we shall see, is precise, and rules out his participation in Cook's Third Pacific Expedition. Anyway, 'Iberian seem'd his boot – his robe the same' and he wears a 'Spanish plume'. He asks to be directed to Albert, and then regales sire and daughter with tales of his 'pilgrimage of taste' which has taken him not only to Spain but to Switzerland, 'gay lilied fields of France' and the top of the Andes. His driving motive, it may be, was simply 'taste' – for 'the rural image' and for 'Nature's savage glories' alike: *Childe Harold* had not yet, in 1809, commenced his *Pilgrimage* and the young man is Rousseauesque, not Byronic.

Gertrude eyes him with 'A strange and troubling wonder'. Albert asks him after 'Young Henry Waldegrave', torn from them when he was 'but twelve years old'. The stranger tries to hide his face but cannot hide his tears. Albert exclaims 'Tis Waldegrave's self'. Gertrude falls 'speechless' on the youth's bosom. Henry exclaims that he hadn't dared disclose his identity when entering Wyoming:

Lest one that knew me might some tidings dire
Import, and I my weakness all betray;
For had I lost my Gertrude and my sire,
I meant but o'er your tombs to weep a day,
Unknown I meant to weep. Unknown to pass away.
(Pt. 2, St. 20)

How did readers find this psychologically credible? Or rather, why
did they want to believe that a much-travelled man could behave like
this? Analogues with 'history painting' again seem relevant. Campbell
is producing the equivalent of a tableau in which the returning Ulysses
is recognised or Lear sees Cordelia again. The absence of explanation
here, as to why Waldegrave left Wyoming and how he has subsisted
on his world tour was noted by critics in 1809, and seen as a fault, but
not as a disabling one, any more than the ludicrous plot of Bellini's *I
Puritani* would debar that opera from success in Paris 25 years later.
Opera, in the conventions of the Romantic era, might seem to have
existed to set up arias (Rossini sets up some wonderful ones in his
Donna del Lago on the basis of the travesty which his librettists gave
him of Scott's perfectly efficient and indeed exciting story-telling in
Lady of the Lake). Just so, Campbell was forgiven narrative inanity
because he set up touching scenes.

Having loved each other as children Gertrude and Henry, of course,
at once marry. The second part of the poem concludes with a passage
which gathers together all the suggestions which charge Gertrude's
mimosa grove with that eroticism to which Hazlitt clearly responded
and which explain the ejaculatory character of his critical remarks in
Spirit of the Age:

And silence brought the soul-felt hour, full soon.
Ineffable, which I may not portray;
For never did the hymenean moon
A paradise of hearts more sacred sway,
In all that slept beneath her soft voluptuous ray.
(Pt. 2, St. 25)

Compared to anything in Scott's verse (and prose) this is, indeed, quite
daring – the word 'hymenean', gently enhanced, conveys the rupture of
Gertrude's perfect innocence as melting bliss. Compared to what Byron
would do with Haideée, it offers nothing at all to present day readers.
But Byron was a very naughty man, and poet. Critics always took
a deep breath, as it were, before acknowledging that 'genius' which
made his writings acceptable. Campbell offered more than Crabbe on
the sensual side without portraying what he might not portray. Indeed
this presentation of wedded bliss, arising as it does from prepubescent
love between Gertrude and Henry merges Christian matrimony with

the innocence which, for the generations after Rousseau, attached itself to childhood.

Part Three opens with the Wyoming idyll enhanced. Not that Gertrude and Henry chat to the shepherd swains or timbrel-directed nymphs: in the whole poem no one in the family of three (as it now is) talks to anyone but Outalissi. With 'her buskin'd youth' beside her, Gertrude parades the groves in 'fancifully wild costume' shading her lovely brow with 'Indian plume'. They are English Christian married persons, they are also noble savages, they are also, of course, Adam and Eve. Dressed as hunters, they cannot bear to shoot birds or to fish in their Peaceable Kingdom:

> Now Labyrinths, which but themselves can piece,
> Methinks, conduct them to some pleasant ground
> Where welcome hills shut out the universe . . . (Pt. 3, St. 4)

However, 'proud oppression' is driving 'Transatlantic Liberty' to arise: that is, what Campbell tactfully calls in a footnote 'The American civil war' breaks out to darken the skies of Eden. Gertrude pleads that they should 'seek fair England's strand' but Henry says he can't 'forsake the cause of Freedom's holy band', nor can she forsake her father whose 'public love' is for Pennsylvania.

One evening Outalissi, aged and famished, bursts in upon the family group. Another recognition scene follows. The white haired Oneida clasps Henry to him – 'my own'. Then he warns them that 'the Monster Brandt' with 'all his howling desolating band' is about to fall upon Wyoming. He, Outalissi, sallies forth to fight him: Brandt slaughtered the entire Oneida tribe, 'I alone am left on earth'. He urges them to seek out a nearby fort held by the American insurgents. At once, the hideous whoops of Brandt's Mohawks are heard. But nearer at hand there is soon the tramp of 'Columbia's friends... of every race the mingled swarm':

> Sprung from the woods, a bold Athletic mass,
> Whom virtue fires, and liberty combines:
> And first the wild Moravian yagers pass,
> His plumed host the dark Iberian joins –
> And Scotia's sword beneath the Highland thistle shines.
>   (Pt. 3, St. 21)

Everyone throngs into Albert's home where Outalissi sings them his battle song. Albert prays for his 'bleeding country' and for the souls of its adversaries. They all then (prudently) head for the fort which has a strangely medieval aspect, with 'arrowy frize, and wedged ravelin'. As they near it, Gertrude, 'safe from present harm', embraces her Henry – but there is an ambush! Albert is shot! So is Gertrude! She makes an affecting speech before she expires – 'ours was not', she justly observes, 'like earthly love'. The 'faithful band' mourn 'their judge and child'. The 'stern warriors' weep. They leave Waldegrave 'prone to the dust', watched only by 'his woodland guide' who casts his 'Indian mantle' over him.

The Spenserian mould at last is broken; each stanza has eleven lines, of varying lengths, and one sees why Hopkins admired Campbell's metrical skill. At first the old chief imagines Henry and himself fighting together in the next day's battle. But where, after that, he wonders, will they go? Henry's home will be haunted with the ghosts of Albert and Gertrude, his own has been depopulated. The last stanza resolves the Ossianic impasse. Henry, tomorrow, will dry his tears in 'glory's fires': meanwhile Outalissi sees his 'father's awful ghost', urging him to 'thirst' for battle and to dry

> The only tears that ever burst
> From Outalissi's soul;
> Because I may not stain with grief
> The death-song of an Indian chief. (Pt. 3, St. 39)

It was probably quite important for the poem's success that the red man sees the white youth as, in effect, his heir. This prefigures the more elaborate and wordy resignation of the good Red Man to White Manifest Destiny in Longfellow's much later *Hiawatha*. Henry's task is to avenge not only his parents, Albert and Gertrude, but also the entire Oneida people. The victory of the rebel colonists, outwith the text, but well known to the poem's readers, seals this vengeance.

The poem's dispensation is at first sight naively Manichean. There are, barring Waldegrave's parents, just five nameable personages. Three Edenically virtuous white Englishpersons and one red Noble Savage are attacked by fiendish evil, the 'Monster Brandt'. But since the narrative has an actual, and, in 1809, recent and well known historical basis, its ideological patternings are in fact complex and, for us, cryptic. Brandt is unleashed by Gertrude's English kin, who are trying to repress her fellow colonists. But the selection of Germans and Spaniards (along with Scots) as typical soldiers in 'Freedom's band' in Part Three of the poem nods towards Britain's allies in the struggle against Napoleon, which was at its height when the poem was published. Anti-British – pro-British – what on earth were Campbell, and his admiring readers, up to when they constructed the best-seller, *Gertrude*?

We should bear in mind four different readerships. The poem was noted all over Europe. Campbell had a large public in England. *Gertrude*, incredible as this may seem now, was popular in the USA. Finally, Campbell was a Scot, and we will find that the most interesting way of reading the poem takes fully into account perception of

Lowland and Highland, Scotland and England, by Campbell and his fellow 'North Britons', and pays attention to the long shadow cast by Macpherson's *Ossian*.

3

In April 1805 Campbell informed his friend Walter Scott, in a letter from his pleasant suburban home in Sydenham:

> There is a Mohawk Indian in town, who whoops the war-whoop to ladies in drawing-rooms, and is the reigning rage of the town this season. He is an arch dog, and plays a number of old Scotch tunes (he was educated in the woods by a Scotchwoman), for Indian opera airs, on his discerning audience . . .[24]

But a letter to another correspondent, of 18 July 1808, is probably as relevant to the genesis of *Gertrude*.

> Of 'Marmion' I think very much – almost as you do; but I do not mean to think of poetry any more: I mean to try to make money and keep a good house over my head in Sydenham.[25]

Coleridge, with *The Rime of the Ancient Mariner*, may be seen as launching the lengthy 'Romantic' narrative poem in English, and Scott had heard *Christabel* recited, though it was not printed till 1816. He over-generously, as was his wont, acknowledged Coleridge as his 'master'. In *The Lay of the Last Minstrel* (1805) he in fact devised his own fusion of the ballad tradition in which he was saturated with the high tone and extensiveness of epic. *The Lay* sold 21,300 copies in five years. *Marmion* was even more popular. Scott's tremendous sales marked a 'revolution in public taste' with profound implications for publishers and authors. Campbell must have been aware, as he wrote *Gertrude* in the autumn of 1808, that he stood a chance of 'making money' out of narrative poetry. In the outcome *Gertrude*, which took sixteen years to reach its ninth edition, did not match Scott's success, and it was somewhat eclipsed, like Scott's narratives themselves, by the rise of Byron and his exotic tales.[26]

However, Campbell had pioneered the trail which Byron followed. Scott's verse tales were set in British 'ballad country'. Campbell took his Spenserian stanzas to a landscape never trodden in verse. Scott's footnotes were historical: Campbell's, like Byron's after him, had to be geographical as well. The British reading public, increasingly bourgeois, evangelical and self-improving, were no doubt almost as grateful for his prose notes as for his poetical flights.

Why did he pick on America? His biographers do not illuminate this choice. He had certainly often thought of the New World. His father had been a business man in Virginia before returning to Glasgow, where his trade was ruined by the American War. Three of Campbell's brothers had emigrated to America – one married a daughter of the famous revolutionary leader Patrick Henry. A cousin was a district attorney under Washington's administration. Campbell, passionate in a general way about 'Freedom' from his student days, took the uncomplicated view that American Independence had been an excellent cause, but American enslavement of blacks was abominable. When an American delegate to the Anti-Slavery Congress in London in 1840 visited the now-elderly bard, Campbell exclaimed, with great warmth, 'I love America very much – and I came very near to being an American myself'.[27]

The Stevenson stanza used in *Gertrude* was modelled on the practice of the Anglo-Scottish James Thomson's *Castle of Indolence*, which Campbell vastly admired. But he had little precedent in the handling of the New World frontier in English narrative. Campbell can hardly have known Robert Rogers' *Ponteach, or the Savages of America* (1766), one of the earliest plays in English written by a North American, and dealing with the Iroquois people who feature in *Gertrude*. Rogers, according to Leslie Monkman, made the historical Pontiac, when he had actually met 'an idealised model of frontier nobility', and 'a foil to the wickedness of frontier whites'.[28]

The Iroquois of the Great Lakes area, dangerous but impressively organised, played a prominent role in the development of European, and settler, conceptions of '*le bon sauvage*', as they did in the wars resulting first from Anglo-French rivalry, then from colonial revolt. As V. G. Kiernan has summarised the large eighteenth-century factual literature about them, their confederacy of five, later six, Nations seemed to embody principles of liberty, equality, fraternity and other modern political conceptions. They had no kings or aristocrats, and no conception of private property except in personal effects. Their warfare, before whites intervened, had not been murderous: no territorial gains had been in view and after injuries had been revenged or desire for prestige satisfied, the Iroquois would demand wampum from their beaten foes – of mostly symbolic value till the Europeans furthered its conversion into currency. The Europeans, furthermore, encouraged, with bounties, the practice of scalping. French, British and Americans employed the Iroquois and their neighbours as auxiliaries and encouraged them to act 'savagely' against white enemies.[29]

Campbell's notes show that he was aware of several factual prose accounts of North American 'Indean' life. His account of Outalissi's stoic restraint of grief could have been derived from various authors who attributed this trait to native Americans: he cites, in his enormous note on the topic, James Adair's *General Observations on the*

American Indians (1775). But for all his parade of 'factual' sources, he saw accuracy as completely irrelevant to poetic success, even as being at odds with it. Byron, in 1821, noting in his journal 'Tom Campbell's defence of *inaccuracy* in costume and description', added that 'his *Gertrude* . . . has no more locality in common with Pennsylvania than with Penmanmawr. It is notoriously full of grossly false scenery...'.[30] Since Campbell really had no overriding interest in depicting Native American life accurately, there would be little point in itemising his use of his documentary sources. It is, however, worthwhile to consider the creative works and cultural tendencies from which he could take bearings in positioning his Iroquois figure 'Outalissi'.

As Hugh Honour notes in his authoritative history of European images of America, Joseph Wright of Derby also drew on Adair when he painted in 1783–5 his notable 'Indian Widow'. Adair describes mourning rites matter of factly: Wright turns the woman into a universal type of grief. This is typical of the age of Ossian, in which 'neo-classical' aesthetics were applied to 'primitive' subject matter so as to produce stripped, chaste images of human nature. As Honour points out elsewhere: 'The poems of Ossian present primitive poetry – and, indeed, primitive life – as the later eighteenth century wished to see it: simple, rugged, unsophisticated and, at the same time, moral, rational and touched by sentiment'. Ossian was actually more useful than Homer to bourgeois taste: Homer was superstitious about amoral Gods, Ossian's supernatural spirits can be construed as merely 'memories, dream visions and premonitions'. Homer is frank about sex: on Macpherson's pages nothing impure impinges.[31] Campbell's 'Outalissi' can be seen as 'neoclassical' in the spirit of the drawings and sculptures of his friend John Flaxman, purifier of Homer. As Redding noticed, writing on Campbell's defence of Flaxman against structures in the *Edinburgh Review*:

> The classic severity of the sculptor, and the purity of his taste, were allied to the poet's own feeling in his best days, those feelings in some respects that led to his defence of Pope against Bowles. There could not be a doubt that Campbell preferred the composite excellence in art to any natural copy of evidence. The ideal was his elysium.[32]

By the first years of the nineteenth century, a new factor was serving to assimilate the 'good' North American 'savage' with the heroes of Ossian: his race was doomed. As Honour remarks, 'Indians' were no longer set viciously or heroically apart from 'the benefits and stresses of the white man's world. They are, rather, the hapless victims of the supposedly irresistible march of material progress. Fortitude and gravity had for long been ascribed to them; but now they have acquired the fatalism and melancholy of the Romantic hero swept along by circumstances over which he has no control'.[33]

While *Gertrude* exemplifies this process well, it is less important in European cultural history than another work which certainly influenced Campbell: Chateaubruand's *Atala* (1800). In this vastly popular prose tale, a half-Indian Christian vows chastity to her dying mother and poisons herself to escape temptation arising from her love for a Christianised Indian, Chactas. *Atala* generated a stage play, was set to music, was illustrated on clocks and plates, and provided a subject for large paintings. In A. L. Girodet-Triosan's canvas of the *Burial of Atala* (1808), the painter, as Honour writes, 'seized upon [*Atala*'s] melange of religious sentiment and erotic impulse and its exaltation of unconsummated passion . . . to create an unforgivable image of love and death. The Chactas of Girodet's picture is a prototype of the melancholy star-crossed European Romantic hero as much as for the nineteenth-century Indian'. Since in the epilogue to *Atala* the narrator meets the very last of Chactas' Natchez tribe lamenting the death of their newborn baby, the parallels with Ossian – and with Outalissi – are unmistakable. But, as Honour points out, while both the 'bloodthirsty' 'savage' and the 'dispossessed and melancholy Indian' appear in *Atala*, and Christianity explains the difference, Campbell rather awkwardly cast as villain of his poem someone who was in fact Christian.[34]

Campbell had recounted the well-known tale of the Wyoming Massacre in his extensive, anonymous piece of hackwork *The Annals of Great Britain* (1807). A standard *Dictionary of American History* will tell us that this was in fact 'a battle in Eastern Pennsylvania' fought on 3 July 1778 between 'Butler's Rangers', a loyalist troop including Tory colonists and Iroquois, and the Connecticut settlers of the Wyoming valley. The able-bodied men of the settlement were serving with Washington's rebel army, leaving only boys and veterans. The local commander, confusingly called Colonel Zabulon Butler, had gathered the families in Forty Fort on hearing of the British approach. Thence he stupidly led a sortie against the foe. His feeble force of about 300, outnumbered four to one, were slaughtered and barely 60 escaped to surrender next day. Major John Butler of the Rangers lost control of his Indian auxiliaries, who ignored the terms of capitulation and destroyed the settler's possessions. This nasty episode was important. It inspired Washington to send General Sullivan to destroy the Iroquois, and generated opposition among the British to the policy of using Indian auxiliaries.[35]

The Wyoming valley, as the foregoing implies, had not been an Eden settled by noble English, Scots, Germans and Andulaisians. It had been a terrain of struggle for several years between 'Yankee' claimants from Connecticut and the Pennsylvanian 'Susquehanna Company' – the so-called 'Pennamite War' in which the notorious Indian-slaying 'Paxton Boys' had played a large part. This was one of the most significant examples of the 'frontier' versus 'tidewater' conflicts in American colonial society much discussed by historians, and it hadn't been resolved in 1778. Resettled from Connecticut after the massacre, Wyoming was awarded to Pennsylvania by congressional commissioners in 1782, so fighting broke out again. The matter was not resolved till 1799.[36]

The Six nations of the Iroquois were divided at the time of the 'Massacre'. Two tribes were neutral. The Oneida, 'Outalissi's' people, sided with the Americans. Three nations, including the Mohawk, served the British. The Mohawk leader, Joseph Brant (1742–1807) was their most remarkable commander. He was an Anglican convert, educated to the point where he could serve as secretary to Guy Johnson, the Superintendent of Indian Affairs under George III. After the Revolution began he worked to get his people to side with the British, was presented at court in London, entertained by Boswell and painted by Reynolds. Commissioned in the British army, he returned to lead Indians in battle with conspicuous courage. He is said to have directed several 'massacres' while harrying New York and Northern Pennsylvania, but not to have been present in Wyoming in July 1778. After the war, he led his people to Canada, helped to establish the 'Old Mohawk Church' there, and translated religious works into Mohawk.[37] Campbell could not have picked on a more prominent 'Indian' as villain for his story.

In January 1822 he had to confess his error in the New Monthly Magazine, of which he was nominal editor. Brant's son had turned up in London and given a lawyer documents to show to Campbell, who responded with an 'open letter'. He claimed that the accusations against Brant in the *Annual Register* of 1779 had stood, as far as he knew, 'uncontradicted' for thirty years, and had been repeated in several books. But now his son had convinced him that Brant was a man of accomplishment, well received in British society by, amongst others, Campbell's hero Charles Fox, and 'personally beloved' by British officers who served with him in America. To the Canadians who had supplied documents, Campbell wrote:

> . . . when they regret my departure from historical truth, I join in their regret only in as far as I have consciously misunderstood the character of Brant, and the share of the Indians in the transaction, which I now have reason to suspect was much less than that of the white man. In other circumstances *I took the liberty of a versifier to run away from facts into fancy, like a schoolboy who never dreams he is a truant when he ram-*

bles on a holiday from school. It seems, however, that I falsely represented Wyoming to have been a terrestrial paradise. It was not so, say the Canadian papers, because it contained a great number of Tories; and undoubtedly that cause goes far to account for the fact. (My italics)

Here Campbell, the lifelong Whig, is squirming around as he wrestles, by implication, with another objection, voiced by Scott and others in 1809, to his poem: that it was unpatriotic to centre it on a massacre discreditable to the British. 'For Heaven's sake', he exclaims, 'let not English loyalty be dragged down to palliate atrocities'. He regrets 'nothing in the historical allusions of my poem, except the mistake about your father'. He adds, in good White Liberal fashion, that:

> If I were to preach to you about European humanity, you might ask me how long the ashes of the Inquisition have been cold, and whether the slave-trade be yet abolished . . . As to warlike customs, I should be exceedingly sorry if you were to press me even on those of my brave old ancestors, the Scottish Highlanders. I can, nevertheless, recollect the energy, faith, and hospitality of those ancestors, and at the same time I am not forgetful of the simple virtues of yours.[38]

The upshot was that Campbell added to his poem a note, always subsequently reprinted with it, exonerating the historical Brant and declaring his own 'Brandt' to be 'pure' fiction. Do his remarks about his own Highland ancestry in his magazine 'letter' amount to more than a tactical manoeuvre by a man striving, not entirely gracefully, to rescue a poem which had been a nice little earner from possible obloquy and oblivion? We shall find that they may have greater significance.

Meanwhile, the letter exposes the question of Campbell's politics. These may be briefly summarised thus: as a Campbell, from the chief Hanoverian clan, he always regarded Jacobitism with complete disfavour, as even such poems as 'Lochiel's Warning' make clear. From first to last he was a Whig. Charles James Fox reciprocated his admiration, and Fox's brief ministry, in 1805, secured the award to him, for life, of a substantial Royal pension. This no doubt helped to complete the rout of his juvenile Republican sympathies; he became an unctuous Royalist. He was also a fervent 'English' patriot, whose 'Mariners of England' was universally known and sung. But he was hotly committed, in print, against black slavery, and very active in person on behalf of exiles after the abortive Polish rising against Russia in 1830. He never deviated from the thoroughbred Whiggery in economic and political matters which he had imbibed from Professor Millar in Glasgow and Professor Stewart of Edinburgh, the academic heirs of Adam Smith, the prophets of Improvement.[39]

4

It is not surprising that Jeffrey praised the poetry of a co-thinker whom he knew and liked personally. But Campbell was admired by many who never met him, and by non-Whigs and anti-Whigs. Jeffrey's criticism of him, along with Hazlitt's, assisted readers to rationalise and verbalise their powerful attraction towards Campbell's verse.

Romantic poetry in its early nineteenth-century heyday was seen as inherently non-partisan. As Jerome J. McGann has put it, 'Amidst the tottering structures of early nineteenth century Europe, poetry asserted the integrity of the biosphere and the inner, spiritual self, both of which were believed to transcend the age's troubling doctrinal conflicts and ideological shifts'. The ideology of Romantic poetry, McGann argues, is that it 'transcends ideology'. However, he detects a shift between the first generation of Romantics and that of Byron, Shelley and Keats. While the earlier poets believed that the imagination could 'effect an unmediated (that is, an aesthetic) contact with noumenal levels of reality' the younger ones take the ideology implicit in such convictions to extreme forms. 'O for a Life of Sensations rather than Thoughts', wrote Keats, echoing Byron's 'the great object of life is sensation'. The shift was 'towards a naked and powerful sensationalism . . . an aesthetic of arresting surface effects, a physique of poetry'.[40]

This analysis might seem to help to make sense of *Gertrude*. It eschews doctrinal and narrative coherence in favour of 'Sensation'. But neither Byron, nor Shelly nor Keats could possibly have accepted the trivialising implication of Campbell's defence of his poem against the younger Brant – that the poet ('versifier') is as free as a schoolboy on holiday. McGann justly observes that Romantic verse was 'everywhere marked by extreme forms of displacement and poetic conceptualisation whereby the actual human issues with which the poetry is concerned are restated in a variety of idealised localities'.[41] But Byron made it quite clear to any alert reader that when he was writing a South Sea fable in *The Island* he was thinking about the struggle for Greek independence: only a fool could mistake *Prometheus Unbound* for a reworking of classical legend purely for its own sake. For that matter, the appeal for British unity – Scots and English against the common foe – which is implicit in Scott's *Marmion*, is complemented by the explicit call for unity as between Whigs and Tories in the famous passage celebrating Fox together with Pitt in death. Campbell is much more timid when he defends *Gertrude* as 'holiday'. Yet this is probably why Jeffrey admired him so much that he made Campbell virtually a touchstone.

The *Edinburgh Review* in the first phase of Jeffrey's long editorship (1802–1829) had to defend itself against charges of sympathy with

France and Napoleon. While Jeffrey proclaimed Napoleon to be 'a most pernicious and detestable tyrant', he and his contributors, as John Clive says, 'never lost their positive view of the achievements of the French Revolution'. As Britain and the USA moved towards the war of 1812, the *Review* argued that peace with America was essential. The journal – like Campbell, who was an early contributor – continued to affirm in principle the values of the revolutionaries of 1776 and 1789.[42] The Whig tradition, however, conflated these with English Liberty – with the values of 1642 and 1688.

Jeffrey was the editor of a review aimed at the new bourgeois reading public but attached politically to the noble self-seen heirs of the aristocratic *coup* of 1688 – 'the Glorious Revolution'. He was uneasily aware, as his *Review* noted with awe in 1804, that there were 'in these kingdoms at least *eighty thousand readers*'. The object of Jeffrey and his colleagues was to reform and uplift these readers, 'imagined' (to quote Ina Ferris) 'as undiscriminating but predisposed to be placed under authority because of a class willingness to grant to texts a special privilege'.[43] The female gender of many of these new readers was a matter for great concern – young women might be corrupted by improper, indelicate reading matter. Yet the *Edinburgh* reviewers were not wedded to any *ancient regime* in publishing or taste.

As followers of Adam Smith they believed in the virtues of a free market in books as in other commodities: as persons seeking reform of political institutions concomitant with Improvement and progress, they could no more believe that Pope, or even Milton, represented the ultimate possible in poetic excellence than they could accept 'rotten boroughs' or oppose the development of steam power.

The notion that Jeffrey was a diehard proponent of classical canons of taste opposed to the new Romantic literature derives from his famous strictures on Wordsworth's views, as expressed in prose, on poetic language. In fact, as has now been abundantly argued (and as even rapid reading of his reviews of poetry shows) he was very positive in his reactions to the new school of poetry. But he was a lawyer, attached by training to sound argument and respect for precedent, he lived and wrote in a country in which all classes were saturated in Calvinist mistrust of sensuality and, as Thomas Crawford puts it his *Review*, 'reflects the dilemma of the Whig Party in the years before the Great Reform Bill – the need to attract the support of radical reformers without at the same time alienating those aristocratic families who had formerly been its staunchest supporters'.[44]

As Crawford goes on to show, Jeffrey had a coherent theory of 'Beauty' related to the arguments of Archibald Alison's *Essays on the Nature of Taste* (1811). Campbell, it should be noted, was a personal friend and devout admirer of Alison and named his second son after that Edinburgh luminary. Jeffrey separated 'natural signs and perpetual concomitants' of beautiful objects from the 'arbitrary and accidental concomitants' which might be associated with them. In private the individual may enjoy the latter as much as the former, but the artist, writing for public consumption, must present:

> Such objects as are the *natural* signs and *inseparable* concomitants of emotions, of which the greater part of mankind are susceptible; and his taste will. . . deserve to be called bad and false, if he obtrude upon the public, as beautiful, objects that are not likely to be associated in common minds with any interesting impressions. (Flaxman's purified Homer meets Jeffrey's criteria.)

Jeffrey sees Beauty as a product of human emotion. It is not a quality inherent in objects – we bestow it on them as we perceive them. He is not far, as Crawford points out, from Coleridge's position that Beauty depends on the 'shaping spirit of imagination'. But he diminishes the significance of imaginative processes by conceiving them to be a form of daydreaming. Campbell's schoolboy-on-holiday can satisfy them. But Jeffrey was also ready to praise Keats and Byron: he believed, as he wrote in 1816, that the Augustans had been 'eclipsed' by his contemporaries: 'Little gleams of pleasantry, and sparkles of wit, glitter through their compositions: but no glow of feelings – no blaze of indignation – no flames of genius'. However, the *Edinburgh* reviewers regretted the tendency of some contemporary poets to express the emotions of the new era in showy and exaggerated ways. The best poetry depended for its effect on the 'just representation of common feelings and common situations'.[45]

It was perfectly consistent in Jeffrey to shed tears over Wordsworth's poems in private while ridiculing him in the *Review*. Later, relieved of the responsibility of editorship, he would weep openly over the pages of the young Dickens. *Gertrude* is an intensely sentimental poem. But it is carefully and chastely composed. According to Jeffrey's principles, it deserves to outlast the more hectic productions of Byron and Scott and the dangerously childish poems of Wordsworth. He enforced these comparisons as new work came his way after *Gertrude*. Scott's flashy style in *The Lady of the Lake* (1810) with its 'nervous diction and irregular versification' lacked the 'elaborate elegance and melody of Campbell'. Byron (1816) for all his unsurpassed 'energy of sentiment' lacked Campbell's 'delicacy'. At the end of his long editorial reign, in 1829, he risked the judgement that Campbell's verse had already outlasted that of his contemporaries:

> Since the beginning of our critical career we have seen a
> vast deal of beautiful poetry pass into oblivion. . . The tuneful
> quartos of Southey are already little better than lumber: – and
> the rich melodies of Keats and Shelley – and the fantastical
> emphasis of Wordsworth – and the plebeian pathos of Crabbe,
> are melting fast from the field of our vision. The novels of
> Scott have put out his poetry... and the blazing star of Byron
> himself is receding from its place of pride. . . The two who have
> the longest withstood this rapid withering of the laurel... are
> Rogers and Campbell; neither of them, it may be remarked,
> voluminous writers, and both distinguished rather for the fine
> taste and consummate elegance of their writings, than for that
> fiery passion, and disdainful vehemence, which seemed for a
> time to be so much more in favour with the public.[46]

When *Gertrude* was in proof, Campbell sent sheets to Archibald
Alison, who passed them on to Jeffrey. The latter at once wrote to
Campbell praising the poem, but pointing out numerous faults. He
notes the inadequacy of the narrative, but says 'the most dangerous
faults' are those of 'diction'. He found 'obscurity in many passages –
and in others a strained and unnatural expression...'. These were faults
due not to negligence but to 'over-finishing . . . Your timidity, or fas-
tidiousness, or some other knavish quality, will not let you give your
conceptions glowing, and bold, and powerful, as they present themselves; but you must chasten, and refine, and soften them, forsooth,
till half their nature and grandeur is chiselled away from them'.[47]

However, Jeffrey hastened to notice *Gertrude* in his *Review* on the
same day that the poem was published. He praised it as 'polished and
pathetic' and proceeded to use it as a rod with which to beat bad
taste out of the stupendous reading public: there were probably by
now more than 80,000 of them, and perhaps 50,000 of them read the
Edinburgh Review. In *Gertrude* there was no 'affectation of singularity or rudeness' (this presumably hits at the *Lyrical Ballads*) nor were
there 'obtrusive and glaring' beauties (like those found, presumably,
in Scott's *Marmion*). Jeffrey then goes on to present his considered
and steady view that the best poetry 'depends for its effect upon the
just representation of common feelings and common situations'. The
'expression of simple emotion' is difficult in 'an advanced state of
society'. Hence some writers (Wordsworth) have been driven to the
'phraseology' of the 'nursery'. It is much more difficult to 'express
natural feelings, than to narrate battles' (like Scott). Jeffrey hopes that
Campbell's previous reputation will help *Gertrude* 'reclaim the public taste to a juster standard of excellence'. Though Jeffrey, with due
honesty, repeats in public the criticisms he had made in private to

the author, he expresses rapture over the poem's presentation of the 'earthly paradise' of Wyoming and the 'singular purity and innocence' of the manners of the inhabitants. Alas, 'no such spot is *now* left, on the whole face of the earth, as a refuge from corruption and misery'. Gertrude's farewell speech to her Henry, Jeffrey avers, is 'more sweetly pathetic than anything ever written in rhyme'.[48] If the poem and its people seem 'natural' to Jeffrey, his notion of human 'nature' must assume in it rather more than the at-a-pinch innate benevolence accorded to it by Hume.

Scott reviewed *Gertrude* for the *Tory Quarterly*. He found 'passages both of tenderness and sublimity, which may decline comparison with few in the English language' and compares the 'exquisite description of Outalissi's sympathy' favourably to the depiction of the Indian in West's *Death of Wolfe*. But in the course of his seventeen page article, he voices not only criticisms identical to Jeffrey's but others which point sharply to the features of the poem which make it now seem ridiculous. No one was better qualified than Scott to appraise the inefficiency of the narrative and Campbell's failure to suggest the crisis of a whole community, concentrating as he does on a 'single groupe' (sic). What Scott had admired in *Pleasures of Hope*, and implies must still be found in this new poem, is 'language alike remote from servile imitation of our more classical poets, and from the babbling and jingling simplicity of ruder minstrels; new, but not singular; elegant, but not trite . . . '.[49]

One senses, reading both Jeffrey and Scott, that Campbell's reputation is important to them not only because he is their friend, but because he has emerged from their own North British circle. The Whig Jeffrey is actually more attracted than the Tory Scott to the prelapsarian, precommercial Arcadia which Campbell presents: though, like Scott, and like Campbell himself, he believes that Progress and Improvement are to be welcomed. Both Scott and Jeffrey admire Campbell's capacity to be romantic without being vulgar. He can be recommended as safely as the pottery of Wedgewood (or the roads of Campbell's friend Telford, who eventually left him a lot of money) to the British middle class public which the reviews seek to educate. Furthermore, he has found a way, though neither reviewer remotely hints at this, of displacing the unease in the heart of the Scottish Enlightenment exposed in the successful promotion of Ossian and expressed again in Scott's poems and novels. Improvement not only destroys the Highland Gael and his way of life. It hacks at the very foundations of poetry, which, as Thomas Blackwell of Aberdeen, 'Ossian' Macpherson's tutor, had pointed out in his seminal *Enquiry into the Life and Writings of Homer* (1735), at its greatest had directly depicted the first hand experience of violent struggle in un-Improved societies. Homer had written in an 'ill-settled' Greece, Dante in an Italy 'torn to pieces' and Milton in a time of '*Civil Rage*'. If the power of Campbell's battle poems (which most critics vastly admired) responded to the current crisis in Europe, did not *Gertrude* suggest that the civilising – improving – power of poetry could also be exercised by a modern writer? The worries expressed by both Jeffrey and Scott about Campbell's over-refinement echo Blackwell's concern that 'what we call *Polishing* diminishes a language', but their commendation of the best effects of his diction may derive from relief that modern verse may be innovative without being childish or hysterical.[50]

5

Campbell left Scotland as a very young man – he was firmly settled in London by 1804, and thereafter revisited his native clime only briefly, and not very frequently. He was typical in his ambivalence towards it of many expatriate Scots of the nineteenth century. In his book *Letters from the South* (1837), about Algeria, he claims to have been 'the first Englishman' to visit Algiers after the French conquest, yet, when he describes the Moorish custom of feasting after a funeral, he writes:

> Your English refinement, I dare say, revolts at the idea... but remember I am a Scotchman, and if you abase these poor people for this custom, you will cast a reflection indirectly on the recent barbarism of my native land. Alas! I fear these Moorish festivities... are decency itself, compared with those which I have witnessed with my own eyes in Scotland.[51]

The 'cultural cringe' is very obvious. Scott and Jeffrey, Lords of literature resident in Edinburgh, might usually retain unself-conscious ease in their own Scottish identities: Campbell, on the make in England, simply could not. He was painfully aware of his accent. Commencing his very successful lectures in poetry at the Royal Institution in 1812, he wrote to Alison that he had taken 'no small pains' to get 'rid of *Caledonianisms* in the utterance'. In 1827 he was still worrying, even if jocularly, over his 'Scotch pronounciationalism'. Yet a little later, travelling in Scotland on the line of the Antonine Wall, looking across to the Highlands, Stirling and Bannockburn, he was moved to write in a letter:

> Much as I am disgusted at many prejudices, which the Scotch mistake for patriotism, yet the sight of those scenes, which spoke of unconquered Caledonia! and of the boundaries which had checked the Rose of England as well as the Eagle of Rome, raised up a native feeling strongly within me, with which even you, English as you are, will sympathise.[52]

He described a trip to Scotland in 1836, when he was made a freeman of Edinburgh, as 'the happiest three [months] of his life', and joked in a letter that all the 'pains' taken by friends to 'Scrape the Scotch accent off my tongue' were being 'thrown away' as he revelled afresh in the 'droll sound of the Scotch words, and the expressive oddity of their phrases'.[53]

One result of his expatriation seems to have been that, whereas Scott was vividly aware of Improvement as a force generated by Scots and applied to Scotland, and showed this in his fictions, Campbell remained stuck at the stage of perception – 'Scotland is primitive, England signifies improvement' – which we have noted in *Pleasures of Hope*. He also seems to have been somewhat obsessive about his status as a Gael, but a Campbell. His last long poem, *The Pilgrim of Glencoe*, reconciles a Campbell with a family of Macdonalds in the very arena where men of the former's clan had massacred folk of the latter's. But it continues to manifest Campbell's conviction that Jacobitism had been sheer folly. His relationship with Walter Scott seems to have been disturbed more by differences over Jacobites and Covenanters (Scott sympathised with Charlie's followers, and the Campbell Earls of Argyll had been arch-Covenanters) than over the current politics of Whig and Tory, *Edinburgh* and *Quarterly*.[54]

We have seen how emigration from Gaelic Scotland is sentimentally acknowledged in *Gertrude*, and how a Gaelic Scot figures in 'Freedom's "shadowy" band' at the end of the poem. It remains to consider how Campbell's poem relates to the complex ideological process by which middle class Scots, who regarded themselves as 'North British' and sang Campbell's 'Mariners of England' at him lustily whenever he appeared at one of their dinners, came to incorporate Highland tartans and Jacobite into their sense of identity, national and personal, at a time when the actual Highlands were in the crisis marked now by the word 'Clearances'.[55]

The causes and effects of that crisis are ineluctably controversial even now. James Loch, commissioner to the Ducal House of Sutherland from 1812 and as such execrated by modern Gaels as an arch-Clearer, was an acquaintance and admirer of the poet who joined the Committee of distinguished persons set up to receive subscriptions for the Campbell Monument in Westminster Abbey.[56] Intellectually, Loch was a characteristic product of the golden age of the Scottish universities, a former pupil at Edinburgh of Dugald Stewart. There is every reason to suppose that Campbell shared his view that the Highlands must be Improved.

Peter Womack has noted that the 'formula of the Highland romance' began in 1746 and can be 'regarded as complete by 1810–11', when a flurry of publications, including most notably Scott's *The Lady of the*

Lake both depended upon and confirmed a settled cultural construction of the Highlands as a 'romantic country', inhabited by a people whose ancient manners and customs were 'peculiarly adapted to poetry'. This romance 'makes out a kind of reservation in which the values which improvement provokes and suppresses can be *contained* – that is preserved, but also imprisoned... Officially Romance and Improvement were opposites: native and imported, past and present, tradition and innovation. But in reality they were twins'.⁵⁷

Thus, for all his libertarianism, Burns had movingly expressed in song the Jacobite tradition of loyalty to chief and King which was transferred, with equal success, to the Hanoverian state as requirements in tartan, skirled the bagpipes, fought and died in every corner of the Empire and every British war in Europe.

In Scott's *Lady of the Lake* – prompted by Britain's Peninsular Campaign against Napoleon – Clan Alpine is protected as the 'apotheosis, not only of naturalness but also of discipline . . . both wild and regimented, spontaneous and docile'. Capitalism rationally needed violence to support it and as Womack acutely points out 'one way of evading this contradiction was to compartmentalise it'. Martial values could be assigned to the 'marginal categories of archaism and ethnicity' where they could be 'externalised as an exotic "survival" from another world'. Meanwhile, the nobility of Scott's Clan Alpine is colourful because it is bathed in the sunset light of their impending historical extinction'. But for the Scottish bourgeoisie, the underdeveloped Highlands had 'the aspect of a residual historical nation – a reminder, certainly, of an economic stagnation they were relieved to have left behind, but also an accreditation, held in reserve, of the national identity which was both required and eroded by their participation in the imperial adventure'.⁵⁸

Scott had a Lowland Tory's relatively uninhibited capacity to identify with the clans, Jacobites and all. Campbell, conscious of his anti-Jacobite, Covenanting Gaelic forebears, was not so free to exploit the potential of the Highland Romance. His attempt to do this in *The Pilgrim of Glencoe* founders, in a, for him unprecedented, access of Crabbe-like common sense, inappropriate both in the author of *Gertrude* and to the land of Fingal's Cave. *Gertrude* can therefore be seen as displacing elements of Highland Romance to an arena where they could be made safe for Gaelic Whiggery. But when they got there, the construction which they generated exposed contradictions in Campbell's famous British patriotism, on which Scott in his reviews harped, and for which the author felt compelled to excuse himself in his open letter to the younger Brant.

In *Gertrude*, the unimproved 'glen' of *Pleasures of Hope* has been transformed by 'improvement' – colonisation – yet through the very presence of utterly innocent colonists has acquired an Edenic character. Upon this Eden the British state unleashes the hellish monster Brandt: Indian auxiliaries perform its hatchet work. But the true spirit of English Freedom embodied in Waldegrave will resist this oppression. American Liberty is identified with the true English ideals. That the actual expression of these ideals has not been, and cannot be, Edenic is well known to both Campbell and his British readers. Improvement, furthermore, necessarily overrides innocence. Hence, the sense of loss implicit in Blackwell's view of poetry, which saturates the work of his pupil MacPherson, eats at the heart's core of the Improving bourgeois, particularly if he is a Scot, still more so if he is Gaelic. It is associated with memories of lost childhood innocence. It is finally fixed in the poem by the death of Gertrude – a child-woman, never exposed to what Jeffrey acknowledged to be the general 'corruption and misery' of advanced society – and by Outalissi's 'death song'.

Just as two aspects of Highland Romance are separated in *Gertrude's* Iroquois, so that Outalissi is awarded Ossianic pathos and failure, 'Brandt' all the martial ferocity shown at the battle of Prestonpans, so bourgeois English values are distributed between the three white characters. Gertrude, of course, represents ideal bourgeois womanhood, living for her father and her husband, and in moments of recreation seeking a beautiful grove in which to read, not Gothic fiction, but the all-transcendent English Shakespeare. Albert represents justice and civic spirit. Waldegrave represents that typically Romantic soul which actively seeks out Beautiful and Sublime vistas so that it may passively receive redemptive images: Byron was going to make something interesting out of this. What Campbell does not do is to show us, through his characters, English Liberty actively in arms, or Improvement actually at work. Brandt's massacre, disposing of Eden, clears a site on which *American* liberty can flourish and *American* improvement will proceed unimpeded after the bad Indians have massacred all the good ones and, in their turn, been killed or extruded.

Scott's verse narratives typically generate ideological harmonisations: forces whose opposition might weaken British unity against Napoleon are symbolically reconciled with the poems' patterns. Byron's romances characteristically generate moral, and hence ideological, suspense: we are not allowed to be sure what we make of heroes whose impressive energies are anti-social. To call Campbell 'confused' in comparison with these more efficient writers would be unjust: what *Gertrude*, through its sheer ineptitude as narrative, achieves, is ideological inertia. If the valley's inhabitants were presented with any particularity, if Waldegrave had any personality, if he and Gertrude waited even a stanza before getting married, conflicts would be implied demanding harmonisation or maintaining an interesting suspense. As it is, we end with Albert and Gertrude nobly dead, Outalissi dying, Waldegrave prone, and no one else in sight. Campbell – successfully as early readers saw it – has displayed in turn Edenic nature, ideal parent-child relations, savage nobility, virginal womanhood, Romantic wanderlust, 'hymeneal' bliss, sublime horrors of war, the pathos of mortality, and savage fatalism. The last word is aptly left to Outalissi since what Campbell is not facing up to is the history of his own people whence he displaces, inertly, on to the noble red man of an extinct tribe. Scott had vivified his own border ancestors in his *Lay* and had shown there was money to be made from that sort of thing. But Campbell, 'timid' as he rightly seemed to both Scott and Jeffrey, transfers his self-contradictions and unease of ancestry to a far shore. Since Jeffrey's self-contradictions partly matched his own, Jeffrey was almost *Gertrude*'s ideal reader. He would be, and yet would not be, Romantic. He was allured by, and distrusted, Romantic verse and its problematic energies. Chaste Campbell's inertia made him seem, to Jeffrey's intellect, at least, supreme among modern poets. But let Jeffrey, reviewing Campbell's *Specimens of the British Poets* (1819) have the last word:

> Next to the impression of the vast fertility, compass and beauty of our English poetry, the reflection that recurs most frequently and forcibly to us, in accompanying Mr Campbell through his wide survey, is that of the perishable nature of poetical fame, and the speedy oblivion that has overtaken so many of the prominent heirs of immortality.[59]

Notes

1. Byron puts it in quotation marks in his 'Detached Thoughts' of 1821–2. The vigilant Leslie Marchand notes its provenance in Campbell (*Byron's Letters and Journals*, Vol 9 (London: John Murray, 1973–82), 17). Campbell, it seems, never forgave Hazlitt for pointing out that his line, 'Like angel-visits, few and far between' echoed Blair's *Grave*: 'Like angels' visits, short and far between'. Cyrus Redding, *Literary Reminiscences and Memoirs of Thomas Campbell*, Vol 2 (London: Skeet, 1860), 220 and William Hazlitt, *The Spirit of the Age in Contemporary Portraits* (London: Colburn, 1825), 192. It has to be said that Campbell improves on Blair.
2. A. D. Harvey, *English Poetry in a Changing Society 1780–1825* (London: Alison and Busby, 1980), 75–6.
3. William Beattie, *Life and Letters of Thomas Campbell*, Vol 3 (London: Hall, Virtue 1850), 383–4, 442–4.

4. Beattie, op. cit., Vol 2, 176.
5. Beattie, op. cit., Vol 1, 415.
6. Redding, op. cit, Vol 1, 267. By 'senate' Redding means the Westminster Parliament. But the US Senate through the century probably heard much Campbell quoted as well; he was familiar across the Atlantic in fourth, fifth and sixth grade readers and in manuals of elocution. See Charles Duffy, 'Thomas Campbell and America', *American Literature* 13 (1942) (Durham, NC), 355.
7. Samuel Taylor Coleridge, *Table Talk* Vol 1, ed. C. Woodring (London: Routledge 1990), 547, cf Coleridge, *Biographia Literaria* Vol 2, J. Engell and W. J Bate (London: Routledge, 1983), 32n.
8. Beattie, op. cit., Vol 2, 326–7: *The Letters of Sir Walter Scott*, ed. W. E. K. Anderson (Oxford: Clarendon Press, 1972), 164.
9. Byron, op. cit., Vol 3, 219–220.
10. Beattie, op. cit., Vol 2, 223, 228, Vol 3, 441.
11. Mary Ruth Miller, *Thomas Campbell* (Boston: Twayne, 1978), 84–5.
12. Miller, op. cit., 23. Since Miller adduces no specific evidence for these effects, beyound reporting her discovery of Campbell's VD in a portion of a letter to a friend which Beattie suppressed, it is hard to assess her contention that the early death, after sudden decline, of Campbell's wife and the strange behaviour, deemed insane, of his son, resulted from the transmission of the disease.
13. *Campbell's Poetical Works*, ed. W. M. Rossetti (London: Moxon, n. d.), IX–XXVII.
14. *The Poetical Works of Thomas Campbell*, ed. W. A. Hill, with a sketch of his life by William Allingham (London: George Bell, 1891), IV.
15. *The Complete Poetical Works of Thomas Campbell*, ed. J. Logie Robertson (London: OUP, 1907), iii.
16. Helen Gardner, *New Oxford Book of English Verse* (London: OUP, 1972): Jon Stallworthy, *Oxford Book of War Poetry* (London: OUP, 1984): John Wain, *Oxford Anthology of English Poetry* (London: OUP, 1990).
17. George Saintsbury, 'Lesser Poets 1790–1837' in A. W. Ward and A. R. Waller, eds., *The Cambridge History of English Literature*, Vol 12 (Cambridge: CUP, 1915).
18. It is really rather odd that the thorough Roderick Watson does not even include *Pleasures of Hope*, so doted on by Scott and Jeffrey, in his chronological table of significant Scottish works (*The Literature of Scotland* (London: Macmillan, 1984). In Douglas Gifford, ed. *The History of Scottish Literature, Vol 3, The Nineteenth Century* (Aberdeen: AUP, 1988) the only reference to Campbell is a passing one: Galt admired him (109). However, there is a recent tradition that Campbell somehow wasn't Scottish, represented in John W. Oliver's contribution on 'The Earlier Nineteenth Century' in James Kinsley,

ed. *Scottish Poetry: A Critical Survey* (London: Cassell, 1955), 233: 'Thomas Campbell, despite his statue in George Square, Glasgow, and despite "Lord Ullin's Daughter" and "Lochiel's Warning", belongs rather to English than to Scottish literature'. Reluctance to read and assess Campbell at all probably underlies dismissal of his Scottish origins and interests. This is venial, but, in literary historians, lazy.

19. J. Cuthbert Hadden, *Thomas Campbell* (Edinburgh: Oliphant Anderson and Ferrier) [1899].
20. Hazlitt, op. cit., 189–191.
21. 'The Pleasures of Hope' in J. Logie Robertson, ed., *Collected Works*.
22. D. M. Moir, *Sketches of the Poetical Literature of the Past Half-Century*, 2nd edition (Edinburgh: Blackwood, 1852), 141–153.
23. All quotations are from Logie Robertson's edition of 1907.
24. Beattie, op. cit., Vol 2, 51.
25. *ibid.*, 151.
26. A. D. Harvey, op. cit., 97–100, 108–9.
27. Beattie, op. cit., Vol 3, 420. See also Charles Duffy, op. cit., 346–7.
28. Leslie Monkman, *A Native Heritage: Images of The Indian in English-Canadian Literature* (Toronto: University of Toronto Press, 1981), 96, 102ff.
29. V. G. Kiernan, 'Noble and ignoble savages', in G. S. Roussear and Roy Porter, eds., *Exoticism in the Enlightenment* (Manchester: Manchester University Press, 1990) 96ff. Kiernan is among few recent scholars to have noted the existence of *Gertrude* as a significant text (109, 114).
30. Marchand. op. cit., Vol 8, 22.
31. Hugh Honour, *The New Golden Land: European Images of America from The Discoveries to the Present Time* (London: Allen Lane, 1976), 135; Hugh Honour, *Neo-Classicism* (Harmondsworth: Penguin, 1968), 64–6.
32. Redding, op. cit., Vol 2, 191.
33. Honour, *New Golden Land*, 220.
34. *ibid.*, 220–5.
35. Francis Dorrance, 'Wyoming Massacre', *Dictionary of American History*, Vol 7 (New York: Scribner's, 1976), 346. For a full account, see William L. Stone, *The Poetry and History of Wyoming* (New York: Newman, 1844) (second edn.), 196–229.
36. Marjorie E. Case, 'Wyoming Valley, Settlement of', in *ibid.*, 346.
37. Allan Johnson, ed. *Dictionary of American Biography*, Vol 2 (London: OUP, 1929), 604. Stone, op. cit., a thorough local historian who spoke to survivors, exonerates Brant, 213 fn.
38. Thomas Campbell, 'Letter to the Mohawk Chief Ahyongwaeghs, commonly called John Brant, Esq. of the Grand River, Uer Canada', *New Monthly Magazine*, Vol 4 (London: Colburn, 1822), 97–101.
39. For a good account of Miller, Stewart, their politics and their influence,

see Anand C. Chitnis, *The Scottish Enlightenment and Early Victorian English Society* (London: Croom Helm, 1986), 1–31.

40. Jerome J. McGann, *The Romantic Ideology: A Critical Investigation* (Chicago: University of Chicago Press, 1983), 67–8, 70, 110, 114–5 etc.
41. *ibid.*, 1.
42. John Clive, *Scotch Reviewers: The Edinburgh Review, 1802–1815* (London: Faber, 1956), 95–104.
43. Ina Ferris, *The Achievement of Literary Authority: Gender, History, and the Waverley Novels* (Ithaca: Cornell University Press, 1991), 24–5.
44. Thomas Crawford, *The Edinburgh Review and Romantic Poetry (1802–1829)* (Auckland: Auckland University College, 1955), 4.
45. *ibid.*, 5–9, 25.
46. Peter F Morgan, ed. *Jeffrey's Criticism* (Edinburgh: Scottish Academic Press, 1983), 73, 84, 102.
47. Beattie, op. cit., Vol 2, 171–3.
48. *Edinburgh Review*, Vol 14, XXVII, April 1809, 1–19.
49. *Quarterly Review*, Vol 1, No 2, May 1809, 241–258.
50. Fiona Stafford, *The Sublime Savage: A Study of James Macpherson and the Poems of Ossian* (Edinburgh: Edinburgh University Press, 1988), 28–32.
51. Thomas Campbell, *Letters from the South*, Vol 1 (London: Colburn, 1837), vi, 284.
52. Beattie, op. cit., vol 1, 544: vol 3, 5, 19–20, 201, 321.
53. Redding, op. cit., vol 2, 259.
54. *ibid.*, Vol 1, 231–4.
55. I do not want to meddle here with the controversies among historians over whether the fate of the Highlands between about 1790 and about 1860 should be regarded as one of attempted genocide or merely a typical episode in the advance of Improvement, enclosure and industrialism. For a judicious overall account, see Eric Richards, *A History of the Highland Clearances*, Vol 1 (London: Croom Helm, 1982).
56. Beattie, op. cit., Vol 3, 441.
57. Peter Womack, *Improvement and Romance: Constructing The Myth of the Highlands* (London: Macmillan, 1989), 2–3.
58. *ibid.*, 55–60, 148.
59. Morgan, ed., op. cit., 26.

John Keats, John Foster, and the Miseries of the World

Geoffrey Carnall

Every reader of the first 300 lines or so of the revised version of *Hyperion* – the so-called 'induction' – must have been struck by the contrast between its tone and temper and that of most of Keats's poetry. There is an urgency, an austerity, a fierce dismissiveness even, for which the odes and the narrative poems have not quite prepared us. The poet is unmistakably in earnest, but not as clear as he might be. The development of the argument presented in the induction is far from straightforward, and critics have been perplexed in their efforts to offer a coherent interpretation. Why exactly should surviving the encounter with death be related to a restless awareness of the miseries of the world? What are we to make of the distinction between the poet and the dreamer? One element in the perplexity, at least, does seem well established. There evidently are what Brian Wicker has called 'unconscious Christian implications' in the offing. John Jones speaks of a 'near-religious atmosphere', and Walter Jackson Bate points out the poem's 'coalescence' of Christendom, Judaism, Egyptian, Greek and Roman antiquity, and even Druidism. The religious dimension of the text has been variously explored by, among others, D. G. James, Stuart Sperry, and Jeffrey Baker.[1] Helpful though these discussions are, there is more to be said about something that would have been obvious to early nineteenth-century readers, and may be less so to our own contemporaries. At the heart of the induction is the death-like agony suffered by the poet. Whatever else it means, one thing is clear: it resembles the experience of many Methodist converts as they felt the pangs of a new birth. John Wesley's journal alone supplies some relevant examples. In 1738 a correspondent wrote to him about his conversion:

> I thought the pains of death were upon me, and that my soul was then taking leave of my body. I thought I was going to Him whom I saw with strong faith standing ready to receive me. In this violent agony I continued about four hours; and then I began to feel the 'Spirit of God bearing witness with my spirit that I was born of God'.[2]

Now, he said, he had angels to guard him to his reconciled other.

The disposition of the figures suggested here is exactly that of Keats's narrative: the struggling poet, the priestess waiting to receive him, the sudden relief as he touches the first step leading to the altar, even the hinted presence of the 'fair angels' who 'on a ladder flew / From the green turf to Meaven' (lines 135–6).

John Barridge's ministry at Everton notoriously generated violent physical symptoms, at the very least indications of acute anguish, 'loud breathing, like that of people half strangled and gasping for life'.[3] One convert was laid lifeless on the ground 'when he soon became stiff... Afterwards his body grew flexible by degrees, but was convulsed from head to foot'.[4] Another also seemed to be dead: 'the only sign of life was the working of his breast and the distortions of his face, while the veins of his neck were swelled as if ready to burst'.[5]

Fuller research might offer up even closer parallels to the suffocating, half-paralysed nightmare described by Keats, but these testimonies will serve. The poet's experience in the Temple of Moneta is partly shaped by an evangelical conviction of sin.

To remark this is not to forget Bate's point that Keats draws upon a variety of religious traditions. Dorothy Van Ghent's reference to the myth of Medusa is pertinent enough, for the poet in *The Fall of Hyperion* does indeed seem to be experiencing petrifaction, even if ultimately no trace will be left of him.[6] But conceding all this, the fact remains that the evangelical connection suggests a fruitful way of amplifying connotations of a kind that would have made immediate sense to readers of the poem if it had been published in 1820. And there is one evangelical writer who relates rather strikingly to the text of the induction: John Foster, in his Essay on the 'Evils of Popular Ignorance', which actually was published in 1820, reviewed in the *Edinburgh Review* alongside the volume of poetry containing 'Lamia', 'Isabella', and the earlier version of *Hyperion*.

Foster was a Baptist minister and journalist, a principal contributor to that most intellectually distinguished of early nineteenth-century religious journals, the *Eclectic Review*. He enjoyed a considerable reputation in his own day, and even in the 1850s George Eliot was mentioning him respectfully while she was denouncing the unamiable evangelicalism of Dr. Cumming.[7] He made his name with a volume of essays first published in 1805, and often revised and reissued in the author's lifetime. If he is remembered at all today it is for the essay in this volume 'On the Application of the Epithet Romantic', which remains an important document in the history of that much-disputed word. In the early years of the nineteenth century it was the essay 'On Decision of Character' which especially made an impression, no doubt because so many people felt themselves to be more like Edward

Waverley than Conrad the Corsair, and wished to remedy the defect. Benjamin Robert Haydon was a zealous admirer of the essay, and in the crisis of his affairs in 1811–12, after his failure to sell his 'Macbeth', turned to it to rouse his spirit and keep up his firmness: 'I read it and reread it, prayed with all my heart, and resolved, come what would, to proceed with a greater work...'.[8] Twenty-five years later, when he wanted to encourage Lord Melbourne, it was Foster's essay that he prescribed.[9] It is possible, even likely, that Haydon would have mentioned Foster's essay to Keats – such was his enthusiasm for it – but there isn't a scrap of evidence that Keats ever looked at it.

If he had looked at it, he would have found much that was congenial at the time he was writing *The Fall of Hyperion* in the summer of 1819. It begins with a fine account of the paralysis to which the human will is ordinarily subject when compelled to contend with a situation without the help of previous example or practice. Enterprises may be formed, but they usually crumble because of self-mistrust and the discouragement of friends. Confidence in one's own judgment rarely survives any real test. But those who do have such confidence, and support it with energy and singleness of purpose, can do extraordinary things. The 'unconquerable mind' earns our respect even when it is the mind of Satan. It become clear as the essay goes on that decision of character is a quality which develops under the stress of isolation and desertion. Satan, turned out of heaven; Marius, in the ruins of Carthage, an outcast from all human society; Spartacus, making a daring attempt against the whole social order of the state where he had been oppressed; Schiller's Karl Moor, cruelly rejected, as he supposed, by his father: all these find in resolute action a compensation for the loss of social support and kindness. 'I do not want any of you, and I am glad that I do not; leave me alone to succeed or die.'[10] These are words that might have been written by the man who was claiming that he equally disliked the favour of the public and the love of a woman: 'they are both a cloying treacle to the wings of independence'.[11]

Foster's piety was distinctly unconventional. He was a fierce radical in politics, and remained one, even if in his old age he found the Chartists indigestible. The 'Essay on the Evils of Popular Ignorance' is charged with indignation against those who take for granted that the common people have to live in a state of deprivation and misery. He scorns the 'circumlocution of delicate phrases' like 'the conservative energies of public institutions' when what is meant is downright force.[12] He is sickened by 'the debasement of great public interests into a detestable private traffic'.[13] As a young man he was in the habit of saying 'we want to put a new face upon things', and he shared to the full the hopes inspired by the French Revolution in its earlier stages. These hopes dwindled in the 1790s, and like the rest of his generation

Foster suffered a severe disenchantment. But he did not lose his determination to put a new face on things. His conversation was always predominantly concerned with the daily life and business of mankind, with its social and political interests. He had a strong aversion to the clerical mode, in particular to the cant language of religion, the peculiar vocabulary in which evangelical piety usually expressed itself. He used to say that he would expunge it from every book by Act of Parliament, if that were possible.

He examines the question of religious language in the concluding essay in his 1805 volume. His rather cumbersome title is 'On Some of the Causes by which Evangelical Religion has been Rendered Less Acceptable to Persons of Cultivated Taste', but the cautious wording disguises a vigorous radicalism. He is prompted by an impulse like that which made Wordsworth frown upon poetic diction, and Jane Austen censure the 'novel slang' of which her niece was occasionally guilty. Foster recoils from epithets 'laid on the outside, and into which none of the vitality of sentiment is found to circulate'.[14] He endeavours at all times to keep his eye fixed steadily on the object, to go behind the word to the thing. He remarks that those accustomed to chime to the sound without apprehending the sense of doctrinal language are often incapable of recognising the doctrines when expressed in different terms, 'and are instantly on the alert with the epithets sound, orthodox, and all the watch-words of ecclesiastical suspicion. For such Christians, the diction is the convenient asylum of ignorance, indolence, and prejudice'.[15] The use of a diversified and natural diction is some guarantee that the mind is really working. It is the daylight of thought. A special vocabulary, a special intonation, altering the whole tone of discourse 'with as formal an announcement as the bell ringing to church', is a sure sign of failure to bring one's whole experience into the discipline of religion.[16]

There is an evident congeniality here with Keats's own hostility to orthodox religion. It is not simply that the church bell is for both an emblem of religions falsity: 'The church bells toll a melancholy sound', as Keats put it in the sonnet 'written in disgust of vulgar superstition'. When Keats formulates his reasons for disliking parsons, it is precisely the lack of wholeness, the absence of the daylight of thought, that he emphasises.

> The notions of Society will not permit a Parson to give way to
> his temper in any shape – so he festers in himself – his features
> get a peculiar diabolical self-sufficient iron stupid expression.
> He is continually acting.[17]

As a Baptist, Foster would in any case elude some of Keats's most contemptuous strictures: at least there was no way in which he could be 'led by the nose by the Bench of Bishops'. But Foster's impatience with evangelical diction reflects a relationship with his own associates which is not at all an easy one. He rebels against the kind of internal censorship which produces a semblance of unanimous conviction among those who are in fact uncertain whether they are agreed or convinced. He was apt to say things which made people look at him 'in such a manner, that you are constrained to recollect and ask yourself whether you have been swearing'.[18] He disliked informal prayer meetings unless they were with an individual or two with whom he could feel 'an entire reciprocation of soul'.[19]

'I cannot', he writes in a notebook, 'love a person who does not recognize my individual character'.[20] 'One is not one's genuine self – one does not disclose all one's self – to those with whom one has no intimate sympathy.'[21] The notebook that he entitled 'A Chinese Garden of Flowers and Weeds' discloses a remarkable freedom of speculation, a Coleridgean delicacy of perception, and a certain preference for the company of cattle and poultry over that of fellow human beings. Brutes, he remarks, have a sense of equality. 'It is observable in a cow, licking another, and requiring a return of the service.' Foster had a strong sense of the individuality of animals, whether of a solitary dog crossing a field, or of an elegant and heroic cock, or of two frisking butterflies like 'rival balled at a ball', or of a cow with her calf.

> The cow advanced her head to look at Foster, and we looked in each other's face, at a very short distance, a long time, and I indulged a kind of wondering about the nature of our mutual consciousness and thought of each other. (By the way, the mutual recognition of beings of any order, is a very strange and mysterious thing.) [22]

On one occasion he passed a considerable time watching a company of hens and chickens basking in the sun (no doubt like Keats when a sparrow came before his window: 'I take part in its existence and pick about the Gravel').[23] Somebody nearby said, 'Foolish man, what can he see about a few hens, that he should be gazing at them all this while?' To which Foster thought of replying, 'Fools, Nature talks with her pupils in a language which you will never understand'.[24]

This exceptionally individualistic evangelical wrote his 'Essay on the Evils of Popular Ignorance' to encourage support for the British and Foreign School Society. He describes the deplorable condition of the mass of the people, who feel that 'what is allotted to most of them…is pressing hardship, unremitting poverty, growing still more hopeless with the progress of time, and of what they hear trumpeted as national glory'.[25] This bitter experience is bound to produce alienation and eventual revolt. Not that Foster expects those who prosper under the system to heed such a warning. In a curious anticipation of *Animal Farm*, he imagines their response

> Go . . . with your mock-tragical fortune-telling, to whoever can believe, too, that one day or other the quadruped of our stalls and meadows may be suddenly inspirited by some supernatural possession to turn their strength on us in a mass, or those of our kennels to imitate the dogs of Actaeon.[26]

These prosperously complacent people are protected by a power of not seeing, an obtuseness which saves them from a good deal of discomfort. 'There is, indeed, a dim general recognition that such things are; . . . but, in the ordinary state of feeling, the mind preserves an easy dullness of apprehension toward the melancholy vision, and sees it as if it saw it not.'[27] Or, as he puts it in the sixth and last section, when the state of the masses is revealed by the exertions of faithful Christians and philanthropists, we might well wish that a misty obscurity should descend on it again, so miserable is the spectacle. Reformers are aware that merely by describing what they see, they will be regarded by some as gloomy fanatics, tinctured with insanity by the influence of some austere creed . . .

> The miserableness (so to express it) of seeing so much misery, (has) lent seduction to the temptations to ease and self-indulgence. Why should they . . . condemn themselves to dwell so much in the most dreary climate of the moral world, when they could perhaps have taken their almost constant abode in a little elysium of elegant knowledge, taste, and refined society?[28]

The temptation needed to be resisted, though, if an eruption of overwhelming violence was to be averted. The eruption might be short-lived, but even 'a short prevalence of the overturning force would have sufficed for the subversion of the proudest, longest established state of privilege'.[29]

Is there not something of a parallel here to the situation of the poet in the paradisal garden, awakening in the Temple of Moneta to be told, after his 'dying into life', that he has survived only because to him the miseries of the world were misery, and would not let him rest?

> All else who find a haven in the world,
> Where they may thoughtless sleep away their days,
> If by a chance into this fane they come,
> Rot on the pavement where thou rottedst half.[30]

The Fall of Hyperion begins with the arresting claim that 'Fanatics have their dreams, wherewith they weave / A paradise for a sect'. Foster is apt to use 'fanatic' and 'fanaticism' with a caustic awareness of how

his outlook will appear to the man of the world. He too indulges in
a fanatic's dream near the beginning of the 'Essay', though it is not
quite a paradise for a sect. He remarks on the vast energies directed to
political and military projects, while the improvement of the people is
totally neglected. The national safety is pleaded in vindication of this
policy, and to argue against it would be 'scouted as the very madness of
fanaticism'.[31] But suppose the national energies were to be redirected,
and foreign perils left to take their chance: the 'fanatic' will not indeed
fancy, in his transient vision, that he beholds Athens revived, with its
bright intelligence all converted to minister to morality, religion and
happiness; but he will, in sober consistency, we think, with what is
known of the relation of cause and effect, imagine a place far surpassing
any actual town or city on earth.[32]

There is at least a hint here of what Keats might have had in mind
when he made Moneta speak of those who 'seek no wonder but the
human face, / No music but a happy-noted voice'.

Foster may appear more of a true fanatic in comments made in
the second section on the ancient cathedrals of England, in particular
Salisbury Cathedral which he evidently had fresh in his memory.

> If he has sensibility and taste, the magnificence, the graceful
> union of so many diverse inventions of art, the whole mighty
> creation of genius that quitted the world without leaving even
> a name, will come with magical impression on his mind, while
> it is contemplatively darkening into the awe of antiquity.[33]

But the protestant, says Foster, will soon reflect that these 'fanes' were
erected to exterminate truth and to fortify a corrupt system. Moneta's
temple, of course, remains a magical impression, unsullied by moral
judgments, and the 'image, huge of feature as a cloud', forms part of
the mysterious rite of an ancient worship into which the poet strays:

> And, coming nearer, saw beside the shrine
> One minist'ring; and there arose a flame.–
> When in mid-May the sickening East wind
> Shifts sudden to the south, the small warm rain
> Melts out the frozen incense from all flowers,
> And fills the air with so much pleasant health
> That even the dying man forgets his shroud;–
> Even so that lofty sacrificial fire,
> Sending forth Maian incense, spread around
> Forgetfulness of everything but bliss,
> And clouded all the altar with soft smoke . . . (lines 95–105)

The cloudiness of the worship and the deity anticipates Foster's
description of popular notions of the divine nature. Foster suggests

that God is thought of as some sort of man, complicated by the sense that he is also a spirit – a sense that may

> somewhat restrain and baffle the tendency of the imagination to a direct degrading definition; but it does so by a dissolution of the idea as into an attenuated cloud. And ever and anon, this cloudy diffusion is again drawing in, and shaping itself toward an image, vast perhaps, and spectral, portentous across the firmament, but in some near analogy to the human mode of personality.[34]

It is no part of my argument that there is a direct connection between Foster and Keats, anything that could be called an influence. What can be said is that there is some convergence in tone. Foster illustrates the vocabulary of earnest social concern available to a writer in 1819. *The Fall of Hyperion* gives an intimation of the Victorian social conscience just as Foster does in his acute awareness of 'two nations' – an expression he deploys many years before Disraeli.[35] It would be pleasant to suppose that there might have been some direct contact between the two men, but the thing is impossible. If only it had been Winchester rather than Salisbury Cathedral that Foster had visited, one might have indulged the conjecture that a meeting took place among its 'superb arches and columns'. It would anyhow make a good subject for an imaginary conversation.

Notes

1. B. Wicker, 'The Disputed Lines in *The Fall of Hyperion*' in *Essays in Criticism* 7, 1057, 41; J. Jones, *John Keats's Dream of Truth* (London, 1969), 111; W. J. Bate, *John Keats* (Cambridge, Mass., 1963), 591–2; D. G. James, *The Romantic Comedy* (London, 1948); S. M. Sperry, *Keats the Poet* (Princeton, 1973); J. Baker, *John Keats and Symbolism* (London, 1986).
2. J. Wesley, *Journal*, ed. N. Curnock (London, 1909–16), II, 110.
3. *ibid.*, IV, 318. May 1759.
4. *ibid.*, 340. July 1759.
5. *ibid.*, 339.
6. D. Van Ghent, Keats *The Myth of the Hero* (Princeton, 1983), 231.
7. George Eliot, 'Essay from Westminster Review, October 1855' ed. T. Pinney (London, 1963), 163.
8. B. R. Haydon, *Autobiography*, ed. M. Elwin (London, 1950), 147 (chap. 9).
9. B. R. Haydon, *Diary*, ed. W. B. Pope (Cambridge, Mass., 1963), IV 365n. July 1836.

10. J. Foster, *Essays*, 4th ed. (London, 1811), 139.
11. *Letters of John Keats*, ed. M. B. Forman, 3rd ed. (London, 1947), 372. Letter to John Taylor, 23 August 1819.
12. J. Foster, 'An Essay on the Evils of Popular Ignorance', 1853 ed., 178–9.
13. *ibid.*, 173.
14. J. Foster, *Essays*, 1811 ed., 331.
15. *ibid.*, 325.
16. *ibid.*, 307.
17. *Letters of John Keats*, ed. M. B. Forman, 3rd ed. (London, 1947), 301. To George and Georgiana Keats, Feb. 1819.
18. J. E. Ryland, *Life and Correspondence of John Foster* (London, 1852), I, 55n. Letter to Rev. T. Langdon, December 1792.
19. *ibid.*, 300.
20. *ibid.*, 186. 'Chinese Garden' 635.
21. 'Chinese Garden' 607, from the MS. in the Baptist College Library, Bristol.
22. *ibid.*, 242, 275, 352, 575; from Journal (also in Baptist College), 13.
23. *Letters of John Keats*, ed. M. B. Forman, 3rd ed. (London, 1947), 69. Letter to Benjamin Bailey, 22 November 1817.
24. 'Chinese Garden', 202.
25. 'Essay on the Evils of Popular Ignorance', 1853 ed., 149–50.
26. *ibid.*, 152. This sentence concludes the third section of the book.
27. *ibid.*, 3.
28. *ibid.*, 245–6.
29. *ibid.*, 181.
30. *The Fall of Hyperion*, lines 150–3.
31. 'Popular Ignorance', 222.
32. *ibid.*, 200.
33. *ibid.*, 48.
34. *ibid.*, 190.
35. *ibid.*, 258. Foster refers to the educated and the uneducated, while Disraeli thinks of the rich and the poor.

Saucy Jack: Byron and Yeats

Jon Curt

> The intellect of man is forced to choose
> Perfection of the life, or the work,
> And if it take the second must refuse
> A heavenly mansion, raging in the dark.
> When all that story's finished, what's the news?
> In luck or out the toil has left its mark:
> That old perplexity an empty purse,
> Or the day's vanity, the night's remorse.[1]

Teaching Byron to undergraduates, Paul had a mischievous habit of sneaking this *ottava rima* stanza into his handouts. Bleary students who had, perhaps, managed to spin through a couple of pages of *Don Juan* in the lift on their way up to his office would curse their luck and bend themselves to the task of fully appreciating the various merits of these 8 lines – replete, they had been told, with all that was best about Byron's style and verve. It was all here, we were told: the cavalier approach to rhyme, the juxtaposition of the philosophical with the mundane, and best of all, that pivotal, rhetorical question: 'what's the news?'. Only the 6th Viscount of Newstead and Rochdale could have penned something as frank and profound as this we affirmed. It has George Gordon written all over it.

Paul would open a bottle of wine or beer, and grin. 'It's Yeats,' he'd say, as he dispensed the hooch, and the bleariest of us would wonder if we had come to the right tutorial. It wasn't fair, it wasn't right, it wasn't even bloody Byron.

For all that Paul was a wag about such things, he never wasted our time and the similarities between a lot of Yeats's later poetry and Byron's most mature work are striking, as 'The Choice' shows quite clearly. At the heart of this similarity lies the *ottava rima* stanza itself. Italian in origin (and therefore automatically appealing to Byron) it was developed in the 14th century for the purpose of telling stories. Travelling 'cantastorie' would entertain crowds at fairs and other gatherings with bawdy and colloquial episodes recited in this eight-line format that facilitated memorising by virtue of the easy rhyme pattern and the 'closure' of the final couplet. The story could go on indefinitely and the real attraction was the digressing and the improvisation of the performer, spinning out a small yarn into a complex and involved saga. Like the ancient oral verse traditions of many cultures, the use of rhyme, especially double-rhyme, helped the teller remember the lines.

Byron came to the *ottava rima* stanza from two directions simultaneously. Firstly from his own reading of Italian poetry in his travels, and secondly through John Hookham Frere's translation of Pulci's *Morgante Maggiore*, published in 1818 as *The Monks and the Giants*. This sprawling and unfinished work is remarkable for the vigour and humour of the opening cantos, relying heavily on the stanza form itself to carry the reader through a fairly insignificant plot. In his introduction to the 1926 edition of the poem, R. A. Waller comments on the Byron's adoption of the 'Whistlecraft' technique:

> (H)e borrowed a form in which the natural flow of his thoughts and feelings was little impeded by the restrictions of a conscious technique. 'The soul of such writing is its license,' he said. There, for his impatient spirit, was its greatest commendation.[2]

In his letters and essays, Yeats repeatedly referred to Byron's energy and spirit and it seemed to baffle him at times that someone like Byron should have become a poet at all. To Cockerell, in 1906, he wrote:

> I have always felt that Byron was one of the great mysteries – a first-rate man who was somehow not first rate when he wrote. And yet the very fascination of him grows from the same root with his faults. One feels he is a man of action made writer by accident.[3]

Here, Yeats seems to have fallen into the trap so carefully laid by Byron in much of his work: the dashing, womanising, fencing, riding, sailing, shooting 'man of action' who almost could not resist surrendering to poetry in the small hours of his sleepless nights.

In his relative youth, Yeats was equally naive about Byron's verse. In a lecture on 'Nationality and Literature' given on 19 May 1893, he sweeps grandly through the Romantic period:

> When the time was ripe the English spirit cast up that lyrical outburst of which Byron, Shelley and Keats were the most characteristic writers. Character, no longer loved for its own sake, or as an expression of the general bustle of life, became merely a mask for some mood or passion as in Byron's Manfred and in his *Don Juan*. In other words, the poets began to write but little of individual men and women, but rather of great types, great symbols of passion and of mood, like Alastor, Don Juan, Manfred, Ahasuerus, Prometheus and Isabella of

the Basil Pot. When they tried, as in Byron's plays, to display
character for its own sake, they failed.[4]

These comments were made in relation to the collapse of the English
'greatness' Yeats found in Shakespeare, but as the opinions of a
fairly young man, they are riddled with inconsistencies. There can
be few poems before or since that concern themselves more with the
'general bustle of life', or in which characters were 'loved for their
own sake' than *Beppo* and *Don Juan*. Likewise, neither of these
poems are principally concerned with passion and mood, and the idea
of yoking the character of Don Juan with Prometheus and Manfred
is surely to miss the point completely. It is also interesting that, at
this early stage of his critical life, Yeats should choose *Isabella* as
the poem most representative of Keats's place in the equation. The
poem is badly flawed, not just in its matter, but more so in its
manner. The stanza Keats used for this studied and self-conscious
narrative was the *ottava rima*, clearly unsuited to the carrying of a
complicated story with many characters and action bordering on the
absurd at times. That he was aware of this is obvious in his own
description of the poem as 'smokeable', but his frustration with the
stanza form he had chosen is just as clear in the way he lurches
violently from the need to advance the story to his desire to make
some comment on the action he is describing. Stanza XXIX shows very
clearly how the *ottava rima* cannot be treated as two quatrains, and
Keats's sheer maladroitism verges on the McGonagall in the last two
lines:

> They told their sister how, with sudden speed,
> Lorenzo had ta'en ship for foreign lands,
> Because of some great urgency and need
> In their affairs, requiring trusty hands.
> Poor Girl! put on thy stifling widow's weed,
> And 'scape at once from Hope's accursed bands;
> Today thou wilt not see him, nor tomorrow,
> And the next day will be a day of sorrow.

Significantly, when Keats decided to write a poem which was all
atmosphere and virtually no action or plot, he chose the more intricate
and laden Spenserian stanza. In *The Eve of St. Agnes*, almost every
stanza is a digression in itself, and as a whole, the poem remains one
of the finest tableaux in literature. That Yeats should have missed this
in his youth is not perhaps surprising but in looking so closely at the
verve and masculinity of Byron he may have missed the way in which
he tampered off and on for many years with the Spenserians of *Childe
Harold's Pilgrimage*, a poem which, for all its weaknesses, he refused
to abandon.

Sixteen years later, confiding in his *Journal*, Yeats realised the way in which great writers often confound their national background rather than reflect it:

> When a country produces a man of genius he never is what it wants or believes it wants, he is always unlike its idea of itself. In the Eighteenth century Scotland believed itself very religious, very moral and very gloomy, and its national poet, Burns, came not to speak of these things but to speak of lust and drink and drunken gaiety.[5]

That Yeats was not only familiar with these verse forms, but also aware of their respective uses, is hinted at in the poem 'The Municipal Gallery Revisited' where all but one of the seven stanzas is in the *ottava rima* form, the exception being the fifth, which has only seven lines. Significantly, the sixth stanza starts with the parenthesised line '(An image out of Spenser and the common tongue)'. This was not a game, but a nod in the direction that certain stanzas suit certain material better than others.

Synge, who is quoted in the poem and whose portrait is the last to be described, provides another connection with Byron, as Yeats saw them in much the same way. Writing of Synge in his *Journal*, to become his memoirs, he wrote:

> There are two types of men of genius. The men who, like Byron, like Goethe, like Shelley have finished personalities, active wills and all their faculties at the service of the will; and men like Goldsmith, like Wordsworth, like Keats who have little personality, little personal will, but fiery and brooding imagination.[6]

Angus Calder, in his short but illuminating book *Byron*, makes the point that Yeats, like Byron, assumed a series of masks throughout his writing career, particularly towards the end, and that this gives us a clue as to how to read both poets:

> The personae of [Byron's] verse, including the varied narrator voices of his tales, are all to be taken provisionally. Byron is not, I believe, saying to himself, 'This is what I know or think or feel: how best can I communicate it?', but asking himself, 'What will happen if I make such-and-such a voice say this? What are the implications of this notion, this conception? What form might suit it, and how can I handle that form?'[7]

This is perceptive stuff and makes the point implicitly that we are as naive to assume that the voice of later Yeats is that of the poet himself, as we are to see too much of Byron the man in *Childe Harold* or

Don Juan. Later, in the same book, Dr Calder makes the simple but important point that 'Yeats admired and learnt from the conversational momentum of [Byron's] syntax'. That this is true has been the main thrust of this essay and it can be left to the words of Yeats himself to finally prove the point. In February 1926 he wrote to H. J. C. Grierson thanking him for a copy of his British Academy lecture entitled 'Lord Byron: Arnold and Swinburne' in which Grierson made many important points about Byron's position in a tradition of colloquial poetry. He linked Byron with Donne, Swift, and especially, like Yeats himself, with Burns, and the lecture finished with the peroration:

> In the house of poetry there are many mansions; and if Byron
> has been over-estimated and under-estimated, English poetry
> would be greatly the poorer without his passionate, humorous,
> in all its register, essentially human voice.[8]

It may be said that Yeats, especially in his later *ottava rima* poems, never really aspired to humour, and wrought his passion from a different metal than Byron, but the essential humanity is there for all to see in the closing stanza of 'The Circus Animals' Desertion', Yeats's last great *ottava rima* poem.

> Those masterful images because complete
> Grew in pure mind, but out of what began?
> A mound of refuse or the sweepings of a street,
> Old kettles, old bottles, and a broken can,
> Old iron, old bones, old rags, that raving slut
> Who keeps the till. Now that my ladder's gone,
> I must lie down where all the ladders start,
> In the foul rag-and-bone shop of the heart.

Replying to Grierson in 1926, he wrote:

> I am particularly indebted to you for your essay on Byron. My
> own verse has more and more adopted – seemingly without
> any will of mine – the syntax and vocabulary of common
> speech ... The over childish or over pretty or feminine
> element in some good Wordsworth–and in much poetry up
> to our date comes from the lack of natural momentum in the
> syntax. This momentum underlies almost every Elizabethan
> and Jacobean lyric and is far more important than simplicity
> of vocabulary .... Byron, unlike the Elizabethans though he
> always tries for it, constantly allows it to die out in some mind-
> created construction, but I think he is the one great English
> poet – though one can hardly call him great except in purpose
> and manhood – who sought it constantly.[9]

Yeats greatly admired Byron and championed him when it was unfashionable to do so. He loved his masculinity, his adventure and his panache, listing him alongside such other men of action as Napoleon, Pericles, Cervantes and Leonardo da Vinci at times, but in his honest humanity and the flexibility of the *ottava rima* stanza, he found the ideal voice for his own later poetry.

Notes

1. Yeats, W. B., 'The Choice', in *Collected Poems*, ed. Augustine Martin (London: Vintage, 1992), 253.
2. Frere, John Hookham, *The Monks and the Giants* (1818), ed. R. A. Waller, (Manchester: 1926), 22–3.
3. Yeats, W. B., *Letters* ed. Wade (London: 1965), 467.
4. Frayne, J. P. and Johnson, C. eds. *Uncollected Prose of W. B. Yeats* (London: Macmillan, 1975), Vol I, 270–1.
5. Spence, J. ed., *The Sayings of W. B. Yeats* (London: 1993), 33.
6. Donoghue ed., *W. B. Yeats: Memoirs* (London: Macmillan, 1972), 203.
7. Calder, Angus, *Byron* (Milton Keynes: Open University Press, 1987), 36.
8. Grierson H. J. C., 'Lord Byron: Arnold and Swinburne', from the *Proceedings of the British Academy* (Oxford: Oxford University Press, 1920), Vol IX, 31.
9. Wade, op. cit. 710.

Additional note:

Many people will recognise the material in this essay as being Paul's. So it is. As an undergraduate he sent me to research the connections between Yeats and Byron and between us we came up with most of the ideas in this piece. Even as an invalid he talked about the time we would sit down together and write this essay. Because it remained a dream to both of us for so long, we referred to it as 'Saucy Jack'. I make no apology for the obscurity of the reference, but if you get it, smile.

Constructing and Reconstructing 'Black Caesar'

Ian Duffield

'An incorrigibly stubborn black'; the phrase introduces an essay beyond all usual boundaries in studies of Australia's transported convicts. Resonating with an important aspect of the work of Paul Edwards, it also serves as an epigraph to some gothically grotesque representations of Caesar's life at Botany Bay. Botany Bay is here used as was commonly done during the period of convict transportation to Australia, not literally but as a metaphor for New South Wales. This penal colony was represented to and by contemporaries as, in social terms, a gothic chamber of horrors; also as an unnaturally topsy-turvey world with bizarre flora and fauna. These representations connect with an aspect of the romantic imagination of the age,[1] although they are not scrutinised in mainstream scholarly discourse on British and European Romanticism.[2]

An influential if controversial revisionary work on Australia's transported convicts, *Convict Workers*,[3] has placed biographical profiles of convicts, and therefore prosopography (in the conventional sense), outside its boundaries. This was prudent in a revisionary quantitative study of the convicts as migrant human capital; that is migrants (albeit forced) with the 'added value' of work skills, work experience and in a high proportion of cases varying degrees of literacy. This task, which involved analysing data on a sample of almost 20,000 convicts, was of sufficient magnitude to make diversions inadvisable. Subsequent studies in convict biography or prosopography, however, have the advantage, if their authors care to take it, of *Convict Workers'* conclusions. These can be used to discern what particular individuals or small groups shared in common, or *vice-versa*, with the mass of convicts. Thus, *Convict Workers'* findings concerning the occupations and literacy of New South Wales convicts have proved invaluable aids in identifying the very different general features in these respects of a couple of hundred Africans transported to Australia from the United Kingdom. Following *Convict Workers*, it was possible to argue that these African convicts were at least a very rough proxy for the much larger African population of the United Kingdom in these and other ways.[4] It was also possible to indicate, for a selection of these convicts, certain aspects of individual lived experience outside that indicated by indent data. This would have been arbitrary as well as diversionary in a vastly larger quantitative study. Unfortunately, in the present instance *Convict Workers* is of more limited assistance. 'Black' Caesar was a 1788 First Fleet convict and thus well outside the book's chronological boundaries of 1817 to 1840. The task, rendered difficult by the paucity of relevant data, of *Convict Workers'* style quantitative analysis of early convict arrivals, has yet to be attempted.

Given the ongoing economic and social transformation of Britain between 1788 and the mid nineteenth century, differences can be assumed in the demographic characteristics (including accumulated human capital) of the 1788 First Fleet convicts and those arriving from 1817 onwards. Caesar was dead before many of these later convicts were born; additionally his origins, as will be later discussed, seem to have been unusual, even among fellow black people in Britain, let alone First Fleet convicts. Nevertheless, the general point holds; *Convict Workers* assists subsequent studies to transcend its boundaries. The *Convict Workers* authors were aware that a small minority of black convicts had existed,[5] although this too was a matter beyond the boundaries of their volume.

John Caesar features recurrently in David Collins's account of New South Wales, published in London in 1798. As a First Fleet Convict, Caesar was, paradoxically, a black founding father of 'White Australia'. Thus, Caesar's life (and that of the other First Fleet blacks) has a tendency to deconstruct the meaning of that term. In modern times, both John Caesar and David Collins, the first Judge-Advocate of New South Wales, reappeared together as fictionalised characters in Thomas Keneally's 1987 novel, *The Playmaker*.[6] Of course, both Collins's and Keneally's Caesars are representations, not the man himself, as is any reconstruction by an historian. Collins, whose account is the richest contemporary source on Caesar, constructed a representation of him as a malign anthropoid. Keneally has reconstructed Caesar along remarkably similar lines though with touches all his own. Juxtaposition of the two texts and others illustrates the point, disturbing to some theoretically naive historians and those who are last-ditch defenders of a rigidly empiricist historical method, that no clear line divides apparently factual historical accounts and works of fiction.

This essay is not a traditional biographical study but an analysis of how Caesar has been represented. It offers, however, elements of a biographical sketch set in an historical and historiographical context. When sentenced, John Caesar was a member of the growing African[7] population of late eighteenth-century London. This had chiefly arisen through the direct and indirect mechanisms of

Britain's massive involvement in the slave trade and plantation slavery. It is not helpful, however, to regard the Africans (or for that matter South Asians) of late eighteenth-century Britain as a minor by-product of historical proceeses mainly occuring elsewhere. The metropole provide the motor for Britain's stake in the slave trade and slavery and the arrival of Africans there, as a consequence, was far more momentous than a mere epiphenomenon. These are matters to which Paul Edwards contributed so richly through his pioneering and long sustained work on black authors and Africans generally in eighteenth- and early nineteenth-century Britain.

In early 1786, when a servant in the Parish of St. Paul, Deptford, Caesar committed theft in a dwelling house and was subsequently sentenced at Maidstone to transportation for seven years. He was then about 22 years old.[8] There were at least ten other First Fleet black male convicts and possibly a black female convict too.[9] As a servant, Caesar was typical of many other blacks in London (and Britain generally), in his time and indeed up to the mid-nineteenth century.[10] Given the poverty and insecurity in which many of Britain's plebeian black population of the 1780s lived,[11] he might better be understood as criminalised rather than criminal. Nevertheless, much still influential Australian historical discourse on the convicts represents them as members of Britain's 'criminal classes', an anti-social and deviant element who were criminal by nature.[12] Positive evidence is lacking about the precise circumstances of Caesar's offence. Nevertheless, Douglas Lorimer has argued that black domestic servants in later eighteenth-century England were still commonly *de facto* chattel slaves, despite the famous Mansfield Judgement of 1772. Many chose running away as a technique of self liberation but were then faced with extreme poverty in insecure liberty.[13] These circumstances are not urged as a plea in mitigation on behalf of Caesar. Even to make such a plea would be to accept the oppressive discourse of the eighteenth-century criminal law, of which mercy was less a property than a prop.[14] To represent Caesar within that discourse would be to reproduce the view that his dominance by it was just, necessary and salutary.

Another discourse from which Caesar must be rescued is that which represents those with dark skins as exotic, savage and 'other', thus negatively defining the 'superiority' of European culture.[15] William Bradley, a naval lieutenant aboard the First Fleet ship *Sirius,* called Caesar a 'Native of Madagascar', in a throwaway line in a narrative perhaps not intended for publication (it was not published until 1969).[16] Treated as a giant unfree labour reserve by the Mascarene plantation economies of the Indian Ocean,[17] later eighteenth-century Madagascar had already been drawn into this function. The Mascarene

Islands (especially the Ile de France, now known as Mauritius), were, however, at that time a French project.[18] However, sea warfare between the British and the French occurred in the Indian Ocean during the American Revolution. Speculatively it is possible that Caesar was a prize captured aboard a French ship and eventually brought to England. Malagasies were certainly rare in late eighteenth-century Britain. There is every supposition that most blacks then in the country (other than South Asians, also then often referred to as blacks) were born either in the Caribbean or North America; or to a lesser extent in Africa; or in Britain itself as the black population biologically reproduced itself.[19] Recent authors have followed Bradley without query. Keneally's Caesar is a Malagasy as is Mollie Gillen's.[20] Even today, Madagascar perhaps has a particularly 'exotic' image to white anglophones; in Caesar's day, when its vast interior was little known to Europeans, far more so. By comparison, African-Caribbean people were then common in the streets of London. Whatever Caesar's birthplace, his identification as a Malagasy seems to ultra-marginalise him even within the discourse of 'exotic, savage, other'. Bradley's view is not quite universal. L. F. Fitzhardinge suggests, without offering evidence, that John Caesar was probably from the West Indies.[21] Collins was content merely to label Caesar as a 'black', which is to say a member of an undifferentiated and essentialised category of semi-human racial inferiors.

Caesar's very name contributes to an 'exotic, savage, other' representation. It defines his subordination as Fido does a dog's to its master. Just as Defoe's Crusoe exhibits and exercises power over his rescued savage by imposing the name 'Man Friday', so slaves and even free blacks were arbitrarily named by their white masters. The name Jacko (which echoes Jackanapes) was so often given by whites to Aborigines in Australia that it came to signify Aborigines in general as grinning, mischievous, parodies of humans. Significantly, Jacko also occurred as a slave name.[22] In the Cape of Good Hope such slave names as April, February, Cupido, America, Windvogel (i.e. 'Windbird') abounded.[23] A notable example is Olaudah Equiano, who only belatedly displayed this, his Igbo name, when a successful abolitionist author. For much of his life he was known as Gustavus Vassa. This was not a compliment to any regal, military or Protestant virtues perceived in him but the arbitrary exercise of the power of a master, Lieutenant Pascal, a naval officer, who cuffed him into submission when he attempted to resist this imposition. Even then, Equiano was merely trying to retain his first slave name, Jacob, which had already been superseded by Michael.[24] Such situations posed for slaves the agonising questions, 'who am I; who am I now supposed to be?' A more obscure but even more complex example is Namoroa, who in 1824 shared John Caesar's

fate of being transported to Australia. Namoroa was recorded as his
'African' name. Later he was called Robbin or Black Robbin by his
master, Major-General Dalrymple, who acquired him in Mauritius
then brought him as a domestic servant to the vicinity of North Ber-
wick, near Edinburgh. On quitting his master's service and moving
to Edinburgh, Namoroa adopted the very Scottish name of Robert
Robertson and was also variously known as Bob and Robert Hewitt
to Edinburgh acquaintances. Finally, in New South Wales, his name
became Robert Nimrod in convict musters.[25] Francophone variants on
the name Caesar occur among blacks transported to Australia from
Mauritius. Thus Mauritius contributed a Charles Cesar sentenced to
transportation for seven years at Port Louis on 21 April 1834 and César
sentenced to transportation for seven years at Port Louis Assizes on
22 June 1842.[26] Caesar and its variants take their place in a particular
sub-set of common slave names, which included Pompey, Scipio and
even Scipio Africanus.[27] These names certainly did not signify that their
bearers were being accorded the cultural respect granted by Europeans
to their canon of great ancient Romans. They signified that their masters chose to represent their power over their slaves in classical terms,
thus legitimising it through a veneer of fake cultural dignity. Whether
or not John Caesar was ever a slave (positive evidence is lacking), his
classical surname hijacked him into the cultural practices of slavery.

Compound Caesar with 'Black', as was often done by his contemporaries, and the wonderful spectacle emerges of a representation which
disempowers by deconstructing itself, as if to warn anyone (especially
'Black' Caesar himself) who might be blockhead enough to take this
be-caesaring seriously. A 'Black' Caesar was a put-down joke against
the man so-named that any white could enjoy. Collins does not ne-
glect to 'Black' John Caesar.[28] Indeed, clapping 'Black' before Africans'
names was a common British practice in the late eighteenth- and early
nineteenth-centuries. One of Caesar's fellow black First Fleeters, John
Williams, was known as 'Black Jack', another as 'Black Jemmy'.[29] A
later transported convict who in his day gained as much notoriety as
Caesar formerly had, was 'Black' John Goff or Gough, leader of two
convict uprisings in rapid succession, one at Port Macquarie in 1825,
another on Norfolk Island in 1826. He ended on the scaffold in Sydney
in 1827. After his death his head was noted by a Sydney doctor, Dr
Bland, as a 'fine subject for the observations of the phrenologist'. Goff's
'otherness' to the assumed white ideal of the species was presumably
what made his skull of such interest to this so up-to-date colonial
medico.[30]

A narrative of sorts can be constructed from Collins on Caesar,
although as Fitzhardinge notes, Collins was more interested in
Aborigines, and more sympathetic to them, than convicts.[31] As Judge-

Advocate, the head, although legally untrained, of the colony's court martial-like criminal court, *ex officio* he had much contact with recidivists, which cannot have improved his opinion of convicts generally. Caesar was at one extreme among habitual offenders and so became a marked man. The penalties he was exposed to – flogging, leg-irons, sentences to remote and uncongenial outposts and the gallows – he cannot have been unaware of. This suggests he had or developed an oppositional and liberational ideology. He foreshadows, therefore, many subsequent persistent offenders in the penal colonies, convicts who paraded their non-compliance by word and deed.[32]

For his first seventeen months in the colony, Caesar escaped the Judge-Advocate's recorded attention. Then, in May 1789, he absconded from the service of an officer (unnamed by Collins), who perhaps had thought that a black servant, as in England, established the social status of his master. Caesar prudently stole provisions, an iron pot and a musket before taking to the bush. Subsequently, robberies increased from the provision grounds planted around the makeshift settlement at Sydney Cove and a theft of lead weights from fishing tackle occurred. Collins supposed Caesar responsible. Thus, he states that the lead weights were taken 'by some person not authorised to kill the game of this country' to make shot, hinting at Caesar by juxtaposition of this remark with his account of Caesar's first escape, as well as at very English notions of property in game.[33] This unpleasantness was briefly put out of mind on June 4, when the King's birthday was celebrated in such style as the colony could muster, including a performance of Farquhar's play *The Recruiting Officer* by a convict cast – as it happens, the event around which Keneally structures his novel. Meanwhile, a close watch was kept and Caesar was at length recaptured, although Collins is vague as to when. Other contemporary evidence states he was in the bush for just over three weeks, a fair run for a first time absconder unfamiliar with the environment.[34] Collins gives no details of the capture[35] but makes it the occasion to comment on the runaway's character:

> The man was always reputed the hardest working convict in the country; his frame was muscular and well calculated for hard labour; but in his intellects he did not very widely differ from a brute; his appetite was ravenous, for he could in any one day devour the full ration for two days. To gratify this appetite he was compelled to steal from others, and all his thefts were directed to that purpose.[36]

Some men were executed in early New South Wales for theft of provisions. To Collins, this was no deterrent to John Caesar, because he was 'such a wretch' and 'so indifferent about death'. As illustration, Collins informs us that while in custody awaiting punishment for thefts committed during his first escape, Caesar let it be known 'that if he should be hanged, he would create a laugh before he was turned off, by playing off some trick upon the executioner'. With evident chagrin, Collins reports that Governor Arthur Phillip (who held the royal prerogative of mercy) was persuaded that 'holding up such a mere animal as an example was not expected to have the proper or intended effect'. Caesar was therefore sentenced to work in fetters on Garden Island, the small islet in Sydney Harbour used for growing vegetables, from which he could supplement his rations.[37] This seems a rational attempt by Phillip at managing a difficult yet hard-working man by a mix of negative and positive incentives. It is clear from all First Fleet accounts that there was a dearth of positive incentives for managing its convict settlers, who were faced with ever-shortening rations, leaving little but coercion as a tool of management. Here, the insights of *Convict Workers* can be put to work.[38] In many ways, the very earliest years of the colony presented similar problems of providing effective incentives to extract labour from the convicts to those that Hazel Marshall, a scholar much influenced by *Convict Workers*, has noted as later occurring on the remote and unsuccessful convict settlement on Melville Island, Northern Australia, between 1824 and 1829.[39]

The formula of better rations plus working in irons in an isolated spot did not serve to tame Caesar, the negative incentives evidently outweighing the positive one of extra fresh food.[40] In late December 1789,[41] he escaped his 'secure' islet prison. For some time previously he had been allowed to work without irons, suggesting satisfactory conduct and labour performance. However, his mind, according to Collins, being 'alike insensible to kindness and to punishment', he took off in a canoe provided 'for the convenience of the other people employed on the island', together with a week's rations. A few nights later he returned in the canoe and made off with his (and in time any other competent absconder's) standard equipment for a free life in the bush, 'an iron pot, a musket and some ammunition'.[42] This time he sustained himself for almost six weeks. Evidently he was improving in bushcraft. He gave himself up in late January 1790[43] at the Rose Hill out-settlement. On surrender, he had several spear wounds. Aborigines had thus unintentionally provided better policing for the penal settlement than it could supply for itself. Later, they were to be recruited as colonial bush constables for their tracking skills.[44] Collins thought Caesar's tale of conflict with Aborigines a cock-and-bull story by a man 'fearful of severe punishment', hardly consistent with the claim that Caesar was 'insensible'. According to Collins, he claimed to have

encountered a small herd of stray government cattle tended by Aborigines. While attempting to drive the cattle off he was attacked. For
Collins, the proof of the mendacity of this story (the wounds apart, as
they could not be denied), was that Caesar was notorious for 'as small a
sense of veracity as honesty', a commonplace eighteenth-century white
prejudice about blacks. At least, these wounds earned Caesar care and
rest under the surgeon at the hospital, Collins implying this was more
than his just deserts.[45]

However, an apparent solution arose to the 'Caesar problem'. Governor Phillip's original instructions included the detachment of some
convicts and marines to settle remote Norfolk Island, a place wrongly
supposed to contain valuable raw materials for naval stores.[46] Settlement proceeded promptly in 1788. However, later reinforcement
of this settlement had more than an economic agenda. It permitted Phillip to rid Port Jackson of its most troublesome convicts, of
whom Caesar was perhaps trouble maker number one. Additionally,
by making Major Robert Ross the second Commandant of the remote island,[47] Phillip escaped daily contact with an abrasive colleague.
Caesar was among the 116 convict men and 68 convict women, together with their 27 children, who were embarked for the island aboard
the *Sirius* and *Supply* on 4 March 1790. Pointedly, Collins contrasts
the departing Caesar with another First Fleet convict also then sent
to Norfolk Island. John Irving, a surgeon, had kept his nose clean in
New South Wales, where his professional expertise was put to work
in the Government Hospital. His 'exemplary conduct' brought him
'the privileges of a free man'; that is, he embarked with a pardon as
assistant surgeon, a member of the island's civil establishment. However, Collins rather spoils the effect by revealing that Caesar too had
been pardoned by the Governor.[48] One of Collins's virtues as a source
is that he sometimes affords us information subversive to his general
drift, though whether out of honesty, thoroughness or blundering is
hard to say.

Caesar then disappears from Collins's narrative for some years.
Norfolk Island was almost impossible to escape from and if he committed further minor offences there, that was a problem for Major
Ross, not the Judge-Advocate. Caesar reappears, without explanation
of his return to Sydney, in Collins's account of July 1794, although
in fact he had been back in Sydney since 21 March 1793.[49] In July
1794, shortly after the execution of two other convicts for burglary –
this conjunction reinforcing a representation of mindless recidivism –
Caesar, 'still incorrigible', took again to the bush, living by 'plundering
the farms and huts at the outskirts' of the settlements but was soon
caught. Although punished 'with some severity', implying a flogging,
'he declared with exultation and contempt, that "all that would

not make him better."'50 For almost another 18 months Caesar is again absent from the Judge-Advocate's account. Then, in December 1795, he entered the climactic phase of his resistance to unfreedom, which ended with his legalised murder at the behest of the colonial state.

Collins places Caesar's last outbreak in the context of increasing violence between colonists and Aborigines. In the mid 1790s the Hawkesbury was a new frontier of white settlement. Aborigines made large-scale raids on its outlying farms in retaliation for expropriation of their lands. In response, a military punitive expedition killed four Aboriginal men, one woman, injured a child and took four others captive. To Collins's naive astonishment, the Aborigines counter-retaliated by 'prosecuting the revenge they had vowed against the settlers for the injuries they had received from their hands'.51 This situation permitted him to yoke Caesar with the Hawkesbury Aborigines as irredeemably savage:

> A savage of a darker hue, and full as far removed from civilisation, black Caesar, once more fled from honest labour to the woods, there to subsist by robbing the settlers.52

In this unlikely circumstance, Caesar committed what to Collins, was his 'one meritorious act'. Collins believed that Caesar had slain the fierce Aboriginal warrior, Pemulwy, a leader of resistance to the colonists from an early date. (In fact Pemulwy had only been seriously wounded and outlived his attacker by some years.) On 10 December 1790 Pemulwy had mortally speared a licensed convict game hunter, John McIntire, who died a lingering death as a consequence. More recently, Pemulwy had seriously, though not fatally injured 'Collins', not the Judge-Advocate but an Aborigine re-named after him, who had become a dependent of the settlement.53 Thus Caesar had avenged Pemulwy's attack on a man whom Collins regarded as a *protégé*. Evidently even an absconded 'savage of a darker hue' had use as a check on Aboriginal resistance. Thus, by December 1795 Caesar had honed his bushcraft to the point where he could ambush a redoubtable Aborigine. This was no mean feat, in view of Aborigines' expert bushcraft, a skill signally lacking among the newcomers on their arrival. By contrast, a military detachment sent to exact reprisals for McIntire's spearing had blundered about the bush. The troops had been easily evaded by the few Aborigines unwary enough to be spotted.54 However, Pemulwy's wounding by Caesar, just as Caesar's earlier wounding by Aborigines, also illustrates that black convicts and Aborigines could find no automatic alliance against the colonial state. Indeed, it is clear that, to Aborigines, black convicts often appeared as merely part of the rapacious intruder society which was ruthlessly dispossessing them. Thus black convicts were probably *pro rata* as much targets for retaliation[55] as whites.

Collins represents a grave internal public order problem as facing the colony by January 1796, in addition to serious conflict with Aborigines. Many government firearms had illicitly passed into the hands of private persons, including convicts and ex-convicts. An order was issued that every private person in possession of a gun must bring it to the commissary, register it and obtain a license. Of 250–300 missing crown firearms, under 50 were duly registered. Collins connects this circumstance with 'almost daily and nightly' robberies. Several men had taken to the bush, armed, although not apparently forming a band; in other words, robbery-under-arms was now rife[56] and the colony was facing a sustained outbreak of banditry.[57] As for Caesar, he sent word 'that he neither would come in, nor suffer himself to be taken alive'. The response was draconian; anyone legally in possession of ammunition who was found guilty of supplying it to 'common plunderers' would be considered an accomplice (and thus, by implication, risk facing trial for a capital offence). Caesar was specifically targeted, thus revealing that he was thought the most dangerous of the robbers at large. The Governor offered a reward of five gallons of spirits to 'whoever would bring him in with his arms' (that is, dead or alive).[58] For a time Caesar evaded the bounty hunters. By now, although six to eight men were at large, everyone, Collins reports, blamed Caesar for the frequent robberies continually reported.[59] As evidence, this is ambiguous. It could be taken to indicate Collins's loathing of Caesar; Caesar's notoriety among officials and officers; even his larger-than-life image among the mass of convicts and ex-convicts; or some combination of these.

Spirits – usually rum – were highly desired by the convicts and ex-convicts of early New South Wales and expensive, their import and wholesaling being monopolised by a ring of officers.[60] Despite the potential for disorder and inefficient work among fighting-drunk or hung-over convicts, payment for extra work with spirits was early found effective in motivating their labour. So it proved for the task of killing Caesar. In early February 1796, a convict called John Wimbow together with another man set off to earn the reward on offer. They found Caesar's hideaway in some brush, concealed themselves until his return at dusk and ambushed him as he emerged on the morning of 15 February 1796. Too late, Caesar perceived the danger and aimed his musket but Wimbow fired first, fatally wounding his quarry. After a few hours Caesar died at the hut of a settler called Rose at Liberty Plains, an ironically named location in the circumstances.[61] Collins's brief obituary is pitiless:

> Thus ended a man, who certainly, during his life could never
> have been estimated at more than one remove above the brute,
> and who had given more trouble than any other convict in the
> settlement.[62]

By denying Caesar's full humanity, Collins reduces his slaughter to an event akin to the necessary eradication of vermin by gamekeepers at the behest of their masters.

Internal contradictions and conflict with other contemporary accounts abound in Collins's representation of Caesar. Thus to have Caesar 'the hardest working convict in the country' and a ravenous brute driven to robbery by ungovernable appetites is self-cancelling. Sustained hard physical labour requires a substantial high calorie diet.[63] As Collins well knew, the convict ration soon dwindled, so inadequate was the First Fleet's provisioning, so uncertain further external supply and so difficult food production from the poor soils of Sydney's environs.[64]

There is a significant deviance between Collins's representation of the reasons for Caesar's voluntary surrender at Rose Hill and those of Tench and Bradley (which in turn contradict each other). Tench attributes Caesar's first two escapes to a desire 'of establishing himself in the society of the natives, with a wish to adopt their customs and to live with them'. He was, however, 'always repulsed by them; and compelled to return in hunger and wretchedness'.[65] A modern reader might conclude that black solidarity was Caesar's motive here, that at first he thought it likely and natural that Aborigines would afford him permanent freedom and human dignity. Tench had been in the West Indies.[66] Perhaps he knew that one form of *marronage* among African-Caribbean slaves was escape and fusion with indigenous free Carib communities (as in Dominica) and assumed something similar was in Caesar's mind. However, as seen, the obstacles to any such plan were formidable. Since Caesar was a putative Malagasy, it is worth noting that in Mauritius, they were considered the most rebellious component in the slave population and were particularly associated with *marronage* in the inaccessible interior hill country, then still thickly forested.[67] Tench avoids sneering at Caesar's motives for surrender at Rose Hill; indeed he conveys a certain human sympathy. However Bradley, in a more extended passage, offers a yet different explanation for this surrender:

> The account he gives of his subsisting himself so long a time
> was, that when he saw a party of Natives with anything on,
> or about their Fire, that he frighten'd them away by coming
> suddenly on them and swaggering with his Musquet, then he

> helped himself to whatever they had left; in this manner he
> made out very well without Ammunition, sometimes robbing
> Gardens. When he lost his Musquet he found it impossible
> to subsist himself, he was then attack'd by the Natives &
> wounded in several places & escaped from a party of them
> through a very thick brush when he surrendered himself.[68]

This suggests not a man who wished to join Aboriginal society but
a master (so long as armed) of cunning stratagems at the Aborigines'
expense, not easy to impose on such people in their own territory.
Caesar's growing confidence in the bush is certainly indicated. Bradley
converges with Tench in silence concerning a pretended attempt to
rescue government cattle as a device for avoiding punishment.

The divergence of these accounts serves perfectly to demonstrate
that what all three offer is not incontestable historical 'facts' (whatever those might be is hard to imagine except in a trivial sense)
but varying representations. It would be pitiful to whine for 'better'
accounts when such an excellent illustration is to hand of a crucial
general point concerning historical evidence. Once that is understood,
there is no fundamental difficulty in extracting meanings from these
representations. Some may yearn, at this point, for the incontestable
authority of Caesar's own voice, not refracted through Collins's text.
Collins's text, however, is not inauthentic because he was Judge-
Advocate, nor are convicts' accounts authentic because they were
transported felons. All are representations requiring interrogation to
extract meaning; all, approached this way, are potentially 'good' evidence.[69] As it happens, occasionally Collins represents Caesar's voice
in a manner which does not disguise its oppositional and liberational
agenda.

For Collins, Caesar was a social isolate, even in relation to his fellow convicts. This can readily be contested. To begin with, Caesar
fathered a currency lass (as native born white Australians were called).
Anne Power, a convict who had arrived aboard the *Lady Juliana* in
1791, gave birth to their child Mary Ann on Norfolk Island, 4 March
1792. Neither returned with Caesar to Sydney in March 1793; for
quite pragmatic reasons, sexual relationships between convicts were
often temporary, as were those of many contemporary plebeians in
Britain.[70] There are no grounds to assume that the relations between
Mary Ann's parents were outside a normal plebeian moral framework
of the period. In this period relations between African men and plebeian white women, whether in Britain or Australia, were nothing out
of the ordinary.[71] Caesar's relations with Anne Power cannot, on the
available evidence, be subjected to retrospective quality control assessment. Nevertheless, the relationship challenges Collins's representation

of Caesar as a social isolate. Caesar's descendants may be around in modern Australia. Mary Anne Power survived to be relocated in Van Diemen's Land with the other Norfolk Island settlers, at the age of 21.[72] She may, therefore, herself have given birth to and raised children and Caesar may have descendants through her in modern Australia.

Collins's representation of Caesar as a social isolate, or even sociopath, is open to challenge on a further front. True, unlike Goff he never appears to have banded with other absconders. The crackdown, however, on suppliers of ammunition to bush robbers implies collaborative relations between these two groups. Caesar and the other bush robbers, by implication, had established black market relations in which stolen items and perhaps game were exchanged for assured supply of the ammunition so crucial to social and material reproduction of their precarious freedom. Seemingly, by 1795/6, bush robbery was no longer merely a means of bare survival for absconders but was generating its own political economy and cultural forms, both of which by definition had a social dimension. If these speculations are well founded, the authorities' apparent *grand peur* in late 1795 and early 1796 is explained. Such black market exchanges threatened an intensifying symbiosis between robbers, outlying assigned convict servants and small emancipist or ex-soldier farmers, in implicit or even explicit opposition to the colony's authorities and dominant officer clique. Something like this appears to have arisen in early Van Diemen's land, where bush banditry with convict and especially small emancipist support soon became endemic.[73] Likewise, Byrne has argued that between 1810 and 1830, a complex political economy and set of cultural practices developed around bushranging in New South Wales. It now emerges that in embryo, all this considerably pre-dated 1810. However, Byrne also convincingly argues that the relationship between bushrangers and those who harboured them, traded with them and kept them informed was double edged. When it suited them, the same small settlers turned against bushrangers for the rewards offered;[74] what might be called the Wimbow factor evidently well pre-dated 1810.

Notwithstanding that point, the bush robber of 1796 carried the germ of the bandit as Robin Hood style community hero, the social bandit, by definition not a social isolate.[75] It would be stretching several points to identify Caesar or his bush robber contemporaries as social bandits, itself a contentious concept whose labyrinthine controversies need not be explored here. Indeed, to post-structuralist readers those controversies are archaic and misplaced. However, Collins's text may unwittingly reveal Caesar's stumblings in the 'bandit-as-subordinate-class-hero' direction, providing a powerful motive for the authorities to arrange his legalised murder before matters got totally out of hand. If this appears far-fetched, Byrne provides evidence that between 1810 and 1830 the colonial authorities, then better established and more powerful than in the embryonic colony of 1788–96, consistently over-estimated the threat posed by bushranging gangs to the entire colonial order.[76] Such fears perhaps had their dress rehearsal in late 1795 and early 1796, when no gangs yet existed. Considering Caesar as a proto-bushranger, if less than a fully fledged specimen, leads to another important point. In due course, Australia's bushrangers were to be-come White Australian popular national heroes, lauded as defenders of the common people and democratic Australian values.[77] With John Caesar as the first significant proto-bushranger, the constructed iden-tity 'White Australia' is further deconstructed. This may partly explain why he was for long virtually forgotten, rather than lack of recorded evidence; if so, a silence and closure of some consequence has been identified in the historiography of bushranging. He would certainly qualify for the title 'the first major proto-bushranger' on grounds of attention drawing/attention seeking, daring, a 'death or liberty' ethos,[78] bush skills and a capacity to undermine and alarm constituted author-ity, all archetypal attributes of the mythic bushranger and some actual ones.

For Collins, one of the early demonstrations of Caesar as a 'wretch', a 'mere animal' indifferent to whether he lived or died, is his jaunty behaviour while waiting execution after 6 June 1789. An established culture of public trial and execution was exported to New South Wales from Britain. As Peter Linebaugh has shown, in eighteenth-century Britain the whole performance from indictment to trial and execution was designedly theatrical and all the players on that stage knew their parts; the accused and condemned, the gaolers, the crowd at the trial and gallows, the judge, jury, hangman and chaplain etc.[79] Among the roles available to the capitally accused and condemned while await-ing trial and subsequent execution was to cut a dash, receive friends, relatives and even sensation-seeking fashionable callers. An excellent example is Jack Sheppard, popular hero of early eighteenth-century plebeian London for his escapes, despite the best efforts of gaolers, locksmiths and manufacturers of fetters.[80] Far from exhibiting any brutish inability to comprehend the gravity of his situation under capi-tal sentence, Caesar played his part as cleverly as Jack Sheppard had. By making it clear that he intended to turn his execution into a farce, he was ruining the show for all who required his fate on the scaffold to be a terrible example to the assembled felonry. A hanging at which the crowd – especially a convict crowd – was brought to a state of subversive derision against the sentencing court, the hangman and the noose, would certainly not produce 'the proper or intended effect'! All this argues Caesar's clear understanding and clever manipulation of the theatre of public execution. The deeds of the later black convict insurrectionary, John Goff, were of far greater extent and gravity for the colonial penal state than Caesar's. Like Caesar, Goff was held by a social and official superior to be detestable and the worst malefactor in the colony.[81] The role Goff played, however, in Sydney's theatre of execution was that desired by the authorities. He held centre stage all right, which was both allowable and inevitable, but in the role of the manly penitent. He acknowledged the justice of his sentence, bade in a firm voice the onlookers to take warning, kissed the rope, leaned on the shoulder of Father Therry, the Catholic priest who attended him, embraced his condemned confederates on the scaffold and prayed heaven for mercy, till the moment of the drop.[82] *That* was 'the proper and intended effect', a well managed execution for the purposes of the colonial state, a terrible warning to the convict onlookers paraded for the occasion.

However, Caesar was not just a plebeian Londoner but a black plebeian Londoner, one among thousands of others. In Deptford, a maritime district, he would certainly have had plenty of opportunity for everyday contact with others of this community originating from all points of the compass.[83] This large black community was not isolated from the wider currents of the Atlantic World. Divided from Africa by the ocean, such communities were also linked by the intricate web of shipping lanes between the main ports of western Europe, the Americas and Africa itself into a fluid, dynamic, subversive, polyglot, multi-national plebeian maritime culture.[84] In Deptford, Caesar was an exemplar. Within this culture African-American and African-Caribbean folk-tales probably circulated. Their trickster-heroes were physically weak animals who confronted and outwitted the powerful and predatory animals with cunning guile.[85] A man who could fool his way out of a hanging and bluff his way into relieving Aborigines of their food,[86] parallels the exploits of Anansi/Nansi, the trickster-hero of the African-Caribbean slaves. Indeed, even his death is folkloric on this paradigm, for slave folk-tale transmitted the useful caution that tricking and humiliating the powerful animals (that is, the masters) was a dangerous game in which the too-clever-by-half courted disaster. Representation of Caesar as a trickster turns him into a type of the African Slave Diaspora culture-hero. The meaning of his life thus becomes of very rich complexity, in contrast to Collins's pasteboard representation of a black sub-human.

Turning to Keneally's modern text, the first after Collins to represent Caesar at all extensively, little has changed over nearly 200 years. Both adhere to the discourse of colonialism, more particularly the racist component of that complex discourse which represents black people as stupid, violent, holding life cheap, and slaves to their appetites. Collins exemplifies what Ranajit Guha has called 'the prose of counter insurgency', in which official accounts (or, as here, the off-duty accounts of officials) of mindless rebelliousness among subaltern elements in a colonial society are negations or even mirror images of mindful subaltern resistance.[87] In Caesar's New South Wales, the Aborigines not yet being subordinated to the colonial project, convicts were the chief subaltern element. Keneally is too uncritically captive to the officer narratives he has consulted and so acts as an unwitting sounding-board for their prose of counter insurgency. To be sure, he offers touches of his own. His text places in Caesar's mouth an extraordinary invented pidgin lingo, which Collins forebears to do. As a sample of this franco-anglophone ooga-booga, Caesar's first words in the novel will suffice, for the rest is of apiece:

> *Ma mère*, you must let go that gentleman. Yes *cherie*, in the name of the Fragrant one. Ease them little arms of yours. This gentleman is *foko* to me, is brother, so ease your arms mammie.[88]

The immediate context does not mitigate the impression created. Lieutenant Ralph Clark has begun auditioning convicts for his production of *The Recruiting Officer*. As if to indicate the extremes of disordered personalities among the convict colonists, it is his hard luck that the first two to offer themselves are a stinking maniacal old woman, Meg Long, and an equally if differently loony Caesar. True, Caesar's voice is described as harmonious; but then natural musicality has almost always been allowed to Africans in racist constructs (good on drums, bad at sums etc.). Soon the text informs us that Caesar 'endlessly' invoked 'the Fragrant one, some sort of Madagascan god' and endlessly indeed, whenever Keneally's Caesar appears, this savage deity is invoked. It later turns out that in Caesar's mind this god is both the 'son of Zanahary', ruler of the dead, and Jesus Christ.[89] Further, at his first appearance, Caesar is represented by the novel's narrative voice as 'very dangerous – the strongest and hungriest of the prisoners'; a hint of the cannibalism so 'typical' of a 'savage', perhaps? The very detachment of the novel's narrative voice conveys impartial authority. After all this we are not surprised that a few lines on it turns out that Caesar is 'renowned among the convict women' because of (what else?) his 'great member' 'but not always welcomed by them, since he took so easily to blows'.[90] It appears that now the hint is that Caesar is a megaphallic black rapist, or at least a woman-beater, again old chestnuts in the racist construct of Africans.[91] Had the slightest suspicion that the historic John Caesar was rapist, woman-basher or cannibal reached Collins, he would certainly have recorded it of one he exhibited such determination to vilify. Record exists of only one First Fleet black convict being involved in a rape; Daniel Gordon *saved* his fellow convict, Lydia Munro, a white woman, from rape by another white convict, William Boggis.[92] Three other First Fleet blacks, however, married white women; consensual relationships within the limits of a society where gender relations were loaded against women. Children resulted from two of these marriages.[93] In view of the low ratio of women to men among the convicts, this tells us that such black male/white female marriages were as easy (or difficult) as any other at that time. For the record, Jane Langley, the 'possible' black woman aboard the First Fleet, 'quite a black complexioned woman' with 'very curly hair', had a child by a white seaman on the voyage out and later married or cohabited with a white marine, with whom she lived till her death in 1828 and by whom she had seven more children.[94] None of these everyday conjugal lives are quite sensational enough for Keneally, though to be fair Mollie Gillen's splendid biographical dictionary of the First Fleet, eclipsing all predecessors in wealth of information, was only published after the novel. However, he can be indicted of a failure of imagination in one direction and an overheated imagination in another. Perhaps for a novelist the first is the more damning accusation although the second might raise more wind. Either way, these two failures are mutually constituting.

Huge black penises and black rape of a white woman, related racist notions of African sexuality, surface elsewhere in the novel. It turns out that Keneally's version of the historical John 'Black Jack' Williams also has a whopping willy. In a peaceful enough encounter with Aborigines, who appear to be puzzled as to Williams' sex, Provost-Marshall Harry Brewer commands him to drop his pants. Not only does this extract 'yelps of praise' from the Aborigines (male and female, one of the men suggestively displaying his bum in response) but Brewer shouts out 'Don't go near my sweetheart with that thing, Jack'. To add to the closet-queen buzz of this passage, a little earlier an Aboriginal male elder has given Williams's chest a feelie, especially the nipples.[95] Keneally's Caesar, before absconding, constantly broods at rehearsals of the play from whose cast he has been excluded. It eventually emerges that after absconding from Garden Island, he has sallied from the bush and savagely beaten Mary Brenham, a young convict player and a redemptive and ultimately redeemed figure in the text. Clark, in the novel and historical sources alike, is her future lover. In the novel, he is already attracted to her. The violent assault on Brenham thus has its dramatic point. The passage, however, is ambiguous as to whether Caesar rapes as well as beats Brenham but is certainly sexually charged.[96] Collins had the decorum to ignore Caesar's sexuality, although reference to Caesar's brutish appetite in his text could be glossed as encompassing libido. Evidence exists, as seen, that Caesar had at least one natural, non-sensational relationship with a convict woman, which produced a natural consequence, a child. Keneally, by contrast, represents his Caesar as a black sex-beast. It will not do to counter that Keneally merely seeks to reproduce the suppositions of late eighteenth-century white males concerning black sexuality. The narrative voice never insinuates this. Eighteenth-century plantocrat racists, indeed, commonly reviled the English lower orders, for their everyday acceptance as natural and uncontroversial of sexual relations, from the casual to cohabitation and marriage, between black men and white women.[97] The frequently xenophobic mobs of England's eighteenth-century cities, however, never rioted against blacks dwelling amongst them on this or any other grounds.

It would be tedious and unnecessary to plod through every appearance of Caesar in Keneally's text. Many of the white convicts and marine other ranks are also represented in the novel as low-life deviants. In the case of the convicts this fits only too well with the 'convict stain' theme in Australia's understanding of its past. As a good Australian nationalist, Keneally sees the beginnings of redemption on Australian soil for most if not all his convict scum. This, however, converges with a variant of the nationalist sub-text of some Australian convict studies, in which it is held that although starting with the most unpromising of human material, a wonderful transformation of Pommie ratbags into dinky-die Aussies naturally occurred in most instances.[98]

If Keneally's Caesar is primitively superstitious, so are most of his other convicts. In a novel extension of the 'criminal class' school, Keneally has most of them votaries and supplicants of an invented dark criminal deity, the 'Tawney Prince' (presumably Old Nick), as a last offering to whom the doomed pay veiled obeisance on the gallows. At the head of this imagined cult, which shares the bogus authenticity of traditional orientalist representations of Thuggee,[99] Keneally's text places the sinister convict woman, Goose. She is sheerly fictional but Keneally's representation of some genuine historical persons (Caesar, Brenham and Clark among many others) serves to show how blurred the line is between the categories, 'fact' and 'fiction'. As play making is an apt enough extended metaphor of the redemptive introduction of order and civility into extreme disorder and deviance, it is surely significant that the two convicts who most practice cults of devilish gods are neutralised at the putting on of the play, the novel's finale. Goose, a mistress of poison, is 'pontiff of the Tawney Prince in this penal reach';[100] Caesar has his personal cult of the 'Fragrant One', a devilish Jesus and lord of the dead. Keneally's Caesar is recaptured during the performance, as if captivated by it. Goose, at the height of her sinister power, is poisoned during the performance, a fate narrowly escaped by Caesar himself (a deliverance he attributes to his dark deity).

It strongly exhibits the continuing hold of colonialist constructs over modern minds that Keneally is so patently captive to them in his fictionalised representation of Caesar. Keneally has taken a major public role in the modern Australian republican movement of which he is a progressive and thoughtful advocate.[101] Crucial to his republicanism is his belief that under the monarchy Australia remains ultimately subjected to the British colonialist project, stultifying the human potential of all its people. He also has every claim to be a major Australian novelist. In the case of *The Playmaker,* however, one fears for the consequences if, like some other of his novels, it is ever transmuted into television or film,[102] for through these powerful mass media the racist representations generated by colonialism could be intensively reproduced.[103]

Here is a last representation of my own devising, a thrawn John Caesar. Circumstances in very early New South Wales were not propitious for his dogged individual resistance to precipitate wider social resistance, although at last he may have edged towards that. In this constrained situation, he could be destroyed but would not yield. For this reason, he seems to me more *thrawn,* as the Scots say, than stubborn, the nearest English equivalent. To illustrate the difference, here is a tale. A prison doctor orders two inmates to take castor oil. One is stubborn, the other thrawn. The stubborn prisoner, an Englishman, repeats over and over that he won't take it, knowing full well that at last he will, which he does. The thrawn man, a Scot, also repeatedly refuses the dose but at last says; 'weel, I jalouse I maun aiblins tak it, but mind mannie, ye'll no' mak me schate.'[104] Likewise, the powers that be in New South Wales could make John Caesar take their castor oil all right. However, as he reportedly responded, 'all that would not make him better'. So at last, unable to risk his exhibition on the scaffold, they procured his death by hired assassins. Apparently there was for long after a popular tradition in New South Wales that the assassins subsequently drank themselves to death with their reward of five gallons of rum. There is a species of thrawn victory for Caesar in this ending; Caesar died rather than submit and, at least in popular memory, his killers deservedly met a more squalid fate than death by gunshot wounds at Liberty Plains.[105]

Notes

1. The commencing quotation of this paragraph is from David Collins, *An Account of the English Colony in New South Wales; With Remarks on the Dispositions, Customs, Manners etc. of the Native Inhabitants of that Country,* Vol. 1 (London, 1798; 2nd ed. with introduction by Brian H. Fletcher, Sydney, A. H. & W. A.

Reed in association with the Royal Australian Historical Society, 1975), 57. This and all subsequent citations are from the Sydney 1975 edition. For the 'Botany Bay' metaphor of New South Wales as a place of horror and disorder, see Richard White, *Inventing Australia; Images and Identity, 1688–1980* (Sydney: Allen & Unwin, 1981), ch. 1. Paul Edwards was no Australianist, but he was a highly original, influential and voluminously published scholar of the literature and history of the African Diaspora, notably that of the Africans of 18th- and early 19th-century Britain. He strongly encouraged my interest in Australia's transported black convicts, when another distinguished Africanist friend thought I had either flipped my lid or deserted the colours. Paul Edwards regarded white [mis]representations of 'bad blacks' as of particular interest; Caesar certainly fits the bill. He was also famous for jokes and pranks. His brilliant lectures on Tennyson, whom he much admired, raised gales of laughter. Once, he persuaded the *Times Literary Supplement* to publish, as an overlooked fragment of doom-laden old English verse, a translation by himself and Charles Jones of the scatological comic ditty commencing, 'Life is but a dismal picture, / Dark and dreary as the tomb' etc. My essay's conclusion is somewhat in the vein of his contribution to R. Simek *et. al.* (eds.), *Sagnaskemmtun; Studies in Honour of Hermann Palsson* (Vienna: Bohlau, 1986). As one Brummie to another, I say 'Ey our Paul, if yer can 'ear us, 'av a good laff at this then'.

2. The literature on early pictorial representations of colonial Australia, however, does take account of the influence of the Romantic Movement on these cultural artifacts. Examples are Tim Bonyhady, *The Colonial Image; Australian Painting, 1800–1880* (Chippendale N.S.W.: Elsyd, 1987); Ian & Tamsin Donaldson, *Seeing the First Australians* (Sydney & London: Allen & Unwin, 1985); H. B. Proudfoot, 'Botany Bay, Kew and the Picturesque Early Conceptions of Australian Landscape', *Journal of the Royal Australian Historical Society*, 65, 1 (June 1979), 30–45; Bernard Smith, *European Vision and the South Pacific, 1768–1850; A Study in the History of Art and Ideas* (Oxford: The Clarendon Press, 1960); Bernard Smith, *Imagining the Pacific; In the Wake of the Cook Voyages* (New Haven & London: Yale University Press, 1992). Paul Carter, *The Road to Botany Bay; An Essay in Spatial History* (London: Faber & Faber, 1987), ch. 8, analyses the reinterpretion and indeed reshaping of Australian landscape in line with European canons of the picturesque.

3. Stephen Nicholas (ed.), *Convict Workers; Reinterpreting Australia's Past* (Cambridge: University Press, 1988).

4. See Ian Duffield, 'Skilled Workers or Marginalized Poor? The African Population of the United Kingdom, 1812–1852', in David Killingray (ed.), *Immigrants & Minorities*, 12, 3 (November 1993), Special Issue on Africans in Britain, 49–87; republished in Killingray (ed.), *Africans in Britain* (Ilford: Frank Cass and Company Limited, 1994), 49–87.

5. As evidence of their awareness of the First Fleet black convicts, see Stephen Nicholas & Peter Shergold, 'Non-British Convicts', in James Jupp (ed.), *The Australian People; An Encyclopaedia of the Nation, its People and their Origins* (North Ryde, 1988), 31–6. Their data for this article came from the database compiled for the production of *Convict Workers*.

6. Thomas Keneally, *The Playmaker* (London & Sydney: Hodder & Stoughton, 1987).

7. African is used in this essay generically, for persons of African birth or descent. As Caesar is said to have been born in Madagascar (see n. 16 below), some may object that he was not an African. However, the people of Madagascar, one of the last major land masses to be colonised by humans, are descended from very various components including East Africans, South Arabians, South Asians and Indonesians. The first three are also present in the Swahili culture of the East African littoral, yet nobody denies that these people are Africans. Africa contains many equally composite cultures and ethnicities and its gene pool is exceptionally diverse. Slaving expanded Madagascar's East African element in the 18th and 19th centuries. Madagascar is a founder-member of the Organisation of African Unity (founded 1963).

8. Mollie Gillen, *The Founders of Australia; A Biographical Dictionary of the First Fleet* (North Sydney: Library of Australian History, 1989), 63.

9. *ibid.,* 424. Another First Fleet black convict, John ('Black Jack') Williams was resident in Deptford – see *ibid.,* 385–6. First Fleet blacks sentenced at the Old Bailey were George Francisco, John Martin, John Mosely, Thomas Orford and James Williams – see accounts in *ibid.,* 134, 239, 255, 269 & 384–5. That 7 of 11 known First Fleet black convicts were convicted in or near London indicates the concentration of England's contemporary black population in the London region. Duffield, 'Skilled Worker or Marginalized Poor?', suggests this continued up to 1852, though declined from 1840. This fostered black communities and a common consciousness among their members. Gillen's 'possible' black female First Fleeter is Jane Langley, also tried at the Old Bailey – see *The Founders of Australia;* 212–3 & 424. A useful survey of the lives of African women in eighteenth-century Britain occurs in Gretchen Gerzina, *Black*

England; Life Before Emancipation (London: Charles Murray, 1995), ch. 3.

10. Norma Myers, 'Servant, Sailor, Soldier, Taylor, Beggarman Black Survival in White Society 1780–1850', *Immigrants & Minorities*, 12, 1 (March 1993), 47–74, esp. 59–60; Duffield, 'Skilled Workers or Marginalized Poor?', 58–64.

11. Black poverty is extensively discussed in Stephen J. Braidwood, 'Initiatives and organisation of the Black Poor 1786–7', *Slavery & Abolition*, 3 (1982), 211–27 and in his major study *Black Poor and White Philanthropists; London's Blacks and the Foundation of Sierra Leone 1786–1791* (Liverpool: Liverpool University Press, 1994), chs. 1 & 2; in Douglas A. Lorimer, 'Black Resistance to Racism and Slavery in Eighteenth-Century Britain', in Jagdish S. Gundara & Ian Duffield (eds.), *Essays on the History of Blacks in Britain; From Roman Times to the Mid-Twentieth Century* (Aldershot: Avebury, 1992), 52–80 & in Lorimer, 'Black Slaves and English Liberty; a Re-Examination of Racial Slavery in England', *Immigrants & Minorities*, 3 (1984), 121–50.

12. To illustrate, A. G. L. Shaw, sees English and Scottish convicts as 'professional and habitual criminals... a disreputable lot'; see *Convicts and the Colonies* (London: Faber, 1966), 165. Lloyd Robson saw the convicts as predominantly 'ne'er-do-wells from the city slums'; Robson, *The Convict Settlers of Australia* (Melbourne University Press, Melbourne, 1965), 158. More recently, Portia Robinson, *The Women of Botany Bay; A Reinterpretation of the Role of Women in the Origins of Australian Society* (Sydney, The Macquarie Library, 1988), 3, represents them without dissent as 'defined by their contemporaries as belonging to "the criminal class"'. The only recent major published study hostile to this view is Stephen Nicholas (ed.), *Convict Workers; Reinterpreting Australia's Past* (Sydney and Cambridge: Cambridge University Press, 1988), which has received many hostile comments on this score; e.g. Ralph Shlomowitz, '*Convict Workers* A Review Article', *Australian Economic History Review*, XXX, 2 (September 1990), 67–88 & 'Convict Workers; Casual or Professional Criminals', *Australian Economic History Review*, XXXI, 2 (September 1991), 106–8. However, three recent Ph.D. theses support it; Hamish Maxwell-Stewart, 'The Bushrangers and the Convict System of Van Diemen's Land 1803–1846', Ph.D. Thesis, University of Edinburgh (1990); Deborah Oxley, 'Convict Maids', Ph.D. thesis, University of New South Wales (1991); Kirsty M. Reid, 'Work, Sexuality and Resistance; the Convict Women of Van Diemen's Land, 1820–1839', Ph.D. Thesis, University of Edinburgh (1995). Oxley's study is to be published by Cambridge University Press. The 'criminal class' view

has been heavily contested by social historians of crime in Britain; an important recent e.g. is Peter Linebaugh, *The London Hanged; Crime and Civil Society in the Eighteenth-Century* (London: Allen Lane The Penguin Press, 1991). The most thoughtful and constructive critique to date of *Convict Workers,* Raymond Evans & William Thorpe, 'Power, Punishment and Penal Labour; *Convict Workers* and Moreton Bay', *Australian Historical Studies,* 25, 98 (April 1992), 90–111, accepts *Convict Workers'* scepticism about the 'criminal class' approach to convict studies.

13. Lorimer, 'Black Slaves and English Liberty', 121–50. Lorimer's opinion is that the Mansfield Judgement was limited in scope and somewhat ineffectual at that. This and his assertion of the continuance of chattel slavery in England after 1772, have been contested by William R. Cotter, 'The Somerset Case and the Abolition of Slavery in England', *History; The Journal of the Historical Association,* 79, 255 (February 1994), 31–56. However, Cotter's late 18th century empirical evidence is weak (lack of references to slaves in the index of the post-1772 *Gentleman's Magazine*!) and his arguments narrowly based on legal positivism and on the frequent citation of Mansfield's ruling by 19th-century British and American lawyers as having freed slaves in England. This attempt to rehabilitate the myth of the Mansfield Judgement is unconvincing. The most recent assessment of the limited nature of the Mansfield Judgement occurs in Gretchen Gerzina, *Black England; Life Before Emancipation* (London: Charles Murray, 1995), ch. 4; however, Gerzina does not seem to be aware of Cotter's article and certainly does not address its arguments.

14. This view of mercy in the 18th century criminal justice system has famously been argued by Douglas Hay, 'Property, Authority and the Criminal Law' in Hay *et. al., Albion's Fatal Tree; Crime and Society in Eighteenth-Century England* (London: Allen Lane The Penguin Press, 1977), 17–64.

15. Of fundamental importance on this topic are Edward Said, *Orientalism* (London & Henley: Routledge & Kegan Paul, 1978) & *Culture and Imperialism* (London: Chatto & Windus, 1993). Other important studies include Theodore W. Allen, *The Invention of the White Race,* Vol. 1, *Racial Oppression and Social Control* (London: Verso, 1994); Michael Adas, *Machines as the Measure of Man; Science, Technology and Ideologies of Western Dominance* (Ithaca & London: Cornell University Press, 1989); Bain Attwood, *The Making of the Aborigines* (Sydney: Allen & Unwin, 1989); B. Atwood & J. Jarrold (eds.), *Power, Knowledge and Aborigines,* special issue of *Journal of Australian Studies* (1992); Etienne Balibar & Immanual Wallerstein, *Race, Nation, Class; Ambiguous Identities*

(London: Verso, 1991); Nicholas B. Dirks (ed.), *Colonialism and Culture* (Ann Arbor: University of Michigan Press, 1992); Stephen Jay Gould, *The Mismeasure of Man* (New York: Norton, 1981); Rana Kabbani, *Europe's Myths of the Orient; Devise and Rule* (London: The Macmillan Press, 1986); Mary Louise Pratt, *Imperial Eyes; Travel Writing and Transculturation* (London & New York: Routledge, 1992); Thomas Richards, *The Imperial Archive; Knowledge and the Fantasy of Empire* (London & New York, Verso: 1993).

16. William Bradley, *A Voyage to New South Wales 1786–1792* (Sydney: Trustees of the Public Library of New South Wales in association with Ure Smith Pty. Ltd., William Dixson Foundation Publication No. 11, 1969), 186.

17. See Gwyn Campbell, 'Madagascar and the Slave Trade, 1810–1895', *Journal of African History*, 22 (1981), 203–27; Gwyn Campell, 'Madagascar and the Slave Trade of the Western Indian Ocean, 1800–1861', in W. G. Clarence-Smith (ed.), *The Economics of the Indian Ocean Slave Trade* (Ilford: Frank Cass, 1989).

18. See Richard Allen, 'Marronage and the Maintenance of Public Order in Mauritius', *Slavery & Abolition*, 4, 3 (Dec. 1983), 214–31; Burton Benedict, 'Slavery and Indenture in Mauritius and Seychelles', in James L. Watson (ed.), *Asian and African Systems of Slavery* (Oxford: Basil Blackwell, 1980), 137–40; Karl No'l, *L'esclavage – L'Isle de France (Ile Maurice) de 1715–1810* (Paris, éditions Two Cities ETC, n.d.); Abdul Sherrif, 'The French slave trade and the resubjection of Kilwa, 1770–1822', in Sherrif, *Slaves, Spices & Ivory in Zanzibar; Integration of an East African Commercial Empire into the World Economy* (London: James Currey, 1987), 41–7; Nigel Worden, 'Diverging Histories; Slavery and its Aftermath in the Cape Colony and Mauritius', *South African Historical Journal*, 27 (1992), 3–11.

19. Gillen, Appendix 3, 424 identifies two of the black First Fleeter convicts as from North America, one as probably a Jamaican, plus accepts Caesar was a Malagasy. The literature on blacks in 18th-century Britain conspicuously lacks reference to Malagasies, abounds in references to Caribbean and North America blacks and notes the presence of others born in Africa and Britain itself. See for e.g. Paul Edwards & James Walvin, *Black Personalities in the Era of the Slave Trade* (London: Macmillan, 1983); Peter Fryer, *Staying Power; The History of Black People in Britain* (London: Pluto Press, 1984); G. Gerzina, *op. cit.*; Norma Myers, 'Reconstructing the Black Past; Blacks in Britain c. 1780–1830', Ph.D. thesis, University of Liverpool (1990); Norma Myers, 'The Black Presence Through Criminal Records', *Immigrants & Minorities*, 7, 3 (No-

vember 1988), 292–307; Folarin O. Shyllon, *Black People in Britain, 1555–1833* (London: Oxford University Press for Institute of Race Relations, 1977) & *Black Slaves in Britain* (London: Oxford University Press for Institute of Race Relations, 1974); James Walvin, *Black and White; The Negro and English Society, 1554–1945* (London: Allen Lane, The Penguin Press, 1973). Duffield, 'Skilled Workers or Marginalized Poor?' 67, identifies the birthplaces of its 195 male convicts transported between 1812 and 1852 as England, 19.5%; Ireland, 1.5%; Scotland, 1.5%; Africa; 7.7%; North America, 33.3%; West Indies plus Bermuda and the Bahamas, 30.8%; Other, 5.6%. The last category includes no Madagascans but 3 Mauritians for whom Madagascan descent is possible. As for Duffield's six female black convicts (see *ibid.*, 71), none was born in Madagascar, one in Mauritius and therefore possibly of Madagascan descent.

20. Gillen, 63.
21. Watkin Tench (ed. L. F. Fitzhardinge), *Sydney's First Four Years. A Narrative of the Expedition to Botany Bay and A Complete Account of the Settlement at Port Jackson* (originally two works, 1st editions, London, 1789 & 1793; this edition, North Sydney: Library of Australian History, 1979), 103, n. 10.
22. Archives Office of New South Wales, *Printed Indents of Convict Ships*, 1838, per ship *Moffat*, lists a black convict called Jacko, sentenced in Antigua on 3 March 1835 to transportation for life. He had already spent time in Van Diemen's Land, where he had arrived aboard the *Lady Nugent* on 12 November 1836.
23. Here is a selection of the names of slaves listed in the Cape Province Archives, CSC/1/1/1/3, *Prison Return To the Supreme Court of the Cape of Good Hope at the Criminal Sessions Closed on [n.d.] of November 1830* Adonis; Salie *alias* Solomon; Isaac; Dianna; Mentor; Phillis; Philander. Note that the bible competes with classical literature as a validating ideological cover for a nasty set of power relations. Similar paste gems from the Cape Province Archives, CSC/1/2/1/10, *Return of all Prisoners in Criminal Cases – Circuit Court of the District of Somerset, 17 October 1832,* include Greet Adventure, Roman Cupido, Windvogel Sturman, Flora, Africa, Appollus and two men called Gallant. The last three were slaves, all the others serflike Khoi servants. The question of slave names is discussed at greater length in Ian Duffield, 'Naming Namoroa', unpublished paper presented at 'Africans and Caribbeans in Britain Writing, History and Society – A Conference in Celebration of Paul Edwards', New College, University of Edinburgh, 21–23 March 1994. That paper, and this present one, acknowledge the crucial importance of Orlando Patterson, *Slavery and Social Death; A Comparative Study* (Cambridge, Mass. & London: Harvard University

Press, 1982), 5 & 55–8, for grasping the significance of names imposed on black slaves by white masters.

24. Olaudah Equiano (with introduction by Paul Edwards), *The Life of Olaudah Equiano or Gustavus Vassa The African* (2 Vols., London, 1789; reprinted London: Dawsons of Pall Mall, 1969), Vol. 1, 93 & 96.

25. Ian Duffield, 'Identity, Community and the Lived Experience of Black Scots from the Late Eighteenth to the Mid-Nineteenth Centuries', *Immigrants & Minorities*, 11, 2 (July 1992), 105–29, esp. 112–115; Duffield, 'Naming Namoroa', further speculates that because of the phonetic closeness of Namoroa to the Portuguese *namorado* (sweetheart – an arbitrary enough name for a slave to have imposed on him), even this may not be a genuine African name. The Portuguese slave ports on the coast of Mozambique supplied a high proportion of Mauritius's mainland African slaves.

26. Archives Office of New South Wales, *Printed Indents of Convict Ships,* 1834, entry for Charles Cesar per ship *Dart,* arrived Sydney from Mauritius 9 July 1834; Archives Office of Tasmania, Con 37/1, *Conduct Registers of Male Convicts Arriving on Non-Convict Ships or Locally Convicted,* 1840–93, No. 152, Caesar, arrived Hobart Town per ship *Agenoria* from Mauritius, 1843. For African-Mauritians in the 1830s and after, see Marina Carter, 'The Transition from Slave to Indentured Labour in Mauritius', *Immigrants and Minorities,* 14, 1 (April 1993), 114–30; Marina Carter & Hubert Gerbeau, 'Covert Slaves and Coveted Coolies in the Early Nineteenth-Century Mascareignes', in *The Economics of the Indian Ocean Slave Trade,* 194–228. The difference between Cesar and Caesar is merely a matter of differing recording of the same name in the N.S.W. convict ship indents, the clerk in the latter case presumably having a smattering of French.

27. A Khoi man of this name born in the Cape Colony occurs in Archives Office of Tasmania, Con 35/1, *Conduct Registers of Male Convicts Arriving Under the Assignment System on Non-Convict Ships and on the Strength in November 1844.* He had apparently arrived in Australia free (possibly as servant to an officer who had previously served at the Cape; his trade is recorded as Groom) and was sentenced at Sydney Quarter Sessions on 13 October 1837 to transportation for seven years and arrived in Van Diemen's Land *per Marian Watson,* 30 October 1837. His V. D. L. Police Number was 799. Khoi were never technically chattel slaves in the Cape Colony but by the 1830s most had become labourers or peons to white masters; see Clifton C. Crais, *White Supremacy and Black Resistance in Pre-Industrial South Africa; The Making of the European Colonial Order in the Eastern Cape, 1770–1865* (Cambridge:

Cambridge University Press, 1992), 28, 40–44, 50–52 & 58. For the transportation of blacks from the Cape to Australia, see L. C. Duly, '"Hottentots to Hobart and Sydney"; The Cape Supreme Court's Use of Transportation', *Australian Journal of Politics and History*, 25, 3 (1979), 39–50 and V.C. Malherbe, 'Khoikhoi and the Question of Convict Transportation from the Cape Colony', *South African Historical Journal*, 17 (1985), 19–39.

28. Collins, *op. cit.*, 371, 378, 381 & 73.
29. Gillen, *op. cit.*, 385–6.
30. Ian Duffield, 'The Life and Death of "Black" John Goff; Aspects of the Black Convict Contribution to Resistance Patterns During the Transportation Era in Eastern Australia', *Australian Journal of Politics and History*, 33, 1 (1987), 36. For a recent analysis of the wider significance of anthropometry in the history of racism and imperialism as well as in South Asia, see Crispin Bates, 'Race, Caste and Tribe in Central India; Early Origins of Indian Anthropometry', in Peter Robb (ed.), *The Concept of Race in South Asia* (Delhi: Oxford University Press, 1995); Clare Anderson, 'The Genealogy of the Modern Subject Indians in Mauritius 1814–1853', forthcoming in Ian Duffield and James Bradley (eds.), *Representing Convicts*, (Leicester University Press, 1996).
31. Fitzhardinge, introduction to Collins, *op. cit.*, xix & xx.
32. For an example of a convict with such a consciousness, see the narrative by 'Jack Bushman' (i.e. the convict Thomas Brooks), *Passages from the Life of a 'Lifer'* (*Moreton Bay Courier*, Brisbane, 2, 9, 16, 23 & 30 April 1859). This narrative was long forgotten till rediscovered by Evans and Thorpe, who draw attention to its importance in 'Power, Punishment and Penal Labour'. Also see Ian Duffield, 'Problematic Passages; "Jack Bushman's" Convict Narrative', publication forthcoming in Duffield & Bradley (eds.) *Representing Convicts*.
33. Collins, *op. cit.*, 57.
34. James Scott, *Remarks on a Passage to Botany Bay 1787–1792. A First Fleet Journal* (Sydney: Trustees of the Public Library of New South Wales in association with Angus & Robertson, 1963), 48–8 has Caesar absconding on 13 May 1789 and being captured on 6 June 1789. This is one of only two First Fleet Narrative written by other ranks; Scott was a Marine Sergeant. His manuscript remained unpublished until 1963. The other such narrative is John Easty's *Memarandom* (sic).
35. *ibid.*, 49, states 'Black Caesar...was taken, About. twelve Oclock At Night by. Saltmarsh a Convict, Close to Mr. Zacharyah Clark's House'. Clark had travelled with the First Fleet as agent to the shipping contractor William Richards and was

appointed commissary i/c issue of provisions soon after his arrival in N.S.W; see Gillen, *op. cit.*, 72. His residence was
surely worth a nocturnal visit by Caesar. The incident shows
how easily the roles of thief and thief-taker were reversible in
early N.S.W., for Saltmarsh had himself received 50 lashes on
11 August 1788 for being found drunk on stolen spirits and
his later record includes two further floggings for theft; *ibid.*,
322.

36. Collins, *op. cit.*, 58.
37. *ibid.*, 58–9.
38. *Convict Workers*, 161–4, discusses the question of discipline and
    incentives in the extraction of labour from convicts.
39. Hazel Marshall, 'Convict Pioneers and the Failure of the Manage-
    ment System on Melville Island, 1824–29', *Push; A Journal of Early
    Australian Social History*, 29 (1991), 29–46.
40. Maxwell-Stewart demonstrates that in Van Diemen's Land the con-
    victs most frequently arraigned for offences were those in isolated
    penal stations, ironed-gangs and road parties, in that order; see 'The
    Bushrangers and the Convict System in Van Diemen's Land', 98,
    figure 4.1. The absconding rate in VDL was highest among convicts
    in road parties, ironed-gangs and at penal stations, in that order;
    ibid., 136, figure 4.11.
41. Bradley *op. cit.*, 186, states Caesar absconded on 22 December 1789.
42. Collins, *op. cit.*, 73. The only item Caesar lacked from the subsequent
    usual (and necessarily stolen) survival kit of convicts who escaped
    into the bush hoping to establish their freedom is a kangaroo dog.
    The significance of kangaroo dogs for early Van Diemen's Land ab-
    sconders is extensively discussed in Marie Fels, 'Culture Contact in
    the County of Buckinghamshire, Van Diemen's Land, 1803–1811',
    *Tasmanian Historical Research Association; Journal and Proceed-
    ings*, 29 (1982), 47–79. Essential equipment of convict absconders
    is also discussed in Duffield, 'Problematic Passages'. There is no evi-
    dence that lurcher dogs suitable for kangaroo hunting accompanied
    the First Fleet, so they were not an option for Caesar to acquire.
43. Bradley, *op. cit.*, 186, gives the date Caesar surrendered himself as
    31 January 1789.
44. For the general importance of Aborigines in the tracking of con-
    vict absconders in N.S.W., see Paula Jane Byrne, *Criminal Law
    and Colonial Subject; New South Wales 1810–1830* (Cambridge:
    Cambridge University Press, 1993), 141–3 & 145. Duffield, 'The Life
    and Death of "Black" John Goff...', 33 & 'Problematic Passages',
    discuss the crucial importance of 'native constables' as trackers
    in apprehending convict absconders; 'Problematic Passages' also
    discusses independent Aboriginal bands as alternately formidable

opponents and invaluable assisters of absconders; Marie Fels, *Good Men and True; The Aboriginal Police of the Port Phillip District, 1837–1853* (Melbourne: Melbourne University Press, 1988) provides a detailed account of a formally constituted and uniformed mounted Aboriginal police force.

45. Collins, *op. cit.*, 76.
46. Judicious analysis of contending views on why Norfolk Island was settled occurs in Ged Martin, 'The Founding of New South Wales', in Pamela Statham (ed.), *The Origins of Australia's Capital Cities* (Cambridge & Sydney: Cambridge University Press, 1989), 37–51. A review of both the literature and the event is given by Frank Clarke in R. Nobbs (ed.), *Norfolk Island and its First Settlement 1788–1814* (North Sydney: Library of Australian History, 1988), ch. 4, 28–36. Also see Malcolm Britts, 'The Commandants', *ibid.*, ch. 6, 70–74; Margaret Hazzard, *Punishment Short of Death; A History of the Penal Settlement at Norfolk Island* (Melbourne: Hyland House, 1984), chs. 1 & 2.
47. Hazzard, *Punishment Short of Death*, 25–6; Gillen, *op. cit.*, 314.
48. Collins, *op. cit.*, 80; for more information on Irving, see Gillen, *op. cit.*, 188–9, in which he is given as John Irvine plus many aliases.
49. Gillen, *op. cit.*, 63, states that Caesar returned to Sydney on the *Kitty* in March 1793, without further information. Collins, 232, mentions the *Kitty's* arrival at Sydney on 21 March 1793 but makes no mention of Caesar disembarking.
50. Collins, *op. cit.*, 319–20.
51. Collins, *op. cit.*, 371. The original raids were on crops and property, probably because the Hawkesbury Aborigines felt the settlers owed recompense for the rich hunting and gathering grounds they had appropriated. The ensuing cycle of violence illustrates both indiscriminate retaliation by whites and the Aborigines' practice of 'reciprocity', in this instance reciprocal retaliation for wrongs committed.
52. Collins, *op. cit.*, 371.
53. For the killing of Pemulwy and the spearing of 'Collins', see Collins, *op. cit.*, 371–2. For the spearing and subsequent death of McIntire, *ibid.*, 117–8 & 122. For the manner in which 'Collins' became a dependent of the settlement and acquired his new name, see *ibid.*, 250–1.
54. *ibid.*, 118–9.
55. Several instances are summarised in Duffield, 'The Life and Death of "Black" John Goff . . . ', 36–7; also see Marshall, 'Convict Pioneers', 29–46. This is not to argue that black convicts, or even convicts generally, were invariably at loggerheads with Aborigines. Recent unpublished research by Richard Walsh of the Department of His-

tory, University of Edinburgh, has revealed remarkable instances of combined operations by absconded convicts and resistant Aborigines on the Hawkesbury River in the late 1790s. Jack Bushman's *Passages in the Life of a 'Lifer'* contains much information on vital assistance given by Aborigines to himself when 'on the run'. The whole question of convict-Aborigine interaction is evidently much more complex than the widely held view that convicts were brutal to Aborigines and that Aborigines retaliated, when able, in kind.

56. Collins, *op. cit.*, 376–7.
57. I avoid calling this 'bushranging' (the usual Australian word for banditry, though not then current) as this is not a satisfactory definitional term. It embraces disparate phenomena under crucially differing political and perhaps moral economies. Caesar may only be a precursor of Ned Kelly in a temporal sense. The most extended and valuable analysis of early bushranging is Maxwell-Stewart, 'The Bushrangers and the Convict System of Van Diemen's Land'. Maxwell-Stewart establishes that V.D.L. bushrangers (and by implication those in early New South Wales?), were not all convict 'bolters'. The best study of bushranging in penal era New South Wales is in Byrne, *Criminal Law and Colonial Subject*, ch. 5, which views bushranging as a complex set of cultural practices, involving the colonial state, its courts, magistrates and judges, the police and the general population, convict and free, as well as the bushrangers themselves. A research project by Richard Walsh at the Department of History, University of Edinburgh, on 'The Birth of Bushranging in New South Wales, 1788–1810', commenced on 1 October 1995 and should elucidate the embryonic circumstances stages of Australian banditry.
58. Collins, *op. cit.*, 377.
59. *ibid.*, 378–9.
60. On the place of spirits in early New South Wales, see N. G. Butlin, 'Yo, Ho, Ho, and How Many Bottles of Rum', *Australian Economic History Review*, 23, 1 (March 1983), 1–27; D.R. Hainsworth, *The Sydney Traders; Simeon Lord and his Contemporaries 1788–1821* (Cassell Australia, 1971), 21–34 & 47–62.
61. Collins, *op. cit.*, 381.
62. *ibid.*, 381; for further information on Wimbow, see *ibid.*, 604, n. 11.
63. Discussed in *Convict Workers*, 183 & 195.
64. Collins, *op. cit.*, 26 reveals that as early as mid-1788 convicts were plundering government livestock and eating their 8 lbs a week flour rations in 3–4 days; for Collins, this was wicked improvidence but it also suggests hunger. By September 1788, it was clear that the first wheat crops around Sydney and at Norfolk Island were a failure and so on 2 October 1788 the *Sirius* departed for the Cape of

Good Hope for further provisions; at once the flour ration was reduced – see Collins, 33–5. In November 1789 rations were reduced across the board to two-thirds; Collins, 68–9. This was after Caesar's first escape but illustrates a trend which reduced the colony to near starvation before fresh supplies arrived. It took several years before N.S.W. produced its own basic food needs although the critical period was over by 1795–6. For a detailed evaluation of the dietary needs and estimated actual diet of convicts who performed the heaviest labour, see Hamish Maxwell-Stewart, '*Convict Workers,* "Penal Labour" and Sarah Island; Life at Macquarie Harbour', forthcoming in Duffield & Bradley (eds.,) *Representing Convicts.*

65. Tench, *op. cit.,* 159, n. *.
66. *ibid.,* 220.
67. Allen, 'Marronage and the Maintenance of Public Order in Mauritius', 227–9.
68. Bradley, *op. cit.,* 186.
69. Evans and Thorpe's views on the authenticity of 'convict voices' are contested in Duffield, 'Problematic Passages', drawing on methods adopted by radical studies of slave narratives and eighteenth-century English criminal biographies. As a courtesy to valued colleagues whose work inspired rather than provoked my response, I have kept Ray Evans and Bill Thorpe informed of this forthcoming publication and provided them with hard copy of my text to enable an early response if they wish. I have received friendly and constructive communications in return. Similar methodological problems exist in interpreting oral evidence; they are excellently summarised in the introduction to Alistair Thomson, *Anzac Memories; Living With the Legend* (Melbourne: Oxford University Press, 1994), 7–13.
70. For the parentage and birth of young Mary Ann Power, see Gillen, *op. cit.,* 63. For convict gender relations, see Marian Aveling (now Quartly), 'The Action of Gender in Early New South Wales', *Push from the Bush,* 24 (April 1987), 31–40 and 'Imagining New South Wales as a Gendered Society', 1783–1821', *Australian Historical Studies,* 25, 98 (April 1992), 1–12; Alan Atkinson, 'Convicts and Courtship', in P. Grimshaw *et. al.* (eds.), *Families in Colonial Australia* (Sydney: George Allen & Unwin, 1985), 19–31; Deborah Oxley, 'Convict Maids', unpublished Ph.D. thesis, University of New South Wales (1991), ch. 6; and for extensive evidence that convict gender relations were not merely nasty and brutish and convict women not generally sluttish whores, Robinson, *op. cit.,* chs. 7, 10 & 11.
71. The best account and analysis of such relations in late eighteenth- and early nineteenth-century Britain is Norma Myers, 'In Search of the Invisible British Black Family and Community', *Slavery and*

Abolition, 13, 3 (Dec. 1992), 156–80. There is no systematic study yet available of gender relations and family formation between black convict men and white women in Australia. However, the author has enough unpublished research data on this matter to be confident that the British pattern was transmitted to Australia. For the *de facto* marriage to a white convict woman of another early N.S.W. male black convict, their six children and numerous subsequent descendants, see Ian Duffield, 'Billy Blue: A Legend of Early Sydney', *History Today* (February 1987), 43–48. I have recently been in correspondence with Ms Wendy Holland, a postgraduate at the Centre for Indigenous Australian Cultural Studies at the University of Western Sydney, Macarthur Campus, concerning her African convict ancestor, born in Sierra Leone. An Australian-born son of this man married an Aboriginal woman in Queensland and Ms Holland is descended from them. This is by no means the first contact I have had with Australians of black convict ancestry though in also having Aboriginal ancestry Ms Holland so far stands alone among Australians known to myself. For information on the marriages of black First Fleeters, see n. 93 below.

72. Gillen, *op. cit.,* 63.
73. Maxwell-Stewart, 'The Bushrangers and the Convict System of Van Diemen's Land', ch. 5, 152–191, 'The Structure of Resistance Banditry, Protest and the Early Economy', comes to this conclusion for V. D. L. 1805–18.
74. Byrne, *Criminal Law and Colonial Subject,* ch. 5, esp. 135–7, 139–44 & 146–8.
75. A very large literature exists on social banditry. E. J. Hobsbawm, *Primitive Rebels Studies in Archaic Forms of Social Movement in the Nineteenth and Twentieth Centuries* (Manchester, 1959), provided the initial theory and case studies of social banditry. Many subsequent publications by Hobsbawm and others have modified his original position and others have challenged it outright. Unfortunately, analytical studies and popular accounts of Australian social banditry crowd around the Kelly Gang in North-East Victoria in the 1870s – early '80s. Examples of analytical studies are F. J. McQuilton, *The Kelly Outbreak 1878–1880; The Geographical Dimension of Social Banditry* (Melbourne: Melbourne University Press, 1979); P. O'Malley, 'Class Conflict, Land and Social Banditry; Bushranging in Colonial Australia', *Social Problems,* 26, 3 (1979), 271–83.
76. *Criminal Law and Colonial Subject,* 143–5.
77. The reality of their daring heroism and of the validity of their claim to epitomise Australian democratic values and loyalties has been entertainingly debunked by Humphrey McQueen, *A New Britannia;*

An Argument Concerning the Social Origins of Australian Radicalism and Nationalism (Ringwood: Penguin Books Australia, 1971), 139–42. The Australian literature cited in n. 74 above sharply diverges from McQueen in arguing that the Kelly Gang were indeed social bandits with widespread subordinate class support. The studies by Maxwell-Stewart and Byrne cited in this paper are certainly not compatible with McQueen's position, which is as crude as the notions he debunks and is based on highly selective use of a limited range of published sources, rather than serious archive research. Research is not neglected in Byrne's chapter and is richly evident in Maxwell-Stewart's full-length study of V. D. L.

78. The 'death or liberty' ethos of early bushranging is discussed in Byrne, *Criminal Law and Colonial Subject,* 129 & 130–31; Duffield, 'The Life and Death of "Black" John Goff'.

79. Linebaugh, 'Tyburnography The Sociology of the Condemned', *The London Hanged,* ch. 3, 74–90.

80. Sheppard's spectacular career is related and analysed in *The London Hanged,* ch. 1, 11–41; also see Philip Rawlings, *Drunks, Whores and Idle Apprentices; Criminal Biographies in the Eighteenth Century* (London: Routledge, Chapman & Hall Inc., 1992), 47–78.

81. Duffield, 'The Life and Death of "Black" John Goff...', 33–4.

82. *ibid.,* 36.

83. Apart from London being the focus of England's then black population, black seamen were a large element of London's and the UK's blacks by occupation. See Myers, 'Servant, Sailor, Soldier, Taylor, Beggarman', 57–8 which finds 26% of her sample of black males recorded in the *Old Bailey Sessions Papers* and the *Newgate Calendars* from 1785–1830 to have been seamen, the largest single occupation group. However, the occupations of 49.6 % of this sample are not recorded in these sources. Duffield, 'Skilled Workers or Marginalized Poor', 58–60, finds 36.4%, the largest single occupational category among his sample of 1812–1852 black male transportees from Britain to have been seamen and an additional 3.1% to have been in waterfront occupations (sailmakers, caulkers, watermen and boatmen). Even without the latter, again seamen exceed any other black male occupational group. In both samples domestic servants are the second largest occupational category.

84. This is brilliantly argued in Peter Linebaugh and Marcus Rediker, 'The Many Headed Hydra Sailors, Slaves and the Atlantic Working Class in the Eighteenth Century', *Journal of Historical Sociology,* 3, 3 (1990), 224–252.

85. For a classic analysis of the historical and cultural significance of such trickster figures, see Lawrence W. Levine, *Black Culture and Black Consciousness; Afro-American Folk Thought from Slavery to*

Freedom (New York: Oxford University Press, 1977), esp. ch. 2.

86. Slave folk-tale tricksters often sucker fellow subordinate animals as well as the predatory powerful animals. The moral is that tricksters can be dangerous to know, if inspirational at a safe distance, for the black oppressed. The same might be said of Australian bushrangers. Whether the Aborigines of very early N.S.W. can be equated with the 'weaker animals' (i.e. of course the slaves themselves) of slave folk tale is a moot point as they generally exhibited great confidence in dealings with whites, and not without good reason, especially in the bush.

87. Ranajit Guha, 'The Prose of Counter Insurgency'. in R. Guha (ed.), *Subaltern Studies II. Writings on South Asian History and Society* (Delhi, Oxford University Press, 1983), 1–42. Although Guha's critique is directed at South Asian peasant resistance, his arguments may be adopted in the present instance. Guha adheres to a Gramscian understanding of subaltern/subalternity.

88. Keneally, *op. cit.*, 6. The language is Al Jolson jostling with a blackface Maurice Chevalier.

89. *ibid.*, 162.

90. This immediately recalls the scurrilous lines of the late eighteenth-century plantocratic racist, Edward Long; 'The lower class of women in *England*, are remarkably fond of the blacks, for reasons too brutal to mention; they would connect themselves with horses and asses if the law permitted them', quoted in Fryer, *Staying Power*, 157. Long's remarks are a telling early instance of the interaction of the discourses of sex, race and class.

91. *The Playmaker*, 7.

92. Gillen, *The Founders of Australia*, 145. I am confident both of Mollie Gillen's painstaking thoroughness as a scholar and that she would not sweep anything under the historical carpet.

93. John Martin married Ann Joy (*per Neptune* 1790) in 1792, marriage terminated by Joy's death in 1806; he remarried to Mary Randall, possibly the daughter of his fellow black First Fleeter John Randall, in 1812 and left property to his five children by her in his will – see *ibid.*, 239. Thomas Orford married Elizabeth Jones *alias* Osborne on 24 March 1788 – see *ibid.*, 269; John Randall married Esther Howard or Harwood on 21 February 1788; she died 11 October 1789 and he then remarried to Mary Butler on 5 September 1790 and they subsequently had two daughters – see *ibid.*, 296. The same source records Martin and Randall as accumulating significant petty property, making them modest colonial success stories. It is no part of the argument of this essay that all black convicts were budding John Caesars or John Goffs.

94. *ibid.*, 212.

95. *The Playmaker*, 81.
96. *ibid.*, 196–201. The historical Mary Brenham became the convict mistress of the historic Lt. Clark and had a daughter by him; see Gillen, *op. cit.*, 47 & 72.
97. Widely discussed in Fryer, *Staying Power*, 146–65. William Hogarth's *Four Times of Day – Noon*, first state, 1747, engraving, both illustrates and utilises, for satirical purpose, earthy and natural sexuality between a black man and a white woman. This pair are the most prominent figures in a plebeian crowd. Both are young and vigorous; the man stands close behind the woman, kissing her cheek which is appreciatively turned to him. His arms are around her waist and clasped to it by hers, his hands fondle her exposed breasts. White liquid streaming from a large pie she is absent-mindedly tilting suggests extreme arousal. On the other side of the picture is a foppishly effete crowd of persons of fashion, some etiolated, others gross. The two most prominent figures are also a man and woman. In contrast to the other side of the engraving and life, they simper at each other at arm's length, the man gesturing affectedly. Both give the air of finding their greatest satisfaction in displaying their expensive and absurdly elaborate clothes, rather than expression of natural desire. There can be no doubt as to which side of the picture Hogarth intends the viewer to sympathise with, which to censure! For an expert analysis of this engraving, see David Dabydeen, *Hogarth's Blacks; Images of Blacks in Eighteenth Century English Art* (Mundelstrup, Denmark: Dangaroo Press, 1985), 63. This work offers a brilliant general study of Hogarth's repeated utilisation of black figures to satirise the pretensions, follies, greed and crimes of the Hanoverian upper classes, thus breaching a previous total silence in studies of Hogarth. That silence is all the more pointed in that Dabydeen's many eminent predecessors agreed on the purposeful placement, 'to yield specific meaning', of every detail in Hogarth's works (see *Hogarth's Blacks*, 9).
98. I tactfully leave it to informed readers to judge if there is any truth in these outrageous allegations. They are in the made in the creatively mischievous spirit of the late Paul Edwards and the Belgian surrealist-anarchist No'l Godin (a.k.a. Monsieur Gloupier). To Godin's sublime example, Keneally owes his novel's *entarté* (or custard-pie-in-the-face) treatment in my essay. Following in the steps of the Belgian master, I award Keneally this delicious punitive treat for his cultural reproduction of pernicious twaddle. The weight of his literary and republican prestige add to the severity of the offence. As a prominent supporter of Australia's delivery from vestigial colonialism, he should take his cream tart like a penitent. Such penitence is, alas, not very likely, as he reputedly adheres to the 'Critics? I

wouldn't feed the bastards!' school of novelists. *Flanneurs du monde scolaire! Aux tartes! Entartez* at will! Over and out – with a sudden duck below the parapet to evade hostile incoming *tartes*.

99. Thuggee (from which, of course, derives the English word thug) was a supposed clandestine criminal cult of the Hindu deity Kali in nineteenth-century India. Its adherents allegedly ritually strangled their victims with a silk scarf by night before robbing them and burying their corpses. It now transpires that the British not only suppressed Thuggee but also virtually invented it, major entrepreneurial official and literary careers being made in the process. See Sanjay Nigram, 'Disciplining and Policing the "Criminals by Birth"', Part 1, *Indian Economic and Social History Review,* XXVII, 2 (1990), Part 2, *Indian Economic and Social History Review,* XXVII, 3 (1990); R. Inden, *Imagining India* (Oxford: Oxford University Press, 1990), 36–48 & 85–93; R. Singha, '"Providential Circumstances"; The Thuggee Campaign of the 1830s and Legal Innovation', *Modern Asian Studies,* 27, 1 (1993), 83–146. The colonialist/orientalist texts on Thuggee, which invented it and till recently were taken as gospel evidence, are innumerable; e.g. W. Sleeman (ed. Vincent A. Smith), *Rambles and Recollections of an Indian Recruiting Officer* (London, 1915); E. Thornton, 'The Thugs or Phansigars', *Foreign Quarterly Review,* 21 (April 1838), 1–32. One can add the nineteenth-century novels, essays and reminiscences of Philip Meadows Taylor, John Master's novel *The Deceivers* (1959, based on Meadows-Taylor's 1839 *Confessions of a Thug*), the Merchant-Ivory film *The Deceivers* (based on Master's novel) and of course in the mass-audience category, *Indiana Jones and the Temple of Doom.* Evidently, although the orientalist construction of Thuggee has been trounced intellectually, in western popular culture it still generates fortunes for the cultural entrepreneurs who repackage it for mass-consumption. Come on, suckers!

100. *The Playmaker,* 299.

101. For an example of his thinking on the necessity for an Australian republic, see Keneally, 'Towards a More Democratic Australia', in Donald Horne *et. al., The Coming Republic* (Sydney: Pan Macmillan Publishers Australia, 1992), 189–94.

102. *The Playmaker* has already generated a play, Timberlake Wertenbaker's *Our Country's Good.* For an analysis of this play and Keneally's novel, see Ruth Brown, 'From Keneally to Wertenbaker; Sanitising the System', forthcoming in Duffield & Bradley (eds.), *Representing Convicts.* Ruth Brown's study proceeds along its own lines, e.g. being informed by the critical theory of Frederic Jameson. Of particular relevance is her perceptive observation that 'Keneally assigns parts to names from historical record and this in itself lends

an air of authenticity... There is an evident fascination with "facts" in the novel: details of crimes the convicts had been sentenced for, their slang, how food was rationed, how Sydney and Manly were so named, and relations between the officers. The question, what evidence was employed in garnering these "facts", might be less important than why they are likely to be accepted without question'. Quite so! Two Keneally novels, *The Chant of Jimmy Blacksmith* and *Schindler's Ark* (now better know by the title of the film version, 'Schindler's List') have been turned into feature films.

103. By contrast, Thomas Keneally's novel *The Chant of Jimmy Blacksmith,* and the film of the same title based on it, are powerful and effective indictments of racist oppression of Aborigines.

104. I am most grateful to Dr. Anne King of the Department of English Language, University of Edinburgh, an authority on Scots linguistics, for telling me this anecdote illustrating the difference between stubborn and thrawn. For those with no Scots, the thrawn man's last words, in translation, could be given as 'well, I suspect I must perhaps take it, but kindly note my good fellow, you will not make me pass a motion'. Unfortunately the pithiness of the original loses somewhat in translation into polite standard English.

105. The tradition concerning the death of John Wimbow and his partner was conveyed to me by the late Russel Ward, a great expert on Australian folklore as well as a great historian. My warmest thanks go to Deborah Oxley and Barrie Dyster for permitting me to submit, *in absentia,* this essay in an earlier form as a paper at their conference 'Beyond Convict Workers', University of New South Wales, Sydney, 27 October 1995; and to Bill Thorpe, for agreeing to present it on my behalf, despite then being snowed under with current work. My thanks also go to various of my final year undergraduate and postgraduate students, especially Richard Walsh, for pointing out guff in earlier drafts. Such guff as remains is all of my own.

Wordsworth in the Tropics Reconsidered: *Michael* and the West African Reader[1]

Paul Edwards

One of the pleasures of teaching English Literature overseas is the occasional discovery that the work can take on new life from the alien environment of the reader, so that the teacher is himself taught, and offered new insights and enjoyments by what is familiar to his pupils. Much of the time, the reverse is the case, the language being too heightened, complex or obscure for readers with an uncertain grasp of English, and the subject matter too remote from their experience and needs. When I began teaching in Ghana in the early 1950s much of the teaching of literature was still a relic of the imposition of English values on a society which for various reasons sometimes found them unacceptable or incomprehensible. If the teacher perceives his task as more than that of propagandist for a culture, it soon becomes clear that the explication of linguistic and cultural puzzles has its limitations as a mode of literary education, and that it is important to find points of contact between the work being read and the experience and values of the reader. I found in Wordsworth's *Michael* a striking example of how this might come about.

In the 'Preface' to the *Lyrical Ballads* Wordsworth, in a grand but perhaps over ambitious zeal for human brotherhood, proposed that poetry should be universal:

> The poet binds together by passion and knowledge the vast empire of human society as it is spread out over the whole earth and over all time . . . [2]

A sublime vision which might appear over-optimistic to the reader conscious of how varied 'the things really important to men' can be. But curiously it might be the modern English reader who could find *Michael* an alien poem, and the African who might read it as a document for his people and his time. The feeling of Michael for his farmland, for instance, expresses something other than simple property ownership.

> I toiled and toiled. God blessed me in my work.
> And 'till these three weeks past the land was free.

- It looks as if it never could endure
Another master . . . (385–9)

He explains its importance to Luke, his son, in this way:

> . . . I still
> Remember them who loved me in my youth.
> Both of them sleep together: here they lived
> As all their Forefathers had done; and, when
> At length their time was come, they were not loth
> To give their bodies to the family mould. (380–84)

The poem is about continuity, the land is the ground of the ancestors, the 'family mould', in which they lie buried and through which contact with them is maintained. For this reason the sale of the land is as inconceivable to Michael as it would be to the Ashanti farmer, who, in the words of Geoffrey Parrinder,

> prays to his grandparents who have cultivated the land, and to Asase Ya, to give help in cultivation, preserve from accidents and snakebite, and give fruitful increase. The real owners of the land, here as elsewhere, are the ancestors, who have laboured there, who watch over the land still . . . [3]

R. S. Rattray's massive study, *Ashanti Law and Constitution*, refers to 'the virtual impossibility of the idea of anything in the nature of alienation of the land', which

> could not be taken away; except for a few feet where an ancestor lay buried, it was wholly dissociated from any particular individual; it therefore could never ordinarily be without some one who was interested in what it produced, because this interest was embodied in a community . . . It belonged absolutely to past, to present, and to future generations as yet unborn. Land could not be sold, land could not be given away, land could not be willed or be the subject of inheritance outside the tribe.[4]

I would not deny that there are differences between the precise conception of land amongst the Ashanti, and in Wordsworth's poem; but my West African students felt closer to the world of the poem and its values than did many of my students in Britain, who were strongly in favour of Luke's following his own fortune in the city, while the African students – many of them from small farming communities, though they themselves were, in the process of education, being assimilated into Ghana's expanding city life – recognised this as a living problematic issue, involving some loss close to home, shared by themselves, which deepened their sense of the poem as tragic. Rattray quotes the Ghanaian J. M. Sarbah on the closely related Fanti law and custom; 'with the exception of the coast towns, where there is much contact with European ideas, private property in the strict sense does not exist'.⁵ Though it might appear that Michael has a stronger sense of personal inheritance and ownership than that described by Rattray, and while he might be seen as, in a sense, one of Wordsworth's solitaries, he is also at the centre of farming community, his cottage lamp is 'famous in its neighbourhood . . . a public Symbol of the life/ The thrifty pair had lived' (135–7) and the poem might be called a memorial inscription, cut upon the 'straggling heap of unhewn stones' (17) to which the questioning eye is drawn, a common tale shared by the community from which it sprang, through the popular medium of its storytellers – 'not unfit, I deem, for the fire-side, / Or for the summer shade' (20–1). Indeed, Wordsworth's reverential sense of belonging to a community of storytellers, 'spread out over the whole earth and over all time' as the 'Preface' says, makes the retelling of the tale itself a communal act.

> For the delight of a few natural hearts
> And with yet fonder feeling, for the sake
> Of youthful Poets, who among these Hills
> Will be my second self when I am gone. (36–9)

This sense of non-urban community was another important factor for my West African students. Their response to Matthew Arnold's post-Wordsworthian *The Scholar Gypsy*, was one of puzzlement. Despite its countryside setting, its subject, a very deliberate withdrawal from community into isolation, made my African students, traditionally bound together in small communities, uneasy. 'Where does this man get his chop,' asked one perplexed student, 'who does his cooking?' and indeed sometimes in my efforts to provide an answer I was reduced to a flurry of eloquent literary handwaving, accompanied by noises about the pastoral tradition.⁶ The classic statement of the irrelevance of the Wordsworthian tradition to tropical audiences is Aldous Huxley's essay, 'Wordsworth in the Tropics':

> Wandering in the hothouse darkness of the jungle, [Wordsworth] would not have felt so serenely certain of those 'Presences of Nature', those 'Soules of Lonely Places', which he was in the habit of worshipping on the shores of Windermere and Rydal . . . There is something in what, for lack of a better word, we must call the character of great forests – even those of temperate lands – which is foreign, appalling, fundamentally and utterly inimical to intruding man.⁷

If Wordsworth's vision were to coincide with Huxley's picture of the 'chaste mild deity who presides over the Gemuthlichkeit, the cozy sublimities of the Lake District', Huxley's criticism might have more substance, but it raises more questions than it claims to answer. We might ask, why does he see the inhabitant of the great rain forests as 'intruding man'? Such a man will not see himself as an intruder: however precarious his life, this is his home and his existence is adapted to it. Huxley calls the supernatural inhabitants of the forest 'devils', but they are gods to the man in the forest, not all to be feared, and even their terrors are less of a threat to whoever submits to the guidance of the spirits of the forest, and honours them in accordance with ancient custom. In secular terms, he knows what to do and how the forest works. Huxley compares the overtones of the word 'river' in English and the jungle. In the latter, he asserts, 'Rivers imply wading, swimming, alligators'. Some of my students met this with amused head-shaking. To them, they explained, rivers meant convenient water supplies for drinking and washing, fish for eating, boats for transport and trade. One added enigmatically that where he came from, people and crocodiles understood one another very well. Huxley had got something wrong – he was after all himself largely a product of cozy English sublimities, and a different jungle.

Yet it is true that the 'chaste mild deity' may well appear a product of complacency when the bliss of solitude can be transformed into a nightmare of lonely isolation – as said above, the forest dweller can live where he does because he is able to form communities, and adapt to his environment, and though the deep woods may not be exactly the horror Huxley (like Mister Kurtz) sees them to be, they are often harsh and inimical. Wordsworth knew this well enough and an aspect of the sublimity of his vision which Huxley ignores comes closer to the ambiguous threat of Blake's tiger than to anything cozy:

> The immeasurable height
> Of woods decaying, never to be decayed,
> The stationary blasts of water-falls,
> And every where along the hollow rent
> Winds thwarting winds, bewildered and forlorn,
> The torrents shooting from the clear blue sky,
> The rocks that muttered close upon our ears,
> Black drizzling crags that spake by the way-side
> As if a voice were in them, the sick sight
> And giddy prospect of the raving stream,
> The unfettered clouds and region of the heavens,
> Tumult and peace, the darkness and the light

Were all like workings of one mind, the features
Of the same fact, blossoms upon one tree . . .
(*Prelude*, VI. 557–569)

Nothing very cozy about that vision! *Michael*, in fact, is a poem whose
landscape does not convey the sense of relaxed contentment under the
benevolent eye of the chaste goddess, the Wordsworthianism of *The
Scholar Gypsy* perhaps, to which Huxley so strongly objects. *Michael*
is properly seen, I think, in the context of a potentially tragic natural
world such as that of the intensely painful 'Ruined Cottage'. Michael's
world is one of mutual interdependency, he himself being 'a public
Symbol' for the community, 'all Who dwelt within the limits of the
vale' (144–5), and at the same time a solitary, living in communion
with an active universe in which 'the winds are now devising work for
me'. (56) 'My lot is a hard lot', he tells us: he and his son 'could stand
against the mountain blasts . . . not fearing toil, nor length of weary
ways' (204–6); there is little 'cozy' in a diet consisting of 'a mess of
pottage and skimmed milk' (102); above all, the landscape is bleak and
harsh, with scanty flocks, thin rocky vegetation, and poised predatory
hawks:

> but they
> Who journey thither find themselves alone,
> With a few sheep, with rocks and stones and kites
> That overhead are sailing in the sky.
> It is in truth an utter solitude . . . (9–13)

Such a landscape cannot be recognised as having much in common with
one in which, to quote Huxley again, 'nature has been nearly or quite
enslaved to man'. The world of Michael has much in common with
what is probably the best known and finest of modern West African
novels, Chinua Achebe's *Things Fall Apart*, its title from Yeats's
'Second Coming', prophetic of shattering social change:[8]

> The falcon cannot hear the falconer,
> Things fall apart, the centre cannot hold,
> Mere anarchy is loosed upon the world . . .

It is a novel about the break up of a way of community life under
shock of the new, the failure of relationships between father and son,
and between neighbouring village communities, a novel written for
reasons resembling those which Wordsworth gives for writing *Michael*,
to honour the land and the spirits of the ancestors. Achebe says:

> The ancestors are sending us signals from the long history
> and experience of bygone days about the meaning of life,
> the qualities we should cultivate and the values which are
> important. Because they are so far away and because we are
> surrounded by the tumult and distraction of daily life they

have to shout and repeat themselves not only in phrase after phrase but myth after myth . . . until the central message goes home . . . It is as though the ancestors who made language and knew from what bestiality its use rescued them are saying to us: Beware of interfering with its purpose . . . [9]

Similarly for Wordsworth:

Emphatically may it be said of the poet, as Shakespeare hath said of man, 'that he look before and after.' Poetry is the rock of defence of human nature, an upholder and preserver, carrying everywhere with him relationship and love.[10]

And, like Michael himself, Wordsworth's task is to find means to carry and sustain these relationships for the sake of past, present and future:

It was the first,
The earliest of those tales that spake to me
Of Shepherds, dwellers in the valleys, men
Whom I already loved, not verily
For their own sakes, but for the fields and hills
Where was their occupation and abode. (21–6)

The poem ends with the great cycle of nature, destruction and continuity, 'the darkness and the light' of the passage quoted from *The Prelude*, returning to the scene of its opening, focusing upon the 'straggling heap of unhewn stones' from which it began, the tragic, uncompleted work of man in the enduring landscape, pointing still to the sense of community in the tale it memorialises, of the father's lost hope, his despair of completing the sheepfold, the 'covenant' as the poem calls it between himself and his son.

. . . 'tis not forgotten yet,
The pity which was then in every heart
For the old man; and 'tis believed by all
That many and many a day he thither went,
And never lifted up a single stone. (462–6)

The tragic events remain in the memory of the living, and the task of the poet is to sustain that memory and convey its lasting significance, as Conrad was to write in the same spirit as Wordsworth:

[The artist] speaks . . . to the latent feeling of fellowship with all creation . . . which binds men to each other, which binds together all humanity – the dead to the living, the living to the unborn.[11]

Like *The Prelude*, the two-book version of which Wordsworth had completed two or three years before composing *Michael*, the poem draws upon 'whatever I find most interesting in Man, Nature, Society, most adapted to poetic illustration'.[12] Insofar as this is his purpose, Wordsworth does not separate 'Nature' from 'Man' or 'Society': as Huxley would have it the dark side of Nature is tragic, and in order to honour the dead and sustain the living the painful tale must be told and retold of the loss of community and land to strangers. In a part of the world where the young men were being drawn from the farms by the appearance of new wealth and new liberty, where the fathers appeared to have little to offer their sons to compete with city lights, the cinemas, the dance halls and the taxis, the sense of physical freedom and choice which the city was seen to offer, *Michael* could become a near-contemporary document, as it was for Wordsworth. But to Huxley, and to many modern British readers in a society already urbanised, it might well appear merely sentimental to lament the loosening of those ties. The poignancy of the poem may be less sharp than for the West African, who is likelier to feel close to Wordsworth's poem, and see in its final lines a record of immediate and terrible events, the loss of common ancestral land, the death of the tribe and the desecration of its graves, so that there is only the poet left to give comfort in the face of an indifferent nature from which the spirits seem to have been driven, or to pay respect to the ancestors and give any meaning to the past.

Notes

1. This essay is a revision and expansion of 'Wordsworth's *Michael* and the African Reader' published in *The Use of English*, XV, 4 (Summer 1964), 275–9.
2. From 'Preface to Lyrical Ballads', in *William Wordsworth (The Oxford Authors)*, ed. Stephen Gill (Oxford: Oxford University Press, 1984), 606.
3. Geoffrey Parrinder, *West African Religion* (London: Epworth Press, 1949), 49.
4. R. S. Rattray, *Ashanti Law and Constitution* (Oxford: Oxford University Press, 1959), 346. See also 361 'All land belonged . . . really to the spirits or the ancestors of the tribe. It was thus held for them, no less than for the living and yet unborn, by the occupants of the various stools [i. e. chiefdoms] who were constituted as trustees for the land . . . '.
5. *ibid.*, 335.
6. I discuss this in 'Hebraism, Hellenism and *The Scholar-Gypsy*' in Durham University Journal, June 1962, 121–7. Illustrating the

problem of assumed 'universality', Indian readers might well not experience such difficulties, in view of Arnold's acknowledged debt to the *Bhagavad Gita*. It is interesting that the seemingly naive question asked by my student about the apparent lack of contact with reality in the life of the Scholar Gypsy was more searching than appeared. It also troubled Arnold's mind, for in a letter to Clough discussed in the article he writes, 'I'm glad you liked my Gypsy Scholar. But what does it do for you?'

7. Aldous Huxley, *Do What You Will* (London: Chatto and Windus, 1949), 113–29.

8. Chinua Achebe, *Things Fall Apart* (London: Heinemann, 1958).

9. Chinua Achebe, 'Language and the Destiny of Man' in *Morning Yet on Creation Day* (London: Heinemann, 1975), 36–7.

10. 'Preface to Lyrical Ballads' in *William Wordsworth*, ed. Stephen Gill, 606.

11. Joseph Conrad, 'Preface to The Narcissus', in *The Nigger of the Narcissus, Typhoon, The Shadow Line* (London: Dent, Everyman Library, 1945), 3–4.

12. Wordsworth to De Quincy, March 6, 1804, quoted in *The Prelude, 1799, 1805, 1850* eds. Jonathan Wordsworth, M. H. Abrams, and Stephen Gill (New York and London: Norton Critical Edition, 1979), 531.

Wordsworth's 'Convulsive Inclination to Laughter': the Narrator's Voice in 'Goody Blake and Harry Gill'[1]

Paul Edwards

In his essay 'My First Acquaintance with Poets', Hazlitt described Wordsworth's appearance and speech:

> There was a severe, worn pressure of thought about his temples, a fire in his eye (as if he saw something in objects more than the outward appearance), an intense high narrow forehead, a Roman nose, cheeks furrowed by strong purpose and feeling, and a convulsive inclination to laughter about the mouth, a good deal at variance with the solemn, stately expression of the rest of his face . . . He sat down and talked very naturally and freely, with a mixture of clear gushing accents in his voice, a deep, guttural intonation, and a strong tincture of the northern *burr*, like the crust of wine.[2]

Laughter is certainly at odds with the solemnity with which, not only Wordsworth's, but most poetry is delivered and received, as fitting the assumed gravity of poetic purpose: yet many a poem in *Lyrical Ballads* displays this inclination to laughter, none more so I believe, than 'Goody Blake and Harry Gill', and the delivery of such poems in the grave or elevated tones of the conventional 'poetry reading voice' can only obscure the more relaxed and cheerful aspects of the work. Humanity is assuredly at the centre of Wordsworth's art, but its music is not always unremittingly sad, though the laughter about Wordsworth's mouth, as in the game he plays with the expectations of his 'gentle reader' in 'Simon Lee', is likely still to lead beyond amusement to thoughtful, sometimes sombre considerations.

In *The Simple Wordsworth* (1960), John Danby uses the poet's comments on *Lyrical Ballads* to demonstrate how accusations of naivety levelled against Wordsworth from the early nineteenth century to our own time, often stem from a failure to see – or rather to hear – poems as dramatic monologues uttered by narrators with their own limitations or axes to grind. Such ideas have been explored further in Stephen M. Parrish's fine study, *The Art of the Lyrical Ballads* (1973). Danby concentrates on three poems of the collection, 'Simon Lee', 'The Idiot Boy' and 'The Thorn', all of which have at one time or another been dismissed as silly-simple, but he pays little attention to 'Goody Blake and Harry Gill', believing that it 'approximates to straight narrative, with a neutral narrator'.[3]

This conclusion is certainly more generous than that of some commentators who appear to take their cue from Wordsworth's remark in the 'Preface' that the poem is 'one of the rudest of this collection'.[4] M. J. C. Hodgart sees it as no more than a naive tale in imitation of the broadside ballad. This appears to be the 'embarrassing fact' in Hodgart's mind when he writes: 'Wordsworth, curiously enough, was less influenced by Percy's *Reliques* or the traditional ballads than by the broadsides.' This embarrassing fact is proved by the way he quotes in his 'Preface' a stanza from 'The Children in the Wood'; and elsewhere his remarks on 'Goody Blake and Harry Gill' show that he was thinking of the broadsides. They did not do Wordsworth any good, but rather encouraged the naivety of his worst poetry.[5]

Hodgart's desire for a more 'elevated' balladry, such as he finds in the traditional ballads, indicates that he misses the point of Wordsworth's trust in common language and everyday incident argued in his letter to John Wilson,[6] the 'Preface' and elsewhere. The assumption that whatever is 'low' must be unsuitable for serious literary purposes was persistently debated throughout the Augustan period, the charge of indecorous lowness being levelled by Dryden against Shakespeare, reinforced by such revisions as his own of *Troilus and Cressida*, and Davenant's of *Macbeth* (1674). In his *Rambler* essay no. 168 (1751), Samuel Johnson makes similar objections to *Macbeth* as those implied by Davenant, and Johnson's objections to 'lowness' in poetry are in turn criticised by Wordsworth in his quotation from Johnson's ballad parody, 'I put my hat upon my head', which precedes the defence of 'The Children in the Wood' in the 'Preface'. The fastidious Addison had defended the ballads 'Chevy Chase' and 'The Children in the Wood' in *The Spectator*, essays 70, 74 and 85 (1711), and stirred up a hornet's nest of ridicule – many of the barbs have been assembled by Wimsatt.[7] The radical nature of Wordsworth's exploration of the language of the ballads went not only against an eighteenth-century critical tradition, but similarly conservative views which persisted in Coleridge's and Southey's criticisms of him. Hodgart's remarks confirm the survival of the tradition in our own century.

But Wordsworth was engaged in a remarkable experiment. As Parrish points out:

'Peter Bell', 'Goody Blake and Harry Gill', and 'The Thorn'
appear to have been 'experiments...written chiefly with a view
to ascertain how far the language of conversation in the middle
and lower classes of society is adapted to the purposes of poetic
pleasure' (1798 Advertisement [to the *Lyrical Ballads*]). But at
another level they are all experiments in narrative technique.
In 'Peter Bell' the poet adopts a colloquial voice much like that
of 'The Idiot Boy' . . . Even more boldly in 'Goody Blake and
Harry Gill', the poet adopts the point of view and the idiom
of a rustic narrator.[8]

However, Parrish sees this narrator as essentially naive, like that of
'The Thorn':

the narrator, unaware that his story only illustrates 'the power
of the human imagination' clearly believes in the reality of
Harry Gill's affliction. He thus reveals something of how his
own imagination works, and the poem verges on the dramatic
monologue form.[9]

Parrish has in mind Wordsworth's comment in the 'Preface':

...the power of verse alone, has contrived to make the plainest
commonsense interesting, and even frequently to invest it with
the appearance of passion. In consequence of these convictions
I related the Tale of GOODY BLAKE AND HARRY GILL,
which is one of the rudest of this collection. I wished to draw
attention to the truth, that the power of human imagination
is sufficient to produce such changes as might almost appear
miraculous.[10]

This gives greater credit to the word 'imagination' despite its proximity
in the quotation to the word 'rudest' than would justify the demeaning
'only...imagination' in Parrish.[11]

    Parrish also has in mind the 'Note' to 'The Thorn' in which
Wordsworth makes it clear that he is interested in the state of mind
of his narrator more than he is telling a story. In one of his letters he
observes that 'in poems of human nature, however short they may be,
character is absolutely necessary etc.; incidents are among the lowest
allurements of poetry'.[12] The 'Note' to 'The Thorn' establishes this as
central to the poet's purpose:

The poem...is not supposed to be spoken by the author's
person; the character of the loquacious narrator will show
itself in the course of the story . . . Superstitious men are always
men of slow faculties and deep feelings; they have a reasonable
share of imagination, by which I mean the faculty which

produces impressive effects out of simple elements, but they are utterly destitute of fancy, the power by which pleasure and surprise are excited by sudden varieties of situation and an accumulated imagery.[13]

I wish to argue that the narrator of 'Goody Blake and Harry Gill' represents a further stage in Wordsworth's experiment. I agree with Parrish that he 'clearly believes in the reality of Harry Gill's affliction', but do not accept that he is 'essentially naive' in his comic representation of it. What is 'real' for Harry is what he believes in, but the narrator of the poem, though he believes in the affliction all right, seems to me sceptical about its source, Harry's naivety, not his own.

Though the narrator may at times use naive expressions – the 'what's the matter' of the opening for instance – this is only one of several postures and guises he adopts in the course of his tale. He might appear to be a plain man telling a cautionary tale to a group of simple farmers, about a man much like themselves who has been struck down by supernatural powers, but though clearly Harry believes in the power of witchcraft, and the audience may believe so too if they wish, the storyteller adopts no such simple view. In Wordsworth's source, Erasmus Darwin's *Zoonomia*, the old woman is said to be 'like a witch in a play', (in any case a fairly ambivalent way of describing her), but in the poem she is not presented as a witch; indeed it is 'God, who art never out of hearing' whom she calls on for aid. Wordsworth's 'Note' to 'The Thorn' says that the poem is about 'some of the general laws by which superstition acts upon the mind'.[14] In this case, that mind is Harry Gill's not the narrator's, who looks on Harry's predicament with an ironic eye, as I shall argue.

Thus in the opening stanza, the first few lines sound naive enough, with their ingenuous exclamatory questions, 'Oh! what's the matter? what's the matter?' and the lugubrious repetitive insistence 'That evermore his teeth they chatter, / Chatter, chatter, chatter still'. Those teeth are still chattering at the end, 'like a loose casement in the wind', but even at the start the audience might catch more than a hint of clowning in the narrator's over-the-top manner. His sense of the absurd is reinforced by the subsequent over-accumulation of waistcoats, coats and blankets piled on Harry's back, and confirmed in the last line, 'coats enough to smother nine', by the word 'smother'. The word is not that of Danby's 'neutral narrator', but in common usage implies a recognition of something ridiculous – 'He was absolutely smothered'. In Harry's huge pile of coats we might find the first of several suggestions of grotesque and comic excess which punctuate the poem, introducing another persistent feature, a narrator who allows his audience to catch glimpses of himself winking and grimacing behind a mask of innocence. We get the note of comic inflation again in the third stanza: 'His cheeks were red as ruddy clover, / His voice was like the voice of three'. However appropriate clover might be as an image of Harry's profession as 'a lusty drover', its colour is more purplish than red, and hints at something potentially apoplectic in this florid, bellowing man. Big Harry is at once set beside the impoverished and underfed Goody:

> Old Goody Blake was old and poor,
> Ill-fed she was, and thinly clad;
> And any man who passed her door,
> Might see how poor a hut she had.

We might notice that the word 'old' is used in two senses, the literal, and the familial, as we might speak of 'Old George' to indicate friendship, not age. And the scene being set is one of social reality, any man might indeed pass her door. The narrator has not only suggested Harry's gross aggressive bulk for comic purposes, he has set it against a common and known world of poverty to make a compassionate social point out of the jest. This social point is developed in the subsequent three stanzas.

The narrator's sense of the absurd returns in the eighth and ninth stanzas. He draws attention again to Goody's poverty and helplessness:

> Now when the frost was past enduring,
> And made her poor old bones to ache
> Could anything be more alluring
> Than an old hedge to Goody Blake.

The ironic word, 'alluring', with its suggestion of luxurious temptations and sensuous delights is qualified by the reality of how little Goody really asks for, 'an old hedge'. This is what Harry fails to see, how little that is which he denies her in her extreme need. The ninth stanza accumulates words which convey a sense that Harry's self-righteous claims to being a victim of theft need to be placed in ironic perspective:

> Now Harry he had long suspected
> This trespass of old Goody Blake;
> And vowed that she should be detected,
> That he on her would vengeance take.

'Suspected', 'vowed', 'detected', above all climactically absurd, 'vengeance', all suggest the inflation of the realities of the situation by Harry. A poor old woman is taking sticks from his hedge, an irritation perhaps, but Vengeance! And the word 'trespass' used to describe Goody's 'crime' has powerful reverberations from 'The Lord's Prayer': 'Forgive us our trespasses that we might forgive them that trespass against us'. Again comically absurd overstatement is given a

graver dimension by its link with 'relationship and love',[15] with popular
religious as well as basic social implications.

Directly on this follows another clownishly melodramatic heating
up of the emotional climate, as big, bellowing Harry (we have been
invited by the earlier physical descriptions of the protagonists to
visualise the scene) tip-toes towards his 'vengeance'. Can we visualise
without laughter the Harry Gill of stanza three as being capable of
'softly creeping' anywhere, on 'tip-toe' too? I am always reminded at
this point of the huge brainless dog of the *Tom and Jerry* cartoons:

> He hears a noise – he's all awake -
> Again? – on tip-toe down the hill
> He softly creeps – 'tis Goody Blake;
> She's at the hedge of Harry Gill.

The poem reaches its climax of comic exaggeration in the penultimate
stanza with Harry, unwarmed by one riding coat, adding a couple
more, 'but not a whit the warmer he'. So both Harry and the narrator
continue to pile things on:

> 'Twas all in vain, a useless matter,
> And blankets were about him pinned;
> Yet still his jaws and teeth they clatter
> Like a loose casement in the wind.

The clatter of his jaws like a rattling window completes a sequence
of ludicrous images of Harry which constitute the comic-ironic
undercurrent to the moral fable.

Now to return once more to Wordsworth's naive narrators as
described in the 'Note' to 'The Thorn', we might recall that one
of their characteristics was a lack of fancy, 'the power by which
pleasure and surprise are excited by sudden varieties of situation and
an accumulated imagery'. It seems to me that the narrator of 'Goody
Blake and Harry Gill' has a distinct talent for accumulated imagery,
'rude' perhaps but robust and effectively working towards deflation:
'varieties of situation' are explored by varieties of tone. The tale
is not simply comic. Parts are narrated in the neutral tone Danby
speaks of, though in view of the context established by the irony, this
might be read more as comic dead-pan than neutral. Parts convey
serious social concern, expressed with righteous energy rather than
irony:

> Sad case it was, as you may think,
> For very cold to go to bed;
> And then, for cold, not sleep a wink . . .

In fact the narrator shows considerable excitement at 'sudden
varieties of situation', particularly so when, for all his irony,

he finds his imagination caught up in the drama of Goody's curse:

> She prayed, her withered hand uprearing,
> While Harry held her by the arm -
> 'God! who art never out of hearing,
> O may he never more be warm!'
> The cold, cold moon above her head,
> Thus on her knees did Goody pray;
> Young Harry heard what she had said
> And icy cold he turned away...

A striking contrast, this, with the comic melodrama of Harry's 'tip-toe down the hill'. This passage ought to have been better received by Hodgart, having as it does more than a hint of the ominous moon that shines in the traditional ballads, such as 'Sir Patrick Spens':

> I saw the new moon late yestere'en,
> Wi' the old moon in her arm:
> And if we go to sea, master,
> I fear we'll come to harm.

But at once the narrator resumes his characteristic manner, and the poem moves towards its bizarre climactic description of Harry laid low under his burden of three riding coats, blankets and pins, his teeth once absurdly 'chattering', now even more so, 'clattering', like an ill-fitting window. The narrator has made it clear that he has not been taken in, but sees the incident as more burlesque than sinister. Whatever has led him to the tense theatrical moment of Goody's curse, it is not simply superstition – that belongs to Harry and perhaps the rustic audience.

Something more like the 'pleasure and surprise...excited by sudden varieties of situation' has brought him to this moment of (almost) high drama, which could not have been achieved by a man with 'slow faculties', a naive narrator.

At this point then we might return to Wordsworth's description of the poem as 'one of the rudest of this collection'. Wordsworth only occasionally uses the word 'rude' in any derogatory sense, and normally means no more than 'unpolished' or 'natural'. It is often found in a context associating it with words 'natural' or 'nature':

> A narrow girdle or rough stones and crags
> A rude and natural causeway . . . '
>
> *(Poems on the Naming of Places*, iv, 1–2)

> Lulled by the sound of pastoral bells,
> Rude Nature's Pilgrims did we go . . .
>
> *(Memorials of a Tour of the Continent*,
> xxxii, 'Elegiac Stanzas' 1–2)

> Therefore, although it be a history
> Homely and rude, I will relate the same,
> For the delight of a few natural hearts.
> *(Michael,* 34–6)

These quotations, particularly the last, would support the view that by the word 'rude' Wordsworth meant nothing more derogatory than that the poem is meant to be heard as told 'naturally'. Wordsworth's concern with the 'living voice' as distinct from 'the trade in classic niceties' is the subject of a revealing passage in *The Prelude*:

> I was a better judge of thoughts than words:
> Misled as to these latter, not alone
> By common inexperience of youth,
> But by the trade in classic niceties,
> Delusion to young Scholars incident
> And old ones also, by that overprized
> And dangerous craft of picking phrases out
> From languages that want the living voice
> To make of them a nature to the heart,
> To tell us what is passion, what is truth,
> What reason, what simplicity and sense.
> *(The Prelude* 1805, VI, 124–134)

And it was this same feeling, that poetry was using a 'dead' language, which led Wordsworth towards these early experiments with 'the living voice', the 'simplicity' of which can tell of 'passion', as well as 'reason', and 'truth' too, and 'sense', all aspects of the narrator's voice in 'Goody Blake and Harry Gill' which carry us beyond naivety.

The 'voice' is colloquial, of course, and only at one moment, when he says, 'Where from sea-blasts the hawthorns lean / And hoary dews are slow to melt', does he seem to me to lose touch with common speech. It is significant that these lines were a late alteration, in the edition of 1837, whereas earlier editions read:

> This woman dwelt in Dorsetshire,
> Her hut was on the cold hill-side
> And in that country coals are dear,
> For they come far by wind and tide.

This displays the 'matter-of factness' of which Southey and Coleridge complained, which appears to have been Wordsworth's reason for making the change here, as in 'The Thorn', though I feel that in this case a further reason might be that they may have seemed rather too flat for the lively narrator of this poem. But Wordsworth had a tendency to deal with these 'flat' expressions by later substituting vaguely 'poetic' language which marks a movement away from, and, it seems, a momentary loss of faith in his experimental principles. The success of 'Goody Blake and Harry Gill' seems to me largely to spring from the achievement of consistency or credibility, apart from the one lapse in the later text, along with variety in the narrator's tone, a consistency which the narrator of 'The Thorn' seems to lack. Take for instance the notorious lines from stanza three of 'The Thorn':

> High on the mountain's highest ridge,
> Where oft the stormy winter's gale
> Cuts like a scythe, while through the clouds
> It sweeps from vale to vale;
> Not five yards from the mountain path
> This thorn you on your left espy;
> And to the left, three yards beyond,
> You see a little muddy pond
> Of water – never dry.
> I've measured it from side to side;
> 'Tis three feet long and two feet wide.

Though at the close of the stanza the supposed 'garrulous narrator' reveals his tediously absurd 'matter of factness', the voice of the opening four lines is that of conventional descriptive verse for which a variety of the 'poetry reading' voice is required which is at odds with the banalities of the closing lines. The 'retired Captain of a small trading vessel…utterly destitute of fancy' would not normally use such expressions as 'Where oft the stormy winter's gale / Cuts like a scythe' etc.: poets go on like that, usually when not at their best. Thus there is a gap in credibility between the voice with which the stanza opens and that with which it closes. In fact if the closing lines are read in an accent appropriate to the character of the man supposedly speaking, say of the English West Country in which the events are set, or the North-East which gave Wordsworth himself the 'strong . . . northern *burr*' noted by Hazlitt, for all their triviality, they become dramatically convincing as the words of a character not wholly in control of the tale he is telling – a plain man doing his best to articulate, but not finding the right words for the powerful emotions he is trying to express. It is true that, as Southey complains, such a narrator may be merely boring, but Wordsworth is experimenting, and we know from the language of Joyce's Dublin, or Pinter or Beckett, what remarkable effects can be achieved through what might be called a rhetoric of inarticulacy. The problem lies less in Wordsworth's use of a 'naive' language as in an inconsistent and so dramatically unconvincing mixture of voices, the one consciously 'poetic', the other of an elderly retired seamen who is driven to describe his feelings but at times loses his way; an ancestor of Conrad's Marlow perhaps? The comparison is by no means extravagant: *Heart of Darkness* can only properly be understood as dramatic monologue, or rather, in view of its pompous opening narrator, dramatic dialogue. There is something very Conradian about parts of Wordsworth's Note to 'The Thorn':

> How every man must know that an attempt is rarely made to communicate impassioned feelings without something of an accompanying consciousness of the inadequateness of our own powers or the deficiencies of language. During such efforts there will be a craving in the mind, and as long as it is unsatisfied the speaker will cling to the same words, or words of the same character.[16]

The hesitancies, repetitions, verbose flourishes, and verbal collapses of Marlow could hardly be better described.

To conclude, while I see 'The Thorn' as an important, but not wholly successful experiment in narrative voice, the narrator of 'Goody Blake and Harry Gill', once one penetrates the surface of naivety, appears a man of some wit and perceptiveness with a sense of humour, and a talent for dramatic storytelling. But part of the drama lies in his ambivalence about the tale he has to tell, and the choice his rustic audience might have about how it might be understood. The owlishly moralistic note of the last two lines is in the tradition, but the moral is not, as so often in the popular ballad, spelt out.

> Now think, ye farmers all, I pray,
> On Goody Blake and Harry Gill.

And Wordsworth invites his audience to do the same. Some member of the audience of the narrator, men like Harry Gill, perhaps, may thrill to a sensational tale of magic. Others, who have recognised the occasional verbal wink, may smile behind their hands. They may, too, recognise 'some of the laws by which superstition acts upon the mind'. In one sense, the moral may seem cautionary at the crudest level: 'watch out for old women with the evil eye'. Or it may be understood as evidence of the immanence of 'God who art never out of hearing', or an appeal for social justice within the community beyond the laws of property. But above all, the narrator's 'inclination to laughter about the mouth' reveals his own sense of the burlesque possibilities of the tale, which nevertheless he does take seriously in terms of social conscience, and above all, as imaginative theatre, as the comedy gives way, for an instant, to the wonder and excitement he feels at the moment of high drama, Goody's curse.

Notes

1. This paper is an expanded and revised version of an article, 'The Narrator's Voice in "Goody Blake and Harry Gill"', published in *English: Journal of the English Association*, Spring 1970 (Wordsworth Bi-Centenary Issue), 13–17.
2. William Hazlitt, 'My First Acquaintance with Poets' (Oxford: Woodstock, 1993), 40.
3. John Danby, *The Simple Wordsworth* (London: Routledge, 1960), 36.
4. 'Preface to Lyrical Ballads' (1802) in *William Wordsworth (The Oxford Authors)* ed. Stephen Gill (Oxford: Oxford U. P., 1984), 611.
5. M. J. C. Hodgart, *The Ballads* (London: Hutchinson, 1950), 149.
6. *Wordsworth* ed. Gill, 620–5.
7. William K. Wimsatt ed., 'Parodies of Ballad Criticism 1711–1787', in *The Augustan Reprint Society* No. 63 (Los Angeles: University of California Press, 1957).
8. Stephen Maxfield Parrish, *The Art of the Lyrical Ballads* (London: Harvard U. P., 1973), 96–7.
9. Parrish, op. cit., 97.
10. *Wordsworth* ed. Gill, 611–2.
11. Precisely what Wordsworth and Coleridge meant by 'Fancy' and 'Imagination' is an old problem. But I think the problem here is that the word 'Imagination' is itself ambiguous, as illustrated by Theseus' speech, in *A Midsummer Night's Dream* 5. 1. 2–28., which fails to distinguish between imagination as illusion – 'such tricks hath strong imagination' etc., and imagination as a creative power – 'And as imagination bodies forth / the forms of things unknown' etc.
12. *The Letters of William and Dorothy Wordsworth: The Early Years 1787–1805* ed. E. de Selincourt, revised C. L. Shaver (Oxford: Oxford U. P., 1967), 234.
13. *Wordsworth* ed. Gill, 593.
14. *ibid.*
15. 'The poet...carrying everywhere with him relationship and love.' 'The Preface' in Gill ed., 606.
16. *Wordsworth* ed. Gill, 594.

Timehri (Composition and Function)

Wilson Harris

The distinctions and inner outer natures (if I may so put it) of composition and function have startled me in the way they have erupted into a new novel – a new imaginative fiction – in which I am deeply engaged as I turn away from it to write this article.

In all the circumstances it would help I think if I were to give a concrete instance that is drawn from the novel itself.

A young man burns a priest's church because he is convinced that the priest is sleeping with his sister. The woman denies this but her brother is sure that she is shielding the priest. In fact the priest is not involved physically with the young woman. But he has fallen in love with her and steadfastly refuses to succumb to the temptation to try to seduce her. He dreams however that she seduces him. Indeed his world is no longer what it was since he came upon the young woman (whose name is June) and her brother Mark. No one, he believes, could suspect the dimensions of his inner turmoil as he pursues his duties as though nothing has happened.

The fiction now raises in this context issues of latency, latent composition, in that the priest in his dreams is gripped subconsciously – an involuntary flame possesses him – by the desire to see his church fired so that he could re-build a new vessel.

When the young man sets fire to the church it seems to the priest that his innermost confusion and meditations are exposed to the public eye. It is as though the crowd which witnesses the fire is looking into him, into a hoard of dreams that he thought was safely locked away within himself.

The fire is a fire. The church is a church. The next day the event will be reported in the newspapers. It is the function of the newspapers to reflect the physicality of events.

Perhaps a quotation from the novel may help now to dramatise, in some degree, the distinction between latent composition and realistic or given or statistical function.

> News! Extraordinary phenomenon! He could not keep to himself the terrifying dream-blaze that arose in the church when

Mark set fire to it. He should have been able to hush it within himself, hide it within himself, as he hid his love of June from the world. But it had blazed out from himself. It was in the headlines. Could a dream blaze out from oneself and became public property? I AM THE DREAM, THE DREAM OF A BLAZING CHURCH, THAT EVERYONE SEES, THAT EVERYONE SEES, THAT EVERYONE KNOWS WITHIN ME, WITHOUT ME. The priest found himself saying that now as he stood in the street within a crowd. He was stricken by his love of June, by his love of the church, and by the fire that Mark lit which had come nevertheless from within himself.

Did he unconsciously desire the fire? Here was a partial meaning to Mark's deed and to his (the priest's) hoard of dreams, a partial meaning to humanity's vulnerability and unsuspecting openness to an eye of itself, beholding itself; an eye half-seeing, half-blind, in its co-relationship with a creator that is visible in the coarse-grained animal / human dreaming soul's extremity of risk, love, responsibility, terror, redemptive self-knowledge . . . The priest was stricken, helpless, in the exposure of his inmost, confused heart, his involuntary meditation on the collapse of his church and the re-building of his church as a new vessel...

Crucial to the latency of composition – in contradistinction to the singularity and the tautology of function (fire is fire, the church is church, etc.,) are the pluralities of involuntary desire for, and implicit involvement in, something that happens and the shock of explicit, eruptive self-knowledge that one is involved in what is happening. That shock is akin to the exposure of a dream one may have forgotten one dreamt. The exposure of the dream seems so true, so vivid, so strangely objective that others – it would seem – must be aware of it. The coarse-grained texture (akin to a certain kind of density) attests the confusion yet profound authenticity and reality of the dream even as it immerses one in the raw material elements of nature (fire, water, earth, sand etc.,) that appear passive at times even as they erupt prodigiously at other times.

There is no true visibility of meaning – one is inclined to say – except through the paradoxes of latency of composition. Institutions, structures, do collapse. Is this a terminal, purely material, process in itself? Is this an end-product in itself of purely deceased ritual and purely material order? Or are there roots to such collapse in the mystery of a living unconscious, dismembered re-membered dream, that gives eloquence to shape and bone and sculpture and grain even as a shell in a desert may still echo with the murmur of vanished oceans that may re-appear in the mind's body within an eruption that evokes parallel realms of consciousness, consciousness it seems in sleeping nature, consciousness it seems in memory and person?

The counterpoint between collapsing order and the re-building of a new vessel – when visualized within latencies of composition – is, I would venture to say, of immense importance. I would like to approach this from within vestiges of enigmatic tradition that may be traced in the landscapes of Guyana and the South and Central Americas.

I have mind, in the first instance, the vestiges of Timehri legend. Timehri is translated by some writers – such as the Australian anthropologist Walter Roth (who travelled extensively in Guyana in the dawn of this century) – as 'the hand of God'. This approach to vestiges of legend (Arawak, Macusi and other Amerindian legend) imprinted on rock faces, and on the landscapes of Guyana, is profoundly evocative. It summons up the sensation of time, of a clock ticking away in rocks and rivers. It suggests mutuality, the hand of the gods in the hand of men. I must confess that for many years I have been fascinated by this spirit of a 'clock'. And it suggests to me legendary (if not strictly scientific) applications to space and time. Do legends of space underpin time or legends of the creation of time space?

That underpinning – which we can never identify absolutely in Amerindian legends – offers us the imaginary prospect of inverse wholeness. The surfaces of place tend to be fractured or broken, the legends imprinted on the fabric of place are weathered and worn but they imply a compositional reach through and beyond themselves, they imply an inverse factor of wholeness.

As such they witness to a core that is numinously exact and true. But even as I say this I need to qualify the assertion. The core of such a reality of exactitude within space or time (or both together in miraculous compression or solidity) cannot be seized or structured. It approaches us nevertheless – we appear to incorporate it into ourselves, it seems to incorporate us into itself – through profiles of myth...

Profiles of the jaguar are significant core truths of Amerindian legend. A curious way to put it, I confess. Until we reflect on the fact that the core truth releases inexactitudes that nourish the spectralities of time and space. The jaguar is not absolute as a physical surrogate of the sun or a psychical surrogate of the sun. The physicality of the jaguar-profile of the sun and the phychicality of the jaguar-profile of the sun loom into such tension that they splinter. The splintering brings about another profile in which the core of the jaguar-sun suffuses the myth with new proportions. There have been five profiles of the jaguar-sun in Aztec (Central American) philosophy. We live – within that clockwork of the ancient past – under the fifth profile of the jaguar now active in space as the sun.

Despite a succession of profiles to break a paranoid fixation with an absolute sun, an absolute core image of a creator or a deity, the Aztec world deceived itself in the end. It began to forfeit the numinosity Shadow in subtle and complex counterpoint to a ruling light that makes increasingly fierce demands on its subjects. Those subjects indeed become victims and their blood is required to feed the sun.

For decades before the arrival of Hernan Cortes, the Spanish conquistador, the Aztecs were haunted by portents of doom, of the devouring complex of the Light that ruled their age. Their rituals and prophecies foretold the return of Quetzalcoatl. It is of interest to note that Quetzalcoatl – the god who had splintered and vanished centuries before – implied two profiles of myth, one pertaining to the Shadow of paradise in the coati-snake (the earth), the other pertaining to the frailty of heaven in the quetzal-bird (the sky). Thus a numinous revisionary logic of linkages between Shadow and Light was at the heart of the Quetzalcoatl legend and its second coming.

Cortes arrived on the very day it had been foretold that Quetzalcoatl would return. His appearance and dress matched the expectations of ritual and prophecy. The core legend of Quetzalcoatl possessed a chasm in itself – a chasm of space between shadow and light – that required the originality of new perspectives if it were to be partially bridged in each century, each generation (if this is possible). The fusion of a core legend, embodied in Quetzalcoatl, with realistic appearance, authorised by ritual expectation, was to fall prey to a profile of myth, and to identify that profile with the mysterious and insoluble exactitude of truth.

The triumph of conventional realism – within five centuries after the conquest of ancient America – entraps us everywhere. There is an archetypal mystery to the pre-Columbian arts. Profiles of myth in the pre-Columbian world may realistically be identified with Japanese, Chinese, African, European features. May I give an instance, which has an element of jest, of comedy? I came upon a small figure with incredible detail in an exhibition entitled BEFORE CORTES which was mounted in the Metropolitan Museum of Art in the autumn of 1970. The figure possesses a corpulence and the commanding air of a sovereign jester. Something about the features – taken with everything else – reminded me of the Tudor King Henry the Eighth. Such is the curious magic of pre-Columbian profiles of myth.

May I return to the questions I have raised of latencies of composition, function, and Timehri vestiges of legend?

Latency suggests, I think, the capacity of art to offer us parallel keys into the mystery of cross-cultural reality.

Such cross-cultural evocation may remain involuntary and hidden from the artist or craftsman himself. In some instances – even when it is perceived by the artist within the imageries that come into play in his work – it may be necessary to endow it with latency in order to give range to tensions in the field and to let other eruptive signals come into play through the eyes of others who enter into a dialogue with the core ramifications of legend. The function, therefore, of imageries – the functional incorporation of one culture by another – gives way, by degrees, to transfigurative dimensionalities. Realism is a function of art. The tendency to perceive it as absolute eclipses transfigurative triggers and sustains patterns of conquest in which cultures strive to ride each other, to claim ascendancy one over the other.

The significance of Timehri legends becomes, I think, increasingly clear.

Each splinter in Timehri is not absolute in realistic terms. The splintered 'clock' miniaturises the hand of time in each detail or crevice. The 'hand' may unlock the age of the rocks or the rivers but such unlocking is a partial capacity. The 'hand' may unlock the action of man upon landscapes, the action of nature upon landscapes, but such action is a partial faculty. The 'hand' may unlock the history of a family, a tribe, that has been broken within conflict, or famine, or flood, or drought. And here the hand secretes parallel keys into various dimensions of the family, dimensions of oral craft that brings to us its spoken cargo of birth certification, marriage certification, death certification; and the way such certification has escalated into painting, sculpture, pottery, dance, theatre . . . But even here the 'hand' resists seizure. For it is rooted in resources that have no absolute function. And as such the 'hand' is empowered century after century to seek – in some creative and original degree – to bridge a chasm between cultures, between the strong and the weak, the rich and the poor, between religions that may incorporate elements in each drawn one from another and still remain antagonistic to each other and in perpetual conflict.

The numinosity of composition miniaturised in splinters of the foundered vessels of civilizations is, I believe, at the heart of the ceaselessly unfinished genesis of the Imagination. It implies, I also believe, a necessity to probe the nature and natures of involuntary cross-cultural traditions in a wholly different way in our Humanities.

The Romantic Non-Picturesque:
Emily Brontë's Yorkshire Landscape[1]

Christopher Heywood

Literary tradition has persistently related the action and the symbolic undercurrents in *Wuthering Heights* to abstract contrasts: human and inhuman, child and adult, storm and calm, good and evil, north and south. These appear cryptically in the text and are frequently discovered in the absence of clarity about whether they were intended. One which has not appeared yet is derived, it appears, from Emily's[2] knowledge of the movement in art and literature known as the Picturesque. Conforming with her persistent interest in symmetry, her narrative is divided into two sets of seventeen chapters.[3] The first is dominated by violence in the lifetime of Catherine I and her brother Hindley. The second traces the painful journey towards emancipation for their children, Hareton and Catherine II. In each half of her story, it appears, Emily exploited her knowledge of the Picturesque and the Non-Picturesque, a contrast coined by William Gilpin.

The relatively featureless moorland landscape of southern Pennine type was thought by William Gilpin and his extensive following in the Picturesque movement, to be a seed-bed of social corruption, industrialisation, and vice. In contrast, the mountain landscapes of the northern Pennines and Lake mountains were in his view the nursery for a pure social morality, based on pastoral values. Illustrating his *Three Essays* (1792) with a contrasted pair of his own paintings, Gilpin shows two similar landscape compositions. A desolate moorland is classified as Non-Picturesque, in contrast to a Picturesque and sparkling mountain landscape.[4] Both pictures have three intersecting hills in a receding pattern. A cold front stalks across the trackless, Non-Picturesque slopes. In contrast, fleecy clouds float beyond the Picturesque trees and crags, and a welcoming path winds among the sheltering hills. Clearly, Gilpin rejected the moorland landscape in favour of the tree-lined crags of a limestone or volcanic formation.

Emily Brontë approached this contrast and its framing ideas in two stages. The poems written in her adolescence and early maturity are about islands in the Pacific named Gondal and Gaaldine. Loves, deaths, battles and betrayals are referred to obliquely, as in early collections of northern verse by Cottle, Herbert, Jamieson, Percy, and Scott. The cryptically invoked events take place against a series of landscapes with mountains, woods, moors, a ruin, and a lake. The name 'Gondal' and its geographical definition, 'a large island in the north Pacific', and 'Gaaldine a large island newly discovered in the south Pacific' appear as manuscript insertions in the Brontë children's copy of Goldsmith's *Grammar of General Geography* (1823), which has survived. The handwriting appears to be Emily's.[5] Goldsmith's description of Japan as a 'populous, and remarkable, Empire' (p. 53) suggests that Japan sat as Emily's model for Gondal. However, the alphabetical position of 'Gondal' adjacent to Goldsmith's entry for Gondar, the ancient capital of Ethiopia, suggests that like Angria, Ashantee, Dongola, Verdopolis, and other names in the Juvenilia shared by Charlotte and Branwell, Emily's fictional islands have African originals. Goldsmith's map of Africa shows their exact or approximate equivalents as Angra Pequeña (the modern Lüderitz), Ashantee, Dongola, Gondar, and the Cap Verde islands (p. 74).

The Gondal story is set among heather-clad slopes on both islands, Gondal and Gaaldine. Although these Pacific islands approximate in geographical position to Japan and Australia, the warfare between Gondal and Gaaldine echoes the conflict between Gondar and its neighbour, the land of the Galla, among whom slave raids and wars were conducted by Ethiopia. The portrayal of ancient Gondar in Bruce's *Travels in Abyssinia* (1776), a work available to the Brontës in the Mechanics' Institute Library at Keighley, appears to have been in Emily's mind in the formation of the Gondal story. The frequent references to slaves, fetters, dungeons and chains in the Gondal poems appear, none the less, to be instances of the general rejection of tyranny by Romantic and pre-Romantic writers. There is room for doubt whether the 'agony' experienced 'When the pulse begins to throb, the brain to think again, / The soul to feel the flesh, and the flesh to feel the chain', in one of Emily's major poems, or the couplet 'We dare not shrink from slavery's chain / To leave our children slaves',[6] refer more than generically to the conditions of enslavement and tyranny since the dawn of history. Matching the tendency to generalise about slavery, the moors, forests, heather, storms, mountains, ruins and lakes in the Gondal poems are general examples from the repertoire of Picturesque effects. There is room for doubt, too, whether the foreshadowings of characters in *Wuthering Heights* in the Gondal series go beyond contrasting the fair and the dark-haired Yorkshire types exemplified by the Earnshaws, the Deans, and the Lintons. They appear under 'Varieties of the Human Species' in Goldsmith's *Geography* as 'the *white* and *brownish* nations of Europe, western Asia, and the north coast of Africa' (p. 91). Emily's tendency to generalise in her poetry culminates in the poem of 1846, beginning 'Why ask to know the date--the clime?', where she suggests that betrayal is a universal condition of life.

The landscape, date, weather, varieties of the human species, and the remedies for a corrupted society, are more pointedly developed in *Wuthering Heights*. In her second stage of work, it appears, Emily drew on memory and experience. Her novel portrays the two Yorkshire landscapes she had seen on her travels and daily life in the mountainous north and the moorland south of the old West Riding. Her novel offers an extended rebuttal to Gilpin's social message. The Picturesque north is portrayed in *Wuthering Heights* as a hotbed of violence, corrupted by its dependence on the Caribbean remittance economy derived from sugar, rum, and slavery. The remedy for slavery is found in a Non-Picturesque moorland landscape, spread like a carpet over an accurately portrayed mountain limestone setting. The moorland south prepares the second heroine for her restoration of order in a disordered pastoral society. In this phase of her work, Emily developed a cryptic method of presenting a continuous story, and relating it to the world she knew. Models for her Picturesque Yorkshire landscape and its corrupted society appear around Cowan Bridge and in the literary traditions of Skipton, Sedbergh, and Tunstall. Her model for the moorland landscape appears around Haworth. North and south in *Wuthering Heights* have symbolic values unsuspected by Elizabeth Gaskell and not understood, it appears, or understood and rejected, by Charlotte. More intensively than in the Gondal cycle, the problem of slavery is identified and named in *Wuthering Heights*, explored through the dark-skinned orphan of Liverpool origin, and developed along lines comparable to those followed by Shakespeare, Aphra Behn, and modern writers on African enslavement from Equiano to our day.

The Picturesque setting around Cowan Bridge had for long been permeated by the problem of slavery by the time the Brontës attended the Clergy Daughters' School. The Caribbean girls at the School named Charlotte and Melanie Hain account, we may suppose, for the Brontës' developed insights into the plantation economy. In Brussels they stood back from the world they had known as children, and gained the strength to depict it from within, with memory and the literature of the region as their means of encompassing the Carus circle around Tunstall, Sedbergh, and Thornton in Lonsdale. All their story material came from within a circle of patronage exercised by the Caruses. A few minutes' walk away from the Clergy Daughters' school, the Welch family of Leck Hall lived in retirement following the dissolution in 1806 of Welch & Co., the largest registered slave trading house in eighteenth-century Liverpool. Edward Guy, a black man baptised at St George's Church in Leck in 1807, across the road from the Clergy

Daughters' School, was the same age as Richard Sutton of Dent, Emily's main model for the character of Heathcliff. Earlier generations of the Carus family had stood as bondsmen to the expansion in Yorkshire of the Caribbean estate of the Sill family of Dent, across Leck Fell.[7] Hallsteads, the small manor at Thornton in Lonsdale, the coach's last stop before arriving at Cowan Bridge by the old coaching road, and apparently the topographical equivalent of the fictional Thrushcross Grange, was for several generations the home of the Foxcroft family, partners in Welch & Co. of Liverpool. A ship's diary of the 16th century records the brutal attack on a West African village by a slave raiding ship owned by the Clifford family of Skipton.[8] Turner's picture of Hornby Castle, illustrating Whitaker's *An History of Richmondshire* (1823), shows a black man on a donkey with a white female partner and five children of various shades, a few miles downstream from the Clergy Daughters' School.[9] Foreshadowing the confusion about Heathcliff's national origin among the bewildered rural residents in *Wuthering Heights*, in the engraving by Radcliffe in Whitaker's *Richmondshire*, the strongly marked African features of the dark boy in Turner's picture are altered into Asiatic eyebrows, nose, hair, and facial outline.

Understandably, since many of the descendants and originals of the actions appearing in veiled or adapted form in *Wuthering Heights* were living when the novel was written, Emily portrayed the rural hinterland of Lancaster and Liverpool slave trading and the economy based on slaveholding in a cryptic or elliptical, allusive form. Evidently she viewed the Picturesque northern Pennines through the lens which had clarified the landscapes explored by Johan Moritz Rugendas in his *Voyage pittoresque dans le Brésil* (1827–39), and by Jean-Baptiste Debret in his *Voyage pittoresque et historique au Brésil* (1834–39). These works casually but eloquently exposed the brutality of plantation society.[10] Perhaps the girls saw them in Brussels. The illustrations by William Blake to *The Narrative of a Five Years' Expedition Against the Revolted Negroes of Surinam* (1795), by John Gabriel Stedman,[11] foreshadowed these protest writings and pictures. Without exception, however, topographical writers had for long portrayed the Non-Picturesque moorland of the southern Pennines as hotbeds of vice, and the Picturesque limestone highlands north of Skipton as the haunt of ancient virtue. This image persists in the description of Haworth in T. D. Whitaker's *Loidis and Elmete*: 'On the whole, Haworth is to Bradford as Heptenstall to Halifax – almost at the extremity of population, high, bleak, dirty and difficult of access'.[12] Overturning this system of ideas, Emily presented her Non-Picturesque moorland as a proving ground for the young Catherine's victory over disruption. Her novel is addressed to the problems of education and slavery or servitude, in relation to order in social and domestic organisation.

The younger heroine overturns the deception, disruption and death resulting from the Earnshaws' rejection of Heathcliff and from her mother's preference for an alluring but violent manorial society.

Viewed against the Picturesque tradition, *Wuthering Heights* turns out to be based on the Romantic and Emancipationist ideal of liberty, within the normal constraints imposed by rural and ecclesiastical life in the north of England. The first part of Emily's story is dominated by a Picturesque, craggy and tree-lined landscape, based on the limestone region lying along the coaching road a few miles to the south-east of Cowan Bridge. Her transparent disguise of that landscape was penetrated by J. H. Dixon, a neglected early reader of *Wuthering Heights*. In a book published posthumously in 1881, Dixon remarked that the reader who knows 'anything of Craven or its scenery [...] will find in that wonderful novel some truly graphic sketching'. He continued: 'Long before we knew anything of the author, we said "This is Craven!" and we knew where to find the bleak and barren moorland solitudes, where the misanthropic hero had his crazy dwelling'.[13] Another early recognition came from Mrs G. Linnaeus Banks: that is, Isabella Varley, writing under her married name. In her novel *Wooers and Winners* (1880), Isabella Banks pointedly invoked Emily's story by portraying a dark-skinned orphan boy from Jamaica who eventually marries the daughter of his adoptive family, the Earnshaws. By placing this action at the foot of Ingleborough hill, on the opposite side from Cowan Bridge, Isabella Banks signalled her penetration of Emily's subject matter, her landscape, and the literary tradition lying behind her novel.[14]

These early recognitions were apparently not known to J. Erskine Stuart, whose remarks on *Wuthering Heights* in his book, *The Brontë Country* (1888), have been overlooked in later discussions of the topography. He arrived independently at conclusions supporting the insights of Dixon and Banks. Stuart noted that the topography and atmosphere in Emily's novel do not resemble those of Haworth and Haworth Moor, a locality, he observed, which will leave the visitor 'woefully disappointed'. He proposed Tunstall as a match for the idyllic, summery atmosphere in *Wuthering Heights*, adding: 'a much more interesting excursion is this, than that to Haworth'.[15] He remained baffled, however, by his impression. Later writers on the problem of the Yorkshire locality in *Wuthering Heights* have maintained silence about the disparity between the landscape around Haworth and the fictional landscape of *Wuthering Heights*.[16] At Haworth, the relatively low-lying gritstone ridges of the southern Pennines slope eastwards to the North Sea. In the novel, high limestone peaks face westwards, rising abruptly above the flat plain of the western seaboard. Dixon clearly recognised Emily's clues, but left it to others to locate the Yorkshire original for her landscape. The two Pennine landscapes, 'the bare limestone country of the fells in which many travellers have found resemblances to the sacred scenes of Palestine and the classic hills of Greece', and the southern 'ridge and furrow type of hill and valley', with 'uncultivated grouse-moor, covered in the wetter places with cotton-grass [...] and in the dryer by heather [...] and crowberry',[17] are defined in Picturesque terms in Whitaker's *Whalley* (1797), *The History and Antiquities of the Deanery of Craven* (1805), *Loidis and Elmete* (1817), and the posthumously published *An History of Richmondshire* (1823). The *Deanery of Craven* was available in the Mechanics' Institute Library at Keighley. It appears to have been known to Emily. Its illustrations include engravings from paintings by J. Griffith, in a style borrowed from Gilpin. Griffith's Malham Cove is among the most remarkable pictures to emerge from the Picturesque movement before Girtin and Turner. In describing Malham Cove, Gordale Scar, and Kilnsey Crag, Whitaker emphasised the Picturesque values of the limestone Yorkshire Dales. Literary material from this tradition is used with wit and irony, founded on independent observation, throughout *Wuthering Heights*. Emily's tour to Bolton Bridge in Wharfedale shows her response to the limestone landscape. T. Wemyss Reid reconstructed Emily's response to the landscape from Ellen Nussey's account of the occasion. He wrote:

> how quick she is to note the least prominent of the beauties around her; she does not talk so much as the rest of the party, but her wonderful eyes, brilliant and unfathomable as the pool at the foot of a waterfall, but radiant also with a wealth of tenderness and warmth, show how her soul is expanding under the influences of the scene.

Emily's language ran beyond words into 'a strange, deep guttural sound which those who know her best interpret as the language of a joy too deep for articulate expression'.[18] The Wharfedale excursion was undoubtedly assisted by Whitaker's *Deanery of Craven*, to which Ellen Nussey refers in her letters to Reid.[19] Emily's interest in Wharfedale is signposted by her use of the names Linton and Thrushcross, both near Bolton Bridge. She appears to have known Frederic Montagu's *Gleanings in Craven* (1838), a humorous tour through Wharfedale and Lunesdale. Foreshadowing Lockwood in *Wuthering Heights*, Montagu paused to acquire stories at first hand from Dales people. A night on the onward journey, spent in the attic of the New Inn at Clapham, at the foot of Ingleborough, ends with a nightmare about a plot by the landlady and her daughter to murder him for his money. He wakes to find the maid knocking at his door with the hot water. His phrasing anticipates Lockwood's in *Wuthering Heights*, where the horrific dream of an encounter at the window is similarly explained. The fictional landscape appearing through asides in the course of Nelly Dean's narrative is founded on descriptions in the books by Whitaker and Montagu, of scenery known to Emily. Nelly explains about the crags observed by the younger Catherine in her childhood: 'they were bare masses of stone, with hardly enough earth in their clefts to nourish a stunted tree' (Ch. 18). On the page facing Griffith's picture of Gordale Scar, Whitaker observes the 'solid mass of limestone, of, perhaps, equal height with [Malham Cove]', and adds: 'Wherever a cleft in the rock, or a lodgement of earth appears, the yew-tree [...] contrasts its deep and glossy green with the pale grey of the limestone'.[20] On the same page he describes Malham Cove as 'an immense cragg of limestone [...] forming a termination at once so august and tremendous that the imagination can scarcely figure any form or scale of rock within the bounds of probability that shall go beyond it'. His phrasing reappears in Montagu's *Gleanings in Craven*. Referring to the same landscape, Montagu notes that in 'the clefts in the rocks' sides, or wherever a lodgment of earth appears, the deep and glossy green of the yew refreshes the eye in its wandering over the pale grey of the vast rock' (p. 102).

Still more strikingly, Emily appears to have drawn on Hutton's *A Tour to the Caves, in the Environs of Ingleborough and Settle* (1781), a work available to her at Ponden House.[21] Lightly modified, Hutton's phrases reappear in Lockwood's discovery of Gimmerton. Hutton notes the isolated farmhouse named Braeda Garth 'on the north side of a high mountain', where he finds a 'shepherd, its solitary inhabitant', who 'with longing eyes looks for returning verdure, when the sun begins to throw his benign rays on the solitary abode'. In this setting with its high winds and 'other instances of tumult in nature', a pure form of pastoral society is maintained: 'Having little intercourse with the luxurious, vicious, and designing part of mankind, they were temperate, substantial, sincere, and hospitable'. The unsuspecting Lockwood reads his newly discovered Picturesque landscape in phrases echoing Hutton's. At first he believes himself to be among people who '*do* live more in earnest, more in themselves, and less in surface change, and frivolous external things' (Ch. 7). Experience shows him, however, the modernity which had engulfed and nearly destroyed this pastoral haven. As a lovelorn but fickle swain, Lockwood echoes Hutton, who discovers in Kingsdale, near the foot of Ingleborough, a refuge for disappointed lovers: 'No monk or anchoret could desire a more retired situation for his cell, or disappointed lover to moralize on the inconstancy of his nymph, and the vanity of the world'. The lovelorn Lockwood is subjected to Emily's sympathetic irony. Hutton's victim of female inconstancy becomes in her hands an inept male practitioner, a 'weak wretch' (Ch. 1) in pursuit of a 'hermit's life' (Ch. 10). Yet he is able to view himself through female eyes: 'what did I do? I confess it with shame – shrunk icily into myself, like a snail; at every glance retired colder and farther; till finally the poor innocent was led to doubt her own senses' (Ch. 1).

Emily removed the varnish from Hutton's picture of pastoral society. Nelly's tale exposes Lockwood to the terrifying aspects lying in wait for the pregnant Isabella. Hutton portrays Yordas Cave in Kingsdale as the refuge for 'a poor woman, big with child, travelling alone up this inhospitable vale to that of Dent, [...] taken in labour, and found dead in this cave'. He jests: 'the gloom and horror increased' and 'the den of Cacus, and the cave of Poliphemus, came into my mind. I wanted nothing but a Sybil conductress with a golden rod, to imagine myself, like Eneas, going into the infernal regions'. Another cave, in Chapel le Dale nearby, reminds him of the 'descent of Eneas to the infernal regions'. Emily answers this complacency with Isabella's active response. She chooses 'perpetual dwelling in the infernal regions' (Ch. 15) rather than bondage to Heathcliff, who excludes her from his world and offers to murder her. She rushes out 'wading through marshes; precipitating myself [...] towards the beacon light of the Grange [...] far rather would I be condemned to a perpetual dwelling in the infernal regions, than even for one night abide beneath the roof of Wuthering Heights' (Ch. 15).

Emily constructed the Gimmerton landscape in phrases borrowed from Picturesque descriptions of the Ingleborough region. They emerge in sparkling form, minted new by her observation and her pointed handling of the language. As though describing a picture by Gilpin, Nelly emphasised the atmospheric ground mist around Wuthering Heights hill: 'Wuthering Heights rose above this silvery vapour' (Ch. 10). The fictional scenery around Gimmerton echoes Hutton's phrasing. Awaiting Edgar Linton's return from church, Nelly Dean hears the 'mellow flow of the beck' through the trees, and reflects on 'the yet absent murmur of the summer foliage, which drowned that music about the Grange, when the trees were in leaf' (Ch. 15). Her phrases are foreshadowed in Hutton's *Tour*, where Leckbeck, the stream or *coln* (*cowen*) flowing under the bridge at Cowan Bridge, appears 'embowered with woods and lofty trees', and 'flows through a chasm amongst rocks at the bottom: imagination is left to conceive the cause of the deep and solemn murmurs beneath'.[22] Ingleborough, the topographical equivalent of Wuthering Heights hill, appears in Ann Radcliffe's *A Journey Made in the Summer of 1794* (1795). Her description of Ingleborough's 'rugged front, the loftiest and most majestic in the scene', of 'the northern fells [...] ever changing with the weather and shifting lights', and of 'those evening clouds on the horizon that catch the last gleams of the sun',[23] foreshadow the younger Catherine's inquiry about 'the brow of that tallest point', and about 'those golden rocks' (Ch. 18). In an aside to Lockwood, Nelly explains that the setting sun has imparted the golden colour to the rocks. The reader, in turn, can see that they must be white or pale grey crags in a limestone landscape from the western Pennines, viewed as Ann Radcliffe had seen them, at sunset.

The limestone landscape in *Wuthering Heights* is subjected to Emily's ironic rejection of it as a haven for the English slaveholding interest. Her Non-Picturesque moorland, laid over it like a magic carpet, lies incongruously at the feet of high limestone crags. It appears first in close detail after the death of the elder Catherine, in 'a corner of the kirkyard, where the wall is so low that heath and bilberry plants have climbed over it from the moor; and peat mould almost buries it' (Ch. 16). This exactly describes the appearance of Haworth churchyard. Beyond the moorland, however, lie the fictional crags. In the Yorkshire Dales, patches of heather moorland are confined to the summits of the limestone crags, their feet and flanks being clothed in meadow, pasture and woodland. At Haworth, conversely, there are no overhanging crags of pale limestone lying beyond the moor. Once installed at the graveside, Emily's moorland holds the stage, and as at Haworth, it has 'shadows and sunshine flitting over it', Nelly's culminatory image for the younger Catherine's expression at the onset of her first marriage crisis (Ch. 27). A series of excursions into the moorland setting closes with the younger Catherine's forthcoming wedding to her maternal cousin on Saturday 1 January 1803. In the summer following her thirteenth birthday she makes her first outing on her pony. She meets Hareton, whom she rejects but will eventually marry. On her sixteenth birthday in early spring she searches for grouse nests. Nelly watches 'her golden ringlets flying loose behind, and her bright cheek, as soft and pure in its bloom as a wild rose, and her eyes radiant with cloudless pleasure'. Among 'hillocks and banks [...] hunting out the nests of the grouse' (Ch. 21), she rushes ahead, calling to Nelly: 'Climb that hillock, pass that bank' (Ch. 21). Thwarted in her relationship with Linton Heathcliff, she retreats within her father's estate, picking flowers and autumn berries (Ch. 22). A clandestine late autumn series of meetings, encouraged by Heathcliff, is thwarted next (Ch. 24). A third series culminates in the excursion on a sultry summer's day in August, when she picks the moorland bilberries for the ailing boy (Ch. 26). A bright summer's day in August brings the sterile marriage to Linton Heathcliff as he races her father to the grave (Ch. 27). Easter brings her rediscovery of Hareton, and the harvest moon brings the news that the wedding day is set for New Year's day.

In the second half of her story, Emily deftly transformed the menacing Picturesque limestone landscape into the Non-Picturesque land she knew and loved. *Wuthering Heights* is a metamorphosis or fairy-tale rendering of that earth-shaking or *withering* idea. The two Yorkshire landscapes are indeed visible in a single glance in clear weather from Withins Height, at the summit of Haworth Moor. The rolling moorland runs northward for some fifteen miles, and is then surmounted by the enchanted whiteness of the limestone Dales, running to the impressive skyline formed by Ingleborough, Cam Fell, Whernside, Penyghent, and Grasssington Edge. In transforming that landscape and its traditions into a fictional narrative, Emily gave the upper hand to the moorland at her feet. The heroine's moorland experiences lead to her victory over the machinations of Heathcliff. He, in turn, understands the ailment afflicting the Picturesque landscape and its society. After an absence of three years, which can only have been spent in the Lancaster and Liverpool slave trade, he returns a wealthy man. Experience enables him to answer Nelly's question 'How has he got rich?' (Ch. 10). He hints but narrowly avoids the obvious explanation: 'The tyrant grinds down his slaves...and they don't turn against him, they crush those beneath them' (Ch. 11).

The Picturesque Yorkshire Dales were the setting for the Brontë sisters' painful experiences at Cowan Bridge, around the foot of Ingleborough. Emily appears to have remained cheerful, however, along lines recognised by her teachers. One of them recalled Emily as 'a darling child [...] quite the pet nursling of the school'.[24] This amplifies her teachers' report of Emily's exceptional reading ability for the age of six years: 'Reads very prettily'.[25] Constantin Heger forecast her novel in his references to her 'powerful reason', her search for 'new spheres of discovery from the knowledge of the old', 'her strong, imperious will', and her 'faculty of imagination'. He found in his brilliant pupil 'a show of argument, that it would have dominated over the reader, whatever might have been his previous opinions, or his cooler perceptions of its truth'.[26] Emily's accurate account of the Picturesque setting around Cowan Bridge justifies that prediction, made after her death, but, it seems, without knowledge of her novel. Written with the strength gained through a masterly command of a region and its literature, *Wuthering Heights* embodies the Romantic ideal of emancipation from past horrors through a restoration of moral values.

Notes

1. Parts of this essay have appeared in my article C. Heywood, 'Emily Brontë's Picturesque and Non-Picturesque Yorkshire', *Sheffield Art*

Review (1994), 3–14. The Editor is thanked for permission to re-use material appearing there.

2. Members of the Brontë family are generally referred to here as Charlotte, Branwell, and Emily.

3. Indications of how Emily pursued symmetry in her narrative appear in C. P. Sanger's pioneering essay, *The Structure of Wuthering Heights* (London: Hogarth Press, 1926).

4. From William Gilpin, *Three Essays* (1792). See Malcolm Andrews, *The Search for the Picturesque* (Aldershot: Scolar Press, 1990), 32 and throughout. Also Alexander M. Ross, *The Imprint of the Picturesque on Nineteenth-Century British Fiction* (Waterloo: Wilfrid Laurier University Press, 1986), xxxvii and throughout (only Charlotte cited); and Peter Bicknell, *The Picturesque Scenery of the Lake District 1752–1855* (Winchester: St Paul's Bibliographies, 1990).

5. J. Goldsmith, *A Grammar of General Geography. For the use of Schools and Young Persons* (London: Longman, 1823), 169, 171. I thank the staff of the Brontë Parsonage Museum and Library for assistance at this and other points.

6. *The Complete Poems of Emily Brontë*, ed. C. W. Hatfield, (New York: Columbia University Press, 1941), 184, 239.

7. See my article C. Heywood, 'Yorkshire Slavery in *Wuthering Heights*', *Review of English Studies*, N. S. 38 (1985), 185–97.

8. See my article C. Heywood, 'A Yorkshire Background for *Wuthering Heights*', *Modern Language Review*, 88 (1993), 817–830.

9. David Hill, *In Turner's Footsteps* (London: John Murray, 1984), 90–98. Also T. D. Whitaker, *An History of Richmondshire*, 2 vols (London: Longman, 1823) 'Hornby Castle from Tatham Church'.

10. Cited in Hugh Honour, *The Image of the Black in Western Art*, vol. 4 (London: Harvard University Press, 1989), part 1, 138–146.

11. Cited in Joan Baum, *Mind-Forg'd Manacles. Slavery and the English Romantic Poets* (New York: Archon Books, 1994), 36–7 and 56–7. I thank Joan Baum for many illuminating insights.

12. T. D. Whitaker, *Loidis and Elmete* (1817), 356.

13. J. H. Dixon, *Chronicles and Stories of the Craven Dales* (1881), 18.

14. Heywood, 'A Yorkshire Background for *Wuthering Heights*', *Modern Language Review*, loc. cit.

15. J. Erskine Stuart, *The Brontë Country* (1888), 98, 69–70.

16. J. F. Goodridge, *Emily Brontë: Wuthering Heights* (London: Arnold, 1964), 62–4; David Daiches and N. Flower, *The Literary Topography of the British Isles* (Harmondsworth: Penguin, 1986), 148.

17. P. F. Kendall and H. E. Wroot, *Geology of Yorkshire*, 2 vols (Leeds: privately printed, 1924), vol. 1, 5, 43–44, 108–24.

18. T. Wemyss Reid, *Charlotte Brontë. A Memoir* (London: Macmillan, 1878), 32–4.

19. Nussey correspondence, Brotherton Collection, Leeds.
20. T. D. Whitaker, *The History and Antiquities of the Deanery of Craven* (1805), 194.
21. Item 1300 in the *Catalogue of Books at Ponden House* (1899) reads *Lakes, a Guide to, in Cumberland, Westmoreland and Lancashire, and Natural Curiosities of Malham-in-Craven*, 1 vol. (1789) (Bradford City Archive Heaton Papers). This is Thomas West, *Guide to the Lakes* (1778), bound in with Thomas Hurtley, *A Concise Account of some Natural Curiosities in the Environs of Malham, in Craven, Yorkshire* (London: Longman, 1786). From the second edition onwards, West's *Guide* included among its Addenda the full text of John Hutton, *A Tour to the Caves, in the Environs of Ingleborough and Settle* (1781). See Bicknell, *The Picturesque Scenery*, op. cit., 33–42. Also my articles C. Heywood, 'A Yorkshire Background', op. cit., loc. cit.; and C. Heywood, 'Yorkshire Slavery', op. cit., loc. cit.
22. Hutton, *Tour to the Caves*, in West, *Guide to the Lakes* (1812), op. cit., 243.
23. Ann Radcliffe, *A Journey Made in the Summer of 1794* (1795), cited in T. H. A. Fielding and John Walton, *A Picturesque Tour of the English Lakes* (London: Ackermann, 1821), 7.
24. Mrs Ellis H. Chadwick, *In the Footsteps of the Brontës* (London: Isaac Pitman, 1914), 75–6.
25. Cumbria Record Office, Kendal Casterton School.
26. Letter to Patrick Brontë, cited in Winifred Gérin, *Emily Brontë. A Biography* (Oxford: Oxford University Press, 1979), 127.

Under the Influence:
Romanticism and Christina Rossetti

Paul Hullah

One discourse which substantially informs the intertextual framework constructing Christina Rossetti's poetry is that arising from her inheritance of certain poetic doctrines purveyed by the Romantics. I would like, here, to clarify Rossetti's position in this respect. As to the revision of Romantic ideology undertaken in Rossetti's writing, the devotional aspect of her verse, coincident with her Anglo-Christian beliefs, is highly relevant.

Christina Rossetti's religious background relied upon a specifically nineteenth-century coupling of Low Church Evangelism (in which tradition her mother had tutored her) and a warmly embraced High Church Tractarianism. During her teenage years, Christina found the Anglo-Catholicism of Pusey, Keble and Newman immensely affecting as a system of belief and, when the female members of the Rossetti family became regulars of the congregation at Christ Church, Albany Street, her conversion to Tractarianism became complete.[1]

As Mayberry points out, whilst Rossetti's religious beliefs were firmly moulded around the central tenets of Tractarianism, her poetry is also conditioned by some 'central aesthetic assumptions' of Newman and Keble in particular, and of the Oxford Movement in general. Literal biblical typology does not predominate in Rossetti's best (we would argue, earliest) devotional poems but baptismal motifs and those of holy communion and marriage are frequently employed as metaphors: the desirability of discipline, submission to divine instruction, asceticism, prayer-like meditation and notions of guilt and penitence increasingly pervade the writings of Rossetti through time which deal explicitly with matters of piety. Whilst Chapman frames a persuasive case for regarding Rossetti as directly a product of the Oxford Movement,[2] Mayberry's qualifying conditions are recognized as pertinent here. Rossetti's finest art is an intertextual synthesis of multiple perspectives, and not simply the unilateral regurgitation of one dominant philosophy which her final devotional productions became. In summary, Mayberry's conditions are these:

> . . . it is at a broad, general level that [Rossetti's] religious
> sensibility is most valuable as a gloss to her poetry...
> In Rossetti's case, the aesthetic implications of the
> [Tractarian] movement had a far greater and long-lived
> influence than did its theological subtleties.[3]

It would be difficult to dispute G. B. Tennyson's statement that Rossetti is a 'far finer poet than her Tractarian predecessors',[4] but the reasons I would offer in support of this claim – those over and above her precise use of diction, metrical ingenuity and innovative employment of Tractarian conventions and motifs mentioned above – are those which need careful attention. Again, the fundamental Tractarian values are plainly evident in Rossetti's verse. These have been classified as 'typology, nature, art, liturgical forms, and above all, the yearning for oneness with God'.[5] More than anything else, the Tractarians invoked a vision of the world as a system of symbols: nature becomes, in this system, a symbolic register through which mouthpiece the divinity – via the processes known as Analogy and Reserve – communicates clues to us of a better, hidden world beyond our own temporal dimension. This sacramental world-view was attractive to the Pre-Raphaelites, who adopted pregnant natural images in their art, both visual and written, offering beauty itself as a work's subject matter in a post-Romantic quest for spiritual permanence. In Keble's *Tract 89*, where both Analogy and Reserve are explicitly defined, the fundamental Tractarian position is formulated:

> In like manner, the Mystical, or Christian, or Theological
> use of [the material world] is the reducing to a particular
> set of symbols and associations, which we have reason to
> believe has, more or less, the authority of the GREAT
> CREATOR Himself.[6]

The belief, adopted in some of Rossetti's earliest lyrics, is that material instances in the natural world are types of elements unseen in the next world (Analogy), this condition being a divine truth that God, being ultimately incomprehensible, could only gradually, indirectly (by Reserve) allow us hints of in this life. 'Thou Sleepest where the Lilies Fade' (*Poems*, III, 221),[7] a two stanza lyric composed before 1853, illustrates Rossetti's early acceptance of the notion that the natural works of God on earth are but fleeting types of the eternal, joyous truths to be experienced in the afterlife:

> Thou sleepest where the lilies fade,
> Thou dwellest where the lilies fade not;
> Sweet, when thine earthly part decayed
> Thy heavenly part decayed not.

Thou dwellest where the roses blow,
The crimson roses bud and blossom;
While on thine eyes is heaped the snow,
The snow upon thy bosom.

This poem works by simple antithetical juxtapositions – 'sleepest . . . dwellest . . . decayed . . . decayed not'. A winter landscape encloses the dead party's tomb and yet perennial spring is simultaneously enjoyed in heaven. Heavenly correlatives of the natural instances on earth (the Analogical process) are seen as permanent universal essences – knowable only through the Reserve exercised by the divinity (Who does not appear in the poem, but remains the unquestioned centre of intelligibility behind it, guaranteeing its conditions, the controller of the whole scheme of things), where death must precede higher knowledge. 'Shadows today, while shadows show God's Will' (*Poems*, II, 331), Rossetti affirms of the Analogical mode elsewhere and, in a late piece from the 'Songs for Strangers and Pilgrims' series published in the 1893 *Verses*, the Tractarian philosophy is unambiguously expressed:

The twig teacheth,
The moth preacheth,
The plant vaunteth,
The bird chanteth,
God's mercy overflowing . . . (*Poems*, II, 332)

Rossetti's inheritance of the Tractarian position is clear, and yet it is only one element of the full equation that her most effective poetry attempts to solve. In her latest, heavily exegetical texts (those published by the S. P. C. K. between the mid-1870s and her death in 1894), Rossetti consistently offers a specifically Tractarian adherence to unity with the Christian deity through unquestioning repetition of devotion. In these later pieces, the fervent artistic quest for personal, individual expression which characterizes Rossetti's best work is finally overtaken by what G. B. Tennyson refers to as 'Keble's bedrock principle that poetry is the expression of intense religious longing'.[8] In this manner, through a self-imposed exile from questioning and doubt, Rossetti was ultimately to achieve that centered pose of stability and coherence which is constantly denied as an available option in her earlier poems.

But it is here my purpose to outline the formative influence that religious belief exercised upon Rossetti's earlier work, and how this brought about tension through a repeated interplay with other values inherited from Romantic thought. G. B. Tennyson urges us to read

Rossetti's 'yearnings' as wholly 'religious' rather than 'psychological',[9] but the two cannot be regarded as mutually exclusive where Rossetti is concerned. In fact, it is the intensely doubtful, ever-renewable debate between post-Romantic, proto-feminist and ascetic Tractarian ideological positions which frequently complicates the already complex intertextual strategies at work in Rossetti's finest work. In a post-Romantic sense (Wordsworth and Coleridge were enormous influences upon Keble in particular)[10] the poetic faculty was the element which allowed us potentially to reconstruct a stable sense of identity from the mutable but sacramentally loaded natural world around us. 'Images' and 'similes', said Keble

> guide us by gentle hints and no uncertain signs, to the very utterances of Nature, or we may more truly say, of the Author of Nature.[11]

Poetry thus becomes a form of religious experience and, as we shall see, this is one distinct energy informing Rossetti's earliest, so-called 'secular' lyrics as well as her many devotional poems. Yet the correspondence in Rossetti's poetry between this divinely allocated role for the artist and the many other ideologies operating upon her as a Victorian woman writer lends her work a lively sense of distrust and self-doubt that is highly appealing in its consequent resistance of complacency, until this tension becomes progressively checked into monotonous exegetical repetition in the devotional poetry and prose with which Rossetti self-consciously chose to conclude her career.

A collision of ideologies then – between the essential quality allocated to nature and the human imagination by Romanticism, and the subjugation of both of these to divine omnipotence demanded by Christian dogma – may be witnessed in Rossetti's work. This markedly conditions many responses within the poetry and carries implications concerning first the redirecting of Romantic ideals and, second, the simultaneous commentary on religious iconography and doctrine enacted by the text. The Romantics aspired towards communion with nature as the ultimate goal with which human imaginative capabilities could be rewarded. Coordination with nature on a successful, reciprocal basis for the individual and, organically, for society is seen as a necessary prerequisite by the Romantics in their endeavors to sustain faith in the primacy of human constructiveness. Wordsworth himself began by elevating this position but, in *The Excursion*, moved towards a form of Christian orthodoxy. Devotional codes, such as those inherited by Rossetti from her vigorous biblical studies, also promote the human imagination, but as a gift from a

God who is a greater universal essence of those particular instances which He has bestowed upon earth for us to construe. Similarly, from a Tractarian standpoint nature is significant not as an infinite end, but as a revelation, a concrete manifestation of a divine, ethereal presence. Cantalupo, distinguishing between this Romantic 'immanence' and Christian 'transcendence', remarks upon Rossetti's perception of the ambiguity:

> Believing that [a] single flower was a type . . . of God's
> love, Rossetti could not accept the implication of some
> Romantic poetry that God was, for example, in the tree
> rather than the tree's maker.[12]

The pre-eminence afforded to human imagination and the world of nature by conventionally expounded ideology is challenged, as it had been by elements of late Romantic thought, as an absolute ideal in the poetry of Christina Rossetti. The sequence (date of composition unknown) of twenty eight sonnets titled *Later Life* (*Poems*, II, 138–50) may be read as illustrative of Rossetti's ambivalent opinion in this area.[13] The cycle begins with a direct, unambiguous declaration of divine permanence and omnipotence:

> Before the mountains were brought forth, before
> Earth and the world were made, then God was God:
> And God will still be God when flames shall roar
> Round earth and heaven dissolving at His nod . . . (I, 1–4)

God is conceived of as the origin of all else in the ontological system the poem begins to construct. God made the 'mountains', symbolizing nature, and so nature is seen not as an absolute but as a sacramental reflection of divine power. God is given as the principle of intelligibility, the centre, guarantee of meaning: 'God was God' and 'God will still be God' – the system of signification generated within this devotional sonnet is one with certainty of reference. But, typically for Rossetti, this complacency is set up as such only rapidly to be analyzed and questioned in terms of its implications. Having established this stable devotional frame of reference, the text immediately steps outside its jurisdiction and offers criticism of the certitudes it implies, presenting religious security as a wholly ambiguous prospect. The absolute certainty promoted by the first sonnet implies a closed system. That the sequence continues at all (for another twenty seven stanzas) represents rejection of that closure. Anxiety is felt in the text as activity, which begins to set itself against the devotional dogma:

> Let us today, while it is called today
> Set out, if utmost speed may yet avail -
> The shadows lengthen and the light grows pale:
> For who through darkness and the shadow of death,
> Darkness that may be felt, shall find a way,
> Blind-eyed, deaf-eared, and choked with failing breath?
> (II, 9–14)

Again, in the spirit of the poems of faith and doubt in Tennyson's *In Memoriam*, this disturbing and compelling image proceeds from a desire to circumvent or escape the stifling clutches of a closed system. The text desires, with 'utmost speed', to set itself apart from an atmosphere of self-satisfying ('today while it is called today') reference. Such a system, in its dogmatic certitude, stifles all possibility of articulation, leaving the text 'Blind-eyed, deaf-eared, and choked with failing breath'. The cycle continues its deconstruction of the devotional epistemological framework it initially promoted, in places – 'If making makes us Thine then Thine we are' – adopting sarcasm as a manner of reproach toward the closed referential process it is moving (literally as the poem continues, and philosophically) away from. By the mid-point of the sequence, its formal centre, the notion of a 'centre' has been wholly rejected. Unity is shown to be a relative, not an absolute idea:

> Our teachers teach that one and one make two:
> Later, Love rules that one and one make one:
> Abstruse the problems! neither need we shun,
> But skillfully to each should yield its due . . .
> Both provable by me, and both by you. (XVI, 1–8)

Indeed, there is a tone of pleasure pervasive here, as the text celebrates its achievement of an exchange. Those redundant certitudes, the notion of closure inherent in the dialectics of the opening sonnet, have given way to open-ended semantic activity:

> Befogged and witless, in a wordy maze
> A groping stroll perhaps may do us good;
> If cloyed we are with much we have understood . . . (XVI, 9–11)

This emphatic desire to dislodge the mechanics of a significatory system built upon certitude and closure must be accompanied by a total decentering process, a rejection of traditional principles of reference:

> I am sick of where I am and where I am not,
> I am sick of foresight and of memory,
> I am sick of all I have and all I see,
> I am sick of self, and there is nothing new;
> O weary impatient patience of my lot! (XVIII, 9–12)

These repeated rejections of potential stability mark something of a turning point in the *Later Life* sequence. The antithetical juxtaposition 'impatient patience' – two oppositional signifiers made to relate directly to one another – marks a complete usurpation of the closed, self-congratulatory system of signification offered earlier in the sonnet cycle from a conventional devotional position. Stability has been demolished by the text, and reconstruction is now attempted, heralded by a turning towards a new frame of reference. With God displaced as a principle of intelligibility, the text looks now to nature.

A *manner* of reconstruction begins. For the poem to continue, it must. The natural world may offer a potential way out of the 'wordy maze' with no fixed centre which the text has come to represent. A 'Winter' landscape is envisaged 'not so drear as was my boding dream', to ensure that the text itself does not become frozen by its own lack of centering principle:

> Still here a bud and there a blossom seem
> Hopeful, and robin still is musical.
> Leaves, flowers and fruit and one delightful song
> Remain . . . (XIX, 7–10)

The isolation of 'Remain' achieved by caesural stopping and the accumulation of qualifying subjects in the preceding line reinforces the aspect of endurance and permanence which the text has now allocated to nature as the quest begins for a new mode of articulation. It is not coincidental that the natural images are closely associated here with 'musical' notions of 'delightful song' as the cycle seeks a new voice. Neither is it by chance that the text turns attention directly away from the 'robin', traditionally the bird of endurance, and the 'hundred solitary birds [which] salute the day' to rest emphasis upon another particular bird from nature – the nightingale:

> One solitary bird salutes the night:
> Its mellow grieving wiles our grief away,
> And tunes our weary watches to delight;
> It seems to think the thoughts we cannot say,
> To know and sing them, and to set them right;

Until we feel once more that May is May,
And hope some buds may bloom without a blight. (XX, 2–8)

This new mode of articulation is conceived in terms of the song of the
nightingale, an important image in Romantic poetry, conveying not
firm belief and confidence in Romanticism unqualified but a strong
note of scepticism, the Romantic agony. In his *Defence of Poetry*,
Shelley likens the poet to this bird:

A Poet is a nightingale who sits in darkness and sings to
cheer its own solitude with sweet sounds . . .[14]

This beautiful image carries the sense of loss which infuses some Romantic texts, a step down from high Romantic dogma, springing from
doubts that the imagination may not be, as Wordsworth terms it in *The
Prelude*, an 'absolute strength', guaranteeing communion with what
Shelley calls 'the eternal, the infinite, and the one'.[15] The nightingale,
immortalised as a symbol in Keats's 'Ode' (and ingeniously remanaged
in Yeats's 'Sailing to Byzantium'), presents an ambivalent image of potentially distressing isolation. In restating this image, Rossetti shows
herself allied to the scepticism already urged by some Romantic texts
towards the Romantic belief in the existence of a vital relationship
between the individual poetic imagination and a broader realm of
existence in the world of exteriors. In *Later Life*, Rossetti's use of the
nightingale also implies scepticism towards this relationship. The text
goes on to study this relationship, making this study a direct response
to its own recent destabilising process. The basis of the search for a
principle of intelligibility becomes the realisation that a *stable* principle will not be forthcoming. The sequence begins to borrow familiar
Romantic codes:

A host of things I take on trust: I take
The nightingales on trust, for few and far
Between those actual summer moments are
When I have heard that melody they make. (XXI, 1–4)

Conveying scepticism towards what many Victorian commentators
dogmatically regarded as Romantic unities, this nightingale image prefaces a direct commentary upon a high Romantic notion –
that of Wordsworth's often ambiguously presented 'spots of time'.
A sceptical stance is adopted by the text 'on trust' towards the
Wordsworthian 'summer moments' of intensity and communion with
the natural world. The sonnet continues, simultaneously inhabiting and

deconstructing Wordsworthian discourse. In doing so, Rossetti shows herself aware of the pitfalls in the reading of Wordsworth as prophet and sage which ignores what we now see as areas of questioning. The 'boy and boat' episode of Wordsworth's *Prelude* is addressed and its inherent uncertainties, overlooked by many nineteenth-century champions of Romanticism, are brought into the foreground of Rossetti's re-reading:

> So chanced it once at Como on the Lake:
> But all things, then, waxed musical; each star
> Sang on its course, each breeze sang on its car,
> All harmonies sang to senses wide awake.
> All things in tune, myself not out of tune . . . (XXI, 5–9)

The poetry here is informed with what appears to be a standard expression of that conjunction achieved in archetypal modes of Romanticism between the innermost self and the natural world of exteriors. But the lines which follow are more of a sceptical commentary upon this platitude than an affirmation. The ultimate Romantic attachment of self and surroundings is suffixed by a tone of calculated detachment:

> Those nightingales were nightingales indeed:
> Yet truly an owl had satisfied my need,
> And wrought a rapture underneath that moon,
> Or simple sparrow chirping from a reed;
> For June that night glowed like a doubled June. (XXI, 10–4)

Later Life here reminds one of Wordsworth's own doubts as to Romantic stability and certitude as to subjectivity, recasting that objection in a reminder of the redundant nature of closed signifying systems – the nightingales 'were nightingales indeed' and June similarly justifies itself as 'like a doubled June'. Aware of the stagnation (illustrated in the sequence's opening sonnet) which such a manner of conjunction can imply, Rossetti here gently mocks post-Romantic, popular Victorian enthusiasm concerning the stable subject. If the object world has been assimilated into the subject sphere, the problem of the object is not solved, but simply placed within a different frame of reference. Representationalism is exchanged for idealism, but the subject/object relation still pertains. Having established stable subjectivity and absolute communion with the natural world, assimilating subject and object, Rossetti immediately attacks this complacent pose by ridiculing its implications. If the problem of the object is no more, then what does it matter which object we settle upon? Anything will signify – 'truly an owl had satisfied my need . . ./ Or simple sparrow' – given Rossetti's desire to inhabit the margins of a Romantically inspired position which once regarded stability as an attainable end.

Later Life makes provocative judgements about systems of signification and, notably, by insinuating an ambivalent interplay between Christian and Romantic ideologies, rejects any notion of a stable subjectivity. By considering signification and articulation as topics, the poem becomes self-referential, its own subject. The rejection of dogmatic readings of Romanticism is emphasised in sonnet XXII which again adopts a Wordsworthian register only to collapse its arguments from within. The famous Alpine scenes of Book Six of *The Prelude* are invoked:

> The mountains in their overwhelming might
> Moved me to sadness when I saw them first,
> And afterwards they moved me to delight;
> Struck harmonies from silent chords which burst
> Out into song, a song by memory nursed . . . (XXII, 1–5)

The contradiction within the image arrives in a manner similar to that effected in the preceding sonnet, simultaneously recalling Wordsworth's own ambivalence in *The Prelude*:

> Tumult and peace, the darkness and the light
> Were all like workings of one mind, the features
> Of the same face . . . [16]

In Rossetti's sonnet, the 'pleasure and . . .wonder' of this spiritual communion are reduced and crystalized into one obvious object-image, the 'forget-me-not' flower. But what power of reference can this image have if the subject-object gap is closed in blissful concordance? If signification closes in certainty of reference what place is left for a 'crown'-ing metaphoric enhancement?

> Yet why should such a flower choose such a spot?
> Could we forget that way which we once went
> Tho' not one flower had bloomed to weave its crown?
>   (XXII, 12–4)

Through establishing affinity in her earliest lyrics with those areas of scepticism and fear of mutability present in Wordsworth and Coleridge, Rossetti has come, by this point, to confront complacent readings of Romanticism with their inherent formative inconsistencies. The poetry actively deconstructs the premises from which it appears to proceed. Notions of stability are dislodged and replaced by a regard for fragmentation, disunity and, finally, relativity. The Romantic assertion of stable subjectivity is upsetting to Rossetti as a woman writer and is thus cancelled in favor of the later ambivalent presentation of selfhood, resulting in a formulation of the self as divided, unstable. Duality abounds – 'we consider what this life we lead/Is not, and is' (XXV, 1–2) – and the irrational is promoted to a level coincident with the rational. The unconscious is recognized as a site of meaning, and this identification colors further the rewriting of Romantic values one finds in Rossetti's poetry. Belsey points out the implications of this attention when she speaks of

> the notion of a unitary and autonomous subject, ultimate
> origin of its own choices. The existence of the unconscious
> puts this notion into question.[17]

Indeed, acute consciousness of self is a pervasive theme in Rossetti's work:

> All my walls are lost in mirrors, whereupon I trace
> Self to right hand, self to left hand, self in every place,
> Self-same solitary figure, self-same seeking face.
> (*Poems*, I, 149)

The idea of the self as irreconcilably divided is present in 'Reflection' (*Poems*, III, 266–8) with its image of the imprisoned autonomous 'soul':

> Gazing thro' her chamber window
> Sits my soul's dear soul;
> Looking northward, looking southward,
> Looking to the goal,
> Looking back without control . . .

The speaker's unconscious, 'my soul's dear soul', is envisaged as 'without control', a site of production of meaning formed around no fixed center, a measure of the irrational. Again, this offers a modification to the Romantic ideals inherited by Rossetti. Imagination itself is thus revalued in Rossetti's poetry.

In a prose work of 1883, *Letter and Spirit*, one can detect, from the creative artist's standpoint, some dissatisfaction with the degree of primacy allocated to imagination, albeit coupled with admission of the imagination's importance.

> To modify by a boundless license of imagination the Voice of Revelation, or of tradition, or our own perceptions, concerning the universe, its Ruler, features, origin, destinies, falls within the range of human faculties.[18]

Imagination is conceived of here, in Coleridgean fashion, as a power with 'boundless license' and yet, in the same breath, is allocated boundaries. It is reliant upon 'our own perceptions' which, in turn, are drawn from a 'universe' with a controlling 'Ruler'. Perception is vouched for as 'other' to imagination and these two exist exterior to a 'Ruler' beyond. But the admission that imagination can 'modify by a boundless license' the data received by means of these other epistemological sites does in fact guarantee imagination the primary status which the devotional aspect of Rossetti's argument is elsewhere at pains to revoke.

> For if (as I have seen pointed out) God is not to be called like His creature, whose grace is simply typical, but that creature is like him because expressive of His archetypal Attribute, it suggests itself that for every aspect of creation there must exist the corresponding Divine attribute.[19]

There is an awkward tone of hollow self-justification about these statements – 'as I have seen pointed out . . . it suggests itself' – which undermines their resolution. The speaker is involved in a blinkered attempt at convincing herself of the validity of the pious dogma she regurgitates. The semi-pantheistic conception of nature and the Platonic view of 'the inadequacy of ought temporal to shadow forth that which is eternal' are clearly at odds with the aesthetic of Romanticism, but this thesis sits uncomfortably with the reverence for human imagination as essentially 'boundless'. An ontological system of existence is generated, and the element which deconstructs this system, necessary to its formation yet simultaneously outside its parameters, is imagination. Rossetti negates the stable concept of subjectivity offered by insensitive interpretations of Romanticism and heralds a re-reading of nature and imagination, thus a re-reading of the nature of reading (perception) itself. Cantalupo is right to declare that Rossetti is 'ambivalent about the Romantic view of nature':

> Clearly she inherits the Romantic concern with epistemology; she wonders 'How do subject and object meet in a meaningful relationship? By what means do we have a significant aware-ness of the world?' Consequently, Rossetti sometimes records the process of reading nature as well as the content of that reading, valuing the flux of her experience of nature, with its misrepresentations as well as its insights.[20]

This is a crucial point. Rossetti's poetry extends inherent Romantic am-bivalence and forms an intertextual investigation of the premises upon which 'certitudes' are founded. It shuns absolutes in favour of relative concepts, aware, as a stanza from 'An Old World Thicket' (*Poems*, II, 123–8) neatly summarizes, that to posit one system of 'truth' is to acknowledge all opposing alternative 'other' possible truths:

> For all that was but showed what all was not,
> But gave clear proof of what might never be;
> Making more destitute my poverty,
> And yet more blank my lot,
> And me much gladder by its jubilee.

Presence denotes absence with Rossetti: it is through absence that pres-ence is often conveyed. The sadness left behind by a departed love, memories, the past, echoes, thoughts of one now dead; Rossetti con-tinually reminds us that being carries with it the possibility of not being, desire implies a lack. Certainty relies upon the possibility of uncertainty:

> We lack, yet cannot fix upon the lack:
> Not this, nor that; yet somewhat, certainly.
> We see the things we do not yearn to see
> Around us and what see we glancing back?
> Lost hopes that leave our hearts upon the rack,
> Hopes that were never ours yet seemed to be . . . (VI, 1–6)

This compelling series of propositions and negations forms the opening to another sonnet of the *Later Life* cycle. It constitutes one of the most concentrated examples, plainly articulated in straightforward etymol-ogy, of the collapsing of certitude in Rossetti's verse. From the very outset, the text is wholly unable to 'fix upon' the concept, 'lack', which forms its fundamental premise, 'We lack'. Grammatical certainty is simultaneously nudged as the verb becomes a noun within a single line. The second line, with its ironic 'certainly', does nothing to assuage the quandary of its predecessor, awkwardly stringing together a staccato succession of partial significations. Perception, given as sight ('We see') is also partially realized and leaves desire, with its implication of lack still pronounced, unfulfilled; 'We see the things we do not yearn to see'. The second attempt at perception is even more unsuccessful than the first as we see 'Lost hopes' that never 'were' but only 'seemed', leaving 'our hearts upon the rack' and the desire informing the poem unfulfilled. Blake has observed how, in Rossetti's poetry, hope is often 'hope deferred', a hope never allowed into being and, thus, not hope at all.[21] Here, we look in vain for 'Lost hopes' in a sonnet which leaves us

> Straining dim eyes to catch the invisible sight,
> And strong to bear ourselves in patient pain? (VI, 13–4)

It is a question unresolved, as we have seen, in terms of the cycle as a whole. *Later Life* gives no single answer since its whole strategy has denied the possibility of such certitude.

In Rossetti's writing, then, we observe conscious scrutiny of the notion of certainty. This represents rejection of the stable subjectivity which some Romantic poetry had appeared to offer as a legacy to the Victorian writer and a marked alliance with the scepticism inherent in late Romantic writing as to that stability. The vital union between language and figure, the distinguishing feature of fully realized Romantic poetry, had successfully constituted a transcendent principle of order compensating for the collapse of natural and historical continuity which plagued the human spirit in the eighteenth century. A poem no longer evoked a pattern outside itself but constituted that pattern from within itself; the world constructed became inseparable from the poetic activity which made it; morality becomes activity, not a code or a system. Imagination assumed a redemptive role, the creative act generating an order inherent within its workings, no longer mimetic of an order outside itself but symbolically constituting that order through union of subject and object, letter and spirit. Hitherto incompatible orders of reality were fused in a spiritual celebration which language could constitute and form. Bloom and Frye have analysed the 'internalization' disclosed in this manner of writing and the programme of spiritual decline and recovery which it began to instil in texts of the Romantic period. The symbolic projection of the internal landscape of the psyche onto that of the external world fused the two realms together in a subject/object unity of sense. Meaning could be generated from the ordering principle of this new stable subjectivity, epistemology was vouchsafed by a new-found manner of certitude.

The second-generation Romantics (Shelley in particular) had already exhibited anxiety towards this confidence in the absolute strength of the imagination – the apocalyptic despair of *Alastor* and the solipsistic unquiet of the *Defence of Poetry*. Rossetti's early lyrics, in a manner becoming increasingly impatient in sustained pieces such a *Later Life*, form a continuity between Romantic ambivalence and Victorian doubt. Initially appropriating areas of Romantic expression and latterly emphasizing the inconsistencies and unease already inherent in those areas through her own discomfort with complacency, Rossetti discloses scepticism towards any manner of surety, self-conscious concern with the subject/object relationship and anxiety as to the very nature of 'reality'. On one level, the easily dogmatized Romantic assertion of stable subjectivity, fusion of subject and object brought about by communion of inner and outer, might be read as an attempt to abolish the problem of the object world. The object is overcome as 'other' by deft relocation within subjectivity and inner consciousness: rather than annihilating the issue, this manipulation simply presents the Victorian poet with the task of redefining the subject/object relationship from within a new framework. In attempting to abolish the problematic object, Romanticism only succeeded in suppressing it inside a fresh epistemological system, thereby summoning later scepticism in poets such as Wordsworth towards such a reductive procedure. The whole nature of reality, not simply the status of one element (the object) within that version of existence, had been qualified by what critics held to be the initial Romantic assertion of stable subjectivity and the battlefield for late eighteenth-century commentators (and those of today) which that area became. Idealism, based upon a fundamental unity of the perceiving mind, had in fact been urged by the Romantics as a new philosophical position.

Many Victorian writers took this Romantic idealism to task not as a model of basic subjectivity (as it had been offered to them) which had internalized and drawn the external object world under its friendly wing, but as a model of total perception and, therefore, still involving the subject/object *relationship* as an essential formative element. Christina Rossetti, undoubtedly, was one such writer.

Notes
1. No proof exists as to whether or not Rossetti read Newman, though she did own a hand-annotated copy of Keble's *Christian Year* and she admired the poetry of Isaac Williams. Her most

'significant and influential' exposure to Tractarian values, how-ever, came from the sermons of the Reverend William Dodsworth, Perpetual Curate of Christ's Church, 1837–50. See Katherine J. Mayberry, *Christina Rossetti The Poetry of Discovery* (Baton Rouge: Louisiana State U.P., 1989), 111 and Antony H. Harrison, *Christina Rossetti in Context* (Sussex: Harvester, 1988), 69.

2. Raymond Chapman, 'Uphill all the Way' in *Faith and Revolt Studies in the Literary Influence of the Oxford Movement* (London: Weidenfeld and Nicholson, 1970), 170–97.
3. Mayberry, 111.
4. George B. Tennyson, *Victorian Devotional Poetry* (Cambridge, Mass.: Harvard U. P., 1981), 202.
5. *ibid.*, 203.
6. John Keble, *Tract 89* in *Tracts for the Times* (London: Rivingtons, 1840) vol. V, 143.
7. All references to Rossetti's poems are from, Rebecca W. Crump ed., *Complete Poems of Christina Rossetti* (Baton Rouge: Louisiana State U. P., 1979–90) 3 vols.
8. Tennyson, 202.
9. *ibid.*, 203.
10. See Harrison, 73, 77.
11. John Keble, *Lectures on Poetry*, translated by E. K. Francis (Oxford: Clarendon, 1912), vol. II, 481.
12. Catherine M. Cantalupo, 'Christina Rossetti the Devotional Poet and the Rejection of Romantic Nature' in, David A. Kent ed., *The Achievement of Christina Rossetti* (Ithaca: Cornell, 1987), 279.
13. Quotations from *Later Life* are given by the number of the son-net in the sequence and the line numbers of that sonnet. *Later Life* was published in *A Pageant, and Other Poems* (London: Macmillan, 1881) but the dates of composition of the sonnets, thought to range from 1860 to 1879, were not recorded by the author.
14. Percy B. Shelley, *A Defence of Poetry* in *Complete Works*, ed. R. Ingpen and W. E. Peck (London: Ernest Benn, 1965), vol. VII, 116.
15. *ibid.*, 112.
16. Wordsworth, William, *The Prelude*, ed. E. De Selincourt (Oxford: O.U.P., 1970), 100.
17. Catherine Belsey, 'The Romantic Construction of the Unconscious' in *Literature, Politics and Theory; Papers from the Essex Conference 1976–84* ed. F. Barker (London: Methuen, 1986), 58–9.
18. Christina G. Rossetti, *Letter and Spirit, Notes on the Commandments* (London: Society for Promoting Christian Knowledge, 1883), 10.

19. *ibid.*, 13.
20. Cantalupo, 282–3.
21. see Kathleen Blake, *Love and the Woman Question in Victorian Literature* (Sussex: Harvester, 1983), 3–25.

Haikai:
Can Romanticism Take a Joke?

Douglas Kenning

> Little flower – if but I could understand
> What you are, root and all, and all in all,
> I should know what God and man is.
> > Tennyson

> My prayer is to die beneath the blossoming cherry,
> in that spring month of flowers,
> when the moon is full
> > Saigyó (1118–90)

> Among evening flowers
> the shy young maiden is heard
> blowing her nose
> > Kobayashi Issa (1763–1827)

For a Japanese, Issa's poem passes beyond contrast into contradiction, and beyond contradiction to synthesis.[1] For Zen, synthesis can be universal (*tai'chi*, 'sincerity') or individual enlightenment, 'liberation' (*satori*). It means harmony (*wa*) and 'truth' and 'can be reached only through the comprehension of opposites' contradictions, paradoxes, the seeking of the polar star in the Southern sky.[2] The mind must seek this wa by not seeking it, the same paradox of Wordsworthian 'wise passiveness' and Keats's 'negative capability':

> Wildly raging sea
> over Sado Island spreads
> quiet the galaxy
> > Matsuo Bashó (1644–94)

There is much that is Romantic – German and English – in this paradox and synthesis.[3]

Romanticism affirms the reality of contradiction that it may be a force for unity; Zen denies its reality. Contradiction, dialectic, and paradox are illusions; Zen uses these, confronts them (in paradoxical questions, *koan*), grasps them like Proteus to show differentiation unreal.

> All melancholy
> I ascend the hill to find
> thorn bushes blooming

Yosa Buson (1716–83)

All traditional Japanese arts seek to express the unity of 'the Leading Principle (Heaven), the Subordinate Principle (Earth)', and 'the Reconciling Principle (Man)'.[4] They converge on the singularity of *satori*, the condition of *wa*. This is what Matsuo Bashó, the greatest of haikai poets, meant in saying, 'There is nothing you see that is not a flower; there is nothing you can think of which is not the moon'.[5]

> Out in the grassland
> free and above earthly things
> the skylark singing

Bashó

'Paradox is the life of haiku', R. H. Blyth tells us.[6] Prior to Byron's 'anti-Romanticism', English Romanticism never found in itself the self-effacement of Zen. Romantic paradox retired into furrow-browed dialectic, rarely knowing that 'convulsive inclination to laughter about the mouth' that Hazlitt (though no one else) claims to have detected in Wordsworth.[7] Yet, though treated by them with po-faced seriousness, contradiction for the English Romantics typically was not extended into the truly serious issues of spirituality and fundamental truth, remaining rather in creative psychology.[8] For Bashó, dialect began in the serious fundamental and spiritual nature of things, but never was dour: 'every truth has a kind of untruth that draws us by its very absurdity . . . its self-contradictory nature'.[9] Though sharing the notion that all things have within themselves the seeds of their own contradiction, and through it their own elevation, Zen, unlike most Romanticism, employed humor as a chief instrument. Its route to harmony was to deflate, to eliminate the self.

Traditional Japanese poetry has deep roots; if anything, Japanese poetry has shaped Japanese Zen rather than the reverse. Behind both lay an aesthetic philosophy of the intimate glimpse at fundamental reality, the narrow focus, the emptied mind. This inner aesthetic defines Japanese Zen, her arts and ethic centering on *chado* ('the Way of Tea') and its attendant aids to reflection: the *tokonoma* (the alcove), *shodó* (calligraphy), *ikebana* (flower arranging), *yakimono* (pottery), *tei-en* (the Japanese Garden), *sumiye* (the black and white scroll painting), *kaiseki ryó ri* (Japanese haute cuisine). The Zen spiritual aesthetic seeks every manner of limitation that the imagination might be most free. So is it in poetry: 'The aim of haiku is to express . . . [t]he idea of becoming with as little material as possible'.[10] There are but 'a very limited variety of subjects considered fit for poetry, and within that limited variety, a limited number of ways of treating them'.[11] There is no broad sweep of events, no grand displays of emotion, no exultation, no great vision, no philosophic speculations, no epic themes, no social reform. The poetry shies demurely from anything suggesting personality or opinion. What in it, then, is Romantic? A Romantic sensibility lurks where it feels with *sabi*, the evocatively flawed, the humble incomplete that is emotionally perfect, and where it rests aware, an unrippled pool of deep feeling. Most of all there is synthesis, whose object is the serene, delicate, melancholic, the philosophic mind retiring into the smallest moment.

Like the original poetry of most cultures, Japanese poetry was born of the toils of the ordinary people. Only the Japanese, however, produced even in these earliest forms a poetry defined in the main by delicacy and restraint, a refined sensitivity to Nature. Yet, such carefulness and precision of thought easily slides into artifice. From the simple and fresh lyricism of such eighth-century collections as *Man'yó shú* ('The Ten Thousand Leaves' [or 'Generations']) and *Nihon Jodai Kayo* ('Collected Japanese Songs'), Japanese poetry hardened into formalism. As the Japanese coalesced into a nation and power centralized, the poetry became monopolized by the court and aristocracy. This court poetry, prior to the influence of Zen, employed Nature to illuminate human concerns (often lapsing into a pathetic fallacy). This did not accord with the self-effacing empathy more natural to the Japanese temper. Heian court poetry (eighth to the twelfth centuries) became almost exclusively social, public recitation with a strong emphasis placed on recondite conceits, technical skill, specific effects, and performance. 'Japanese poetry, bent toward aestheticism, had taken the progressively sterile path of concentration on form'.[12] When the court moved to Kamakura (AD 1185), the now tenuous link to true feeling further dissipated and the poetry became vitiated and rigid.

The term *waka* (now a general term for traditional Japanese poetry) originally referred to the poetry of the Heian court. Out of it, in reaction to its calcification, came *renga*, linked poetry, an irreverent (*mushin*) revolution away from waka's stilted and costive formalism. This was a familiar Japanese dialectic: a national character tending to humor and unserious self-effacement pulling against the serious pretensions of a 'religious' sense of nation and a (Confucian) social instinct expressed as deference to higher or prior authority. This worship function of Japanese poetry and the conformist pressures of the social ethic turned renga itself formulaic, class and rule-bound, and serious (*ushin*), which then necessitated the birth of haikai in the sixteenth century to parody it.

Haikai remained linked to poetry. Since the pre-Heian times, Japanese poetry was a social affair as much in the composition as in the reading (performance): 'collaborative creation, evaluation and appreciation . . . is the lifeblood of Japanese poetry'.[13] Linked poetry involved of a group of poets sitting together (*za*) and linking their lines in a set sequence. *Tanka*, the five-line, thirty-one syllable stanza (at once autonomous and linked), remained the most popular form of renga. The object of each poet was to complete the tanka begun by his predecessor. He would do so either by adding two (seven-syllable) lines to an initial three lines (of five-seven-five syllables) or by adding three lines to complete an opening two. The lines to which he links were themselves the completion of a tanka begun by the poet seated to the right of his predecessor. Progressing through the sequence by this overlapping, added lines should avoid narrative development, but rather take off on a new tangent by reinterpreting the immediately previous lines in a strikingly new way. They would have to offer this inventive turn while simultaneously keeping emotional coherence and following the complex rules governing the progression of themes and the hundreds of rules for linking specific images within the composition as a whole. In a linked poetry evening, each poet would be under a time constraint as well.[14] A *kasen* produced at such an evening would be thirty-six stanzas in two broadsheets, front and back.

The latitude for striking off in new directions every third or fourth line was considerable, given a language where gender, number, subject, object, and referent typically are not specified. Further, the language – even the daily language, much more the poetic – is by nature evocative and symbolic. For example, medieval waka played strongly on the sensual associations in the Japanese word for 'color' (*iro*). Various colors became codes for sexual pleasures, seasons, flowers, facial emotions, and racial coloring, in a more direct way than the English language associates color with these areas. Flowers through their associated colors came to stand for certain female eroticisms or other states of charged emotion,[15] while the adjective *iroppoi* acquired the further meaning of 'seductive' or 'erotic'. Gradually, the poets sought transcendent expression, not by rising above the sensual but by taking the sensual with them: the direct experience of colors, specific things of Nature (e.g. seasonal flowers, the moon, certain insects and birds) as representative of a manifold of things beyond themselves, a symbolic language such as Shelley sought.[16]

The technical rules (*shikimoku*) governing imagery and structure set by waka and later by renga in its 'serious' style were equally intricate, sacrosanct, and esoteric.[17] The set structural rhythm of expression through time (in read or spoken texts) is *jo-ha-kyú* ('introduction – development – fast close'). In renga, each of these parts is a specific length or number of stanzas (though overlapping a bit as the emotional flow demands), where the tone and the closeness or distance of the relations between the subjects subtly is altered. Every stanza has a motif, drawing from a menu of established motif categories (*fushimono*, e.g. living things, growing things, manufactured things, natural scenes, social class distinctions, times of the day, etc.), each one evoked by one or more words out of a symbolic language. Certain subjects (subgroups under a motif) have especial reverence and their own governing rules. For example, in a kasen there has to be one flower stanza per sheet, the first in the seventeenth stanza (the eleventh stanza on the back of the first sheet) and the second flower in the thirty-fifth stanza, the fifth and penultimate stanza on the reverse of sheet two. This last is nearly invariable, even in haikai. There must be a moon stanza on each sheet face except the last. The formal position of a moon or flower stanza is in the penultimate line of a sheet face, but where the moon or flower would conflict (on the back of the first sheet), the flower, the rarer thing, has pride of place and the moon moves to the fourteenth stanza, the eighth on the second side. Named flowers, like named insects, are kept very rare, never more than one in a hundred stanzas (normal flower stanzas speak only of *hana*, 'flower'). Similar regulations apply to thousands of identified words and hundreds of possible relations between them. Each reference, be it a specific flower, creature, place, or the moon itself, resonates with a certain amount of power, which must be orchestrated for the harmonious flow of the verse. The underlying rhythms and ultimate references of the motifs and images evoke specific seasons, and their use is restricted to these seasons. The seasons are the touchstones of all Japanese aesthetics. Each *jo-ha-kyú* structure (a dramatic rhythm equally applicable to single phrases or entire collections) is governed by an established sequence of seasonal stanzas. This reflects the understanding that the progress of the seasons themselves is a *jo-ha-kyú* dramatic text scripted by the gods. Shinto pantheism pervades all, and its symbolic language must be revered. In this sense, poetry itself serves religion, is devotional text, and the intricate Procrustean canon that is the waka and renga of medieval aristocratic poetry shows it in cabalistic service.

In a liberal climate this is fertile soil for parody and revolt. As might be expected, even during the Heian period, some independent minds took a contrary course. Saigyó was the late Heian poetic exponent of that Japanese native genius which later was to reshape Zen to its Japanese form. Saigyó wrote *jukkai*, poetic lamentations on the solitary self, in contrast to the courtly waka of his time. He spoke to universal human loneliness, a yearning for companionship that has always endeared him to his readers. His poetry at first was subjective, of the poet and the poet's response to the scene, rather than the scene itself. In later works, the fusion grew closer, and the poet began to vanish into the scene.

In the sixteenth century, it was the rise of a commercial middle class which loosened artistic license, giving rise to *haikai* (which means 'light', 'unserious', 'free'). Yet, the loosening of rigor and seriousness spurred a powerful defense of the notion of poet-as-holy man and poetry-as-divine mysteries. Matsunaga Teitoku (1571–1663) appears as not the first, but the first nationally honored haikai poet. As a writer of haikai, Teitoku rode the rising wave of sentiment ostensibly to popularize the cabalistic world of Japanese verse. Yet, to be accepted fully as a great and serious national poet, he needed an 'induction into the mysteries' of Japanese poetic composition by apprenticeship with the current poetic 'high priest', Tanemichi.[18] Of course, this training was highly esoteric. It included 'spending months memorizing the secret traditions of how to pronounce the names of the successive emperors and the reign-names (*nengó*)' and studying the traditions surrounding that most revered early Heian waka collection, the *Kokinshū* (ca. 920), which set the template for Japanese poetry for a millennium. He remained seduced by the esoterica and far from the exoteric spirit of Zen.[19]

The strong 'religiousness' of Japanese poetry shows in the very similar treatment accorded Confucian texts and scholarship during this period. Kept from the 'blasphemy' of translation out of the Chinese, these texts were 'transmitted mainly as secret traditions', defended 'jealously' by the ruling families, who would ensure 'passing them only to their eldest sons . . .'.[20] The translation of some of the Confucian texts into Japanese in 1599 was a watershed in religious reform and reflects the spirit of this haikai age. Religion and poetry, in fact, did not move in parallel, but as one. William LaFleur bases his look into 'Buddhism and the literary arts of Japan' on the assumption that 'the medieval period of Japan is best viewed in terms of a strong conflation of the religious and literary dimensions of human experience'.[21] Japanese philosophy always had found its expression, even its values and dimensions, in literature. Until modern times, it had no separate existence. Imported Asian religions the Japanese also folded into literature (in a less functional way also into the other arts). Behind literature, shaping the way a people think, lay the Japanese language, a language which frames thought in pragmatic, worldly terms, and thinks in continuous, not patterned or compartmentalized time. So can time and its events be collapsed into a few syllables of poetry in the present tense. (*Nó* is one vehicle for this poetry, a drama ever true to its origin in sacred rite.) This 'conflation' of religion and philosophy into literature is helped by the characteristic vagueness, the suggestiveness of the language. As the nexus of religion, art, and ethics, literature (especially poetry) forms 'the central core of Japanese piety'.[22] With the pre-eminence of Zen among the dominant military classes from the mid sixteenth century, and the appearance of such Tea masters as Rikyú (1522–91) life and art merged to form a purely Japanese secular religion.

Yet, this was not a 'religion' to appeal to the new moneyed classes, rising as they were from the lowest rung on the social ladder. Naturally, as irreverent haikai grew in popularity with this new bourgeois class, it grew in disfavor with the defenders of poetry's sacred office. Teitoku generally advised young poets to avoid such base subjects as the sexual organs, defecation, and the making of money.[23] So Teitoku was caught in the middle. Though a prolific composer of haikai, his desire to remain respectable, especially as a holder of the 'secrets', a defender of the empyrean of Japanese poetry, caused him to insist his name be left off some early collections of his haikai published by his followers. And once he had accepted the mantle of the national haikai poet, Teitoku sought to codify the form, to establish, for example, when and how often *haigon* were to be employed (e.g. '"Devil", "woman", / "tiger", or "wolf" may appear / one a thousand verses / even on the front page, but / only once in a session').[24] So would he make the revolutionary respectable (as always happens to the revolutionary), doing to haikai what his predecessors had done to renga, and reflecting a desire of himself and his followers to keep such an unruly form (contemptuous of religion and thus socially dangerous) under restraint. Studiously he avoided the vulgarity that irreverent humor was prey to (especially as displayed in some of the haikai of Moritake, 1559–1647). In one notable case, he strongly objected to lines by Só kan (in *Shinzó Inu Tsukobashú*, 'New Dog's Collection of Linked Poetry') about someone farting while his parent is dying. With commendable Confucian values, Teitoku felt it could have been 'superior' verse if only it had been someone else's parent. In editing this work, he added linking verses which reinterpreted the farting so that it is done by a baby weasel whose parent is being killed by a cat.

In the main, the humor in early haikai was not especially challenging or revolutionary, only it showed a lowering of the spirit of reverence a religion requires. Teitoku's humor was often forced or sophomoric:[25]

> Now even the mist
> seems to be rising in spots
> Year of the Tiger

Early haikai humor could turn on a poetic conceit, as in this case. More typically, the poem would pivot on one word, called a *haigon*, planted specifically to stretch or break the convention of what is permissible in verse. This word would suffice to drop the poem into the world of ordinary people and daily life. Or the humor would rise from a general spirit of irreverence, especially to a 'sacred' image:

> Is that the reason
> why everyone is napping
> the autumn moon?

That is, 'the morning after' consequence of a typically Japanese late-night moon-viewing party.

The entire movement of haikai away from renga is encapsulated in the phrase *haikaika*, or 'haikai change', where the formal and very serious symbolic images of renga are turned on their head, returned to the commonplace. This was the first poetic 'revolution' of haikai, one begun even before Teitoku (though long resisted even by its practitioners), one reflecting the spirit of the middle class social revolution touching all the arts by the seventeenth century.[26] 'Haikai change' was meant to surprise in its lowering the subject matter of renga (e.g. from crickets to lice, from cranes to warblers, from carp to loaches, from samurai to pedlars).

> In the light spring rains
> thoughts of Tamino Island
> with this loach pedlar
>
> Bashó

These lines resonate only when it is understood that Tamino Island represents the sublime themes of the monsoon rains and cranes, rather than spring rains and loaches.[27] The haikai change, this humbling of very lofty images, gives these lines their energy, but only with the Bashó generation did this 'surprise' serve a Zen-like purpose to illuminate. Issa shows this irreverence for the beloved images:

> Oh get it for me
> that big pretty autumn moon
> the child pleads crying

As does Bashó:

> A little warbler
> shits on the New Year rice cake
> at the end of the porch

Both poets treat a revered image shabbily: the moon and a sacred Shinto offering. For Bashó, however, irreverence is not enough. His poem also celebrates a harbinger of spring appearing at the New Year (the Chinese New Year in February), an allusion he deepens infinitely by playing on the word *en*, 'porch', which can also mean 'fate' or 'destiny'. Now the warbler becomes a frail wisp of the spirit of life appearing out of the dead of winter to make a defiant gesture at the determinist universe. Yet the gesture would have no religious (synthetic) power were it not also funny.

Bashó's *Sarumino* ('The Monkey's Straw Raincoat', 1691) is a collection entirely of *hokku* (the seventeenth-syllable, three-line, beginning stanza of a sequence).[28] Writing a sequence only of hokku is itself revolutionary and a haikai change. Further, Bashó reverses the established and sacrosanct ranking of the seasons. He and his collaborators shift the flower and moon stanzas from their accustomed places and play loosely with the relation between stanzas. Bashó was the greatest of haikai poets because he most successfully synthesized *yúgen* (deep sublimity) with its contradiction that is haikai humor. In the kasen, *Ichinaka wa* ('Throughout the Town'), the opening hokku (the first three lines below) was granted to Bonchó (d. 1714), as the usual courtesy to the guest of honor of the linked poetry evening. He opens with proper seriousness, even with spirituality. The image here is of the Buddhist and Christian Romantic (but distinctly not Japanese Zen) dualism of the earthly and the spiritual. The moon above the smelly city evokes the Buddhist lotus blossom, a spiritual allegory for the enlightened soul rising out of the muck of life into perfect nirvana:

> Throughout the town
> above the sea of smelly things
> floats the summer moon
>
> > Bonchó

To Bashó is given the second (the *waki*) stanza, to complete the full tanka by adding two lines of seven syllables as linked poetry requires. No doubt in the good-natured fellowship that marked these poetic sessions, he took the opportunity to puncture Bonchó's air of sublimity. Yet, only with spirituality assured would he drop us into the haikai change of the sweaty laments from the stifling streets:

> Throughout the town
> above the sea of smelly things
> floats the summer moon
> how hot it is, how hot it is
> comes the cry from every house
>
> > Bashó

Bashó defined this new sort of haikai as loneliness, elegance, and madness. First, 'Its feeling can be called loneliness'. In subject matter, it 'plays with refined dishes but contents itself with humble fare'. The new poets would keep and use the sacred images (such as the seasonal references, *kigo*, like cherry blossoms and the bush warbler for spring, fireworks for summer, the moon and the Milky Way for autumn, and other conventions). They would retain the recondite allusions to classic Japanese and Chinese literature, the common coinage of their education. Yet poetry embraced all subjects now and the prevailing spirit was *okashimi*: the odd, the low, the humorous. The poet Shikó (1665–1731) said: 'Haikai broadens art to that which is below average'. Second, and closely related, 'Its total effect can be called elegance'. In point of view, it 'lives in figured silks and embroidered brocades but does not forget a person clad in woven straw'. These two elements recall *Lyrical Ballads*, claiming for the common man a place in the most elevated of poetic styles. Still, haikai arrives at the social/political nexus from the opposite direction; again echoing Zen, by means of haikai change, it 'does not elevate a humble person to heights . . . [but puts] an exalted person in a low place':[29]

> Busy New Year's eve
> they notice great grandfather
> sleeping on his arm
>
>   Chó wa

Third, 'Its language can be called aesthetic madness. Language resides in untruth and ought to comport with truth. It is difficult to reside in truth and sport with untruth'. Here is the Romantic insistence on the falsity and inadequacy of language. In Issa's poem above, not only the irreverence shown to the moon, but the simple language counts as a haikai change. This includes but goes beyond Wordsworth's own seeking of the language and subjects of men. It uses the fact that language is inadequate to the demands of vision ('words are no help!', Shelley cries), and further plays with the tension between the elevation expected of linked verse and the low subjects it treats. As Bashó says: 'The profit of haikai lies in making vulgar speech right'.[30]

Accepting, therefore, the haikai 'lowering' of poetry, the seventeenth-century Bashó poets then rescued it from the trivial, as Teitoku could not. It took their generation to find that delicate balance of the best Japanese poetry to float momentary experience very lightly over the gulf of the eternal. Freed from Teitoku's timid reverence and from the contrary extreme of the superficial, lame humor of populist 'Danrin'-style haikai, depths opened beneath the lightest of touches:

> The Rose of Sharon
> along the side of the road
> eaten by my horse

This slightly comic scene frames gently the poet's sudden recognition and regret. At the moment of its destruction, the flower meets the eye of the one who alone can know its aesthetic voice in pure whiteness, to accept its message, in a sense to fulfill its purpose. The poet's discourse with 'a Beauty that must die' is deepest because of its transience. So Bashó affirms the special revelatory nature of the poet's eye, the spirituality that that eye gives to the aesthetics of Nature and the greater depth of feeling transience gives both to beauty and to experience. Then, he allows the horse to comment most pragmatically, most like a Sancho Panza, on the pretensions of abstracted vision. This is a haikai which seeks in itself the vision and then becomes the object of its own parody. Zen self-effacement rescues this poetry from the stifling subjective Ego of Romanticism.

So, if their haikai ignored Teitoku's rules and parodied renga, finding popularity with the new bourgeoisie, still it endures only because they honored, even deepened, traditional Japanese spirituality and its images, exorcising mere gamesmanship. Humor now helped to refresh the haikai 'reformation', a refocus on the tradition of poetry as religious text. In a manner perhaps parallel to Zen, poetry (renga, haikai, and later haiku) acts both as *zazen* (the basic Zen meditation) and as Zen *kó an*, the paradoxical questions (impenetrable catechisms) asked by a Zen master to push the supplicant past logic and intellect.

Teitoku had felt that even haikai must remain reverential. Drawing on an ancient claim for divine sanction of Japanese poetry, Teitoku made plain its purpose as ministry:

> In Japan the gods, initiating the art of poetry written in thirty-one syllables, created the tradition of our country. This, we are told, was because they knew that while a man is beguiling himself by writing poetry he does not allow the three poisons [traditionally, greed, wrath, and folly] to rise within him. Should we not be most grateful for this art?[31]

Note that even the form itself has divine sanction.

His verse abounds with evocations and allegories to Buddhism and Confucianism, yet a spiritual depth is as wanting as is true humor. Even as Teitoku published his definitive haikai rule book, *Gosan* (1651), a seven-year-old Bashó was beginning studies that would rediscover inner distances plumbed by Saigyó while opening poetry to the selfless infinite spaces sought by Zen. It was a revolution and reformation with strong echoes in Romanticism.

As Bashó said of himself, he 'resembles a priest but is soiled by the dirt of this world; and he resembles a layman but has a shaven head'.[32] Saigyó had chosen when twenty-three to become a recluse:[33]

> A man whose mind is
> at one with the empyrean
> enters a spring mist
> and begins to wonder whether
> he might step out of the world

Saigyó returned repeatedly to this *contemptus mundi* theme, which he helped establish as the tradition. An admirer of Saigyó, Bashó adopted self-consciously the role of wandering poet. Yet, more than just 'a kind of Nature troubadour', more than a kind of mendicant friar, he accepted the robes his admirers thrust upon him of saint and seer.[34] The quality of the recluse was *wabi*, defined as asceticism, cultivated simplicity, poverty as a virtue, of which Bashó, though born into the samurai class, became the living definition. This was the fashion in poetry and Zen worship. Yet, it was a communal reclusion, which is both characteristically Japanese and in the universal tradition of the wandering holy man and his disciples. The role merged the tradition of poet-as-holy recluse with the communality of linked poetry. Bashó's stepping into this tradition was exactly the strong move a serious poet must make.[35]

In this way, the poet retains his traditional Japanese role as holy man, divine scribe of holy texts. More than 'art for art's sake' in the sense of art as self-justified, Bashó had entered fully into the more deeply 'religious' life-as-art moral aesthetic of Japanese tradition. There was little in him of formal religion (however deeply he was steeped in the Buddhist-Confucian iconography and ethic). His was the Japanese aesthetic expressed in poetry as *sabi*, which affirmed that there is not beauty but where beauty is not: the aged cup, the old, the decayed. The poet Ton'a (fourteenth century) defined *sabi* in saying, 'It is only after the silk wrapper has frayed at top and bottom, and the mother-of-pearl has fallen from the roller, that a scroll looks beautiful'.[36] The Heian court poets had begun a tradition of admiring the 'noble' peasant, the virtuous rustic. Bashó's ethic was *fúga no michi* ('the way of elegance'), which has nothing to do with class or its rejection, but rather implies a *sabi* grace in simple living and returns us to the Buddhist spiritual sense of *wa* it calls *tai'chi*, ('sincerity'). It recalls Wordsworth's 'Animal Tranquillity and Decay'. Shuichi Kato quotes Bashó about himself that 'his life was run through by the single thread' of art; he spent it 'following no religious law, observing no popular customs'.[37]

In a sense the spiritual vision this brings also seems Romantic. 'Shinken's Essay in Chinese Prose and Verse' (1690) from Bashó's collection *Sarumino* comments on the poet's fusion of imagination with Nature. Note that it is the scenery which has found the passively wise poet: 'I realized that he possesses the soul of reclusion and that in his writing the scenery has found a person to know it rightly. So it is that this person and the natural scene have taken on full existence in their mutual relation'.[38] Or as Van Gogh observed, the Japanese poets 'live in nature as though they themselves were flowers'. Shinken expresses this view of Bashō in verse. The place described is the poet's tiny, austere mountain hut (what he called his 'Unreal Hermitage'):

> To the south of Lake Biwa there rises the peak of Mt. Kokubu
> Where old pines cluster and the green is shade is fresh.
> A modest hut stands there, no more than a few steps square,
> And in it lives a superior person, nourishing his being.
> His rich expression constantly brocades the hills and streams,
> So that the scenery becomes spiritualized into a poetic castle.
> This area has always been known for its famous places,
> And now because of him this spot has unusual splendor.

An English Romantic might give the poet's imagination the active power to transform a scene. Here the poet's humble and passive presence alone spiritualizes the place. The Romantic poet 'transfers his poetic state to the objects; he does not dissolve himself into the nature that surrounds him; on the contrary, he absorbs nature by the prodigy of his imagination . . .'.[39] In contrast, at its best, the Bashō revolution is a dissolution of the poet, imagination and all. Most famously, Bashō's revolutionary frog splash has nothing of the poet, not even implied feeling. It is total 'negative capability':

> The old pond
> a frog jumps in
> the water's sound

We can ask, 'Is it poetry?' Byron might respond rhetorically, rather, 'Is it not the thing itself?':

> Fleas are here and lice
> and now the horse is pissing
> outside my window
>
>   Bashō

This is direct experience for its own sake; it is idle to search for meaning or reference. Even beyond humor, it is, as much as words can be, 'the thing itself'. In the mundane, not through it as in Romanticism, do we experience the eternal. In Zen, 'what is is – which is the final act of experience'.[40] *Shó fú*, the poetry of direct perception, unadorned, uninterpreted, is the second great poetic 'revolution' of haikai, and it is Bashó's own. It represents his final, most mature poetic. Bashó did not seek Zen, no more than the young Romantics did he trust formal religion, but this is of a Zen perception regardless. Perhaps it would be more true to step back one causal level and say that it speaks of the Japanese earth-bound pragmatism that reshaped Zen to itself as it made its own poetry into a spiritual aesthetic. The frog poem is the great penetration to this, a haikai change into reality that is at once a cosmic turn out to the sublime. Most of what Bashó and the others wrote continued to be on a less sublime, less direct level (mostly haikai and hokku with the expected clever references, allusions, and witty humor) but the mould had been broken.

The parallel here remains with late or 'anti'-Romanticism. 'Do not, I beg you', says Goethe, 'look for anything behind phenomena. They themselves are their own lesson'.[41] *Chanoyu*, the Tea Ceremony, is the ultimate Zen immersion into direct experience. Here is the bridge between direct experience and the worship that is Zen and Japanese poetry, as affirmed by Tennó Dó go (AD 748–807): 'If you want to see, see right at once. When you begin to think, you miss the point'.[42] From another post-Romantic, Ruskin, comes, 'The greatest thing a human soul ever does in this world is to see something, and tell what it saw in a plain way . . . To see clearly is poetry, prophecy, and religion – all in one . . . [it is to be] a Seer'.[43] This is transparent, truly passive sight, not through the prisms of a restless, Protestant, Ego.

This is not to say the Japanese poet must not funnel the impressions through his mind. Further, poets normally must work through memory, distancing themselves even more from the experience. Still, though he cannot be the pure recorder of experience he would wish to be, in his final and most sublime stage of his career Bashó would hope to avoid the interpreting, hence distorting power of Wordsworthian memory. In the most direct way, he says, 'you should put into words the light in which you see something before it vanishes from your mind'.[44]

In a general way, nonetheless, a haikai or haiku is a Wordsworthian 'spot of time', a quasi-religious moment of purely private revelation into 'the life of things'. Formal linked poetry, renga, was very unRomantic in being a communal art, what in Europe might have belonged in a coffee shop or among the Spectator Club, more clever than profound. The Bashó poets kept the communality, but still touched the sublime. This requires both an intense seriousness as well as a more than European sense of a shared cultural coherence. Though a spiritual synthesis, seriousness here still carries a smile of recognition as the moveless Eternal and muddy life link in verse under the same mortal rain:[45]

> The strolling pedlar
> cries out nicknames for his wares
> as he passes by
> just cover from a shower
> is man's life in endless flux
>
>   Yasui (1658–1743)

> Just cover from a shower
> is this world in endless flux
> sleeping at noon
> the figure of the heron
> poised nobility
>
>   Bashó

Notes

1. The joke in Issa's poem of course is in the contrast of the evocative blossoms and the very human act. For the Japanese, the contrast would be contradiction and could hardly be wider, as flowers have almost sacred resonances, while the act of blowing one's nose in public is an almost unforgivable *faux pas*. Then there is a verbal pun: *hana de* means 'among the blossoms', while *hana kamu* means 'to blow one's nose'. This double meaning (*kakekotoba*) for *hana*, rhythmically harmonized together on the line, bridges a vast gap. This poem is hugely funny (or shocking) to most Japanese.
2. Kakuzo Okakura, *The Book of Tea* [1906] (Tokyo: Kodansha, 1989), 68.
3. . . .and much that is not, but a Zen / Romanticism comparison is not the subject of this paper.
4. Okakura, 121.
5. quoted in R. H. Blyth, *Haiku*, vol. 1 (Tokyo: Hokuseido, 1949), 267.
6. 211.
7. 'My First Acquaintance With Poets', *William Hazlitt: Selected Writings* (London: Penguin, 1970), 59.
8. e.g. *Biographia Literaria* XIV.
9. quoted in Blyth, 218.
10. Blyth, 242–43.
11. Donald Keene, quoted in A. M. Janeira, *Japanese and Western Literature: A Comparative Study* (Tokyo: Charles E. Tuttle, 1970), 33.

12. Janeira, 30.
13. Ooka Makoto, *The Colors of Poetry: Essays on Classic Japanese Verse* (Oakland, CA: Katydid, 1991).
14. The spirit of this we may see in the *Kyokusuinoen* Ceremony, still popular on the first Sunday in March. Poets in Heian era costume sit at spaced intervals along a stream under cherry blossoms. A cup of *sake* (rice wine) floats slowly along the stream, and each poet must compose a poem on a tablet before the cup reaches them. If they are successful, they may sip from the cup, to the appreciation of thousands of spectators.
15. e.g. the red camelia blossom (*tsutsuji*) drops to the ground in a manner of a cap and since medieval times has been directly associated with beheading. With the decline of this practice in modern times the image has become more generally that of an omen of untimely death.
16. The heart of the symbolic language was *hana* ('flower', as embodied in the perfection of the cherry blossom) referring to the pure ideal of *renga* aesthetics. It expressed not just the facile emotions in sympathy with transient beauty, but an essence of pure beauty (though more prized for being a 'Beauty that must die') to which the artist strives, but which ever eludes even as it informs all striving. It is what Zeami meant by the pure 'flower' of Nó performance.
17. A reasonably complete discussion of *shikimoku* is given by Hiroaki Sato in *One Hundred Frogs: From Renga to Haikai in English* (New York: Weatherhill, 1983), chap. 1.
18. Donald Keene, *Landscapes and Portraits: Appreciations of Japanese Culture* (Tokyo: Kodansha, 1971), 74.
19. Keene, 74.
20. Keene, 80.
21. *The Karma of Words: Buddhism and the Literary Arts of Japan* (Berkeley: U. of California P., 1983), 149. His italics.
22. Joseph Kitagawa, *Kúkai as Master and Savior*, quoted in LaFleur, 150.
23. Sato, 60.
24. *Teimon Haikai Shú*, I, 102, quoted in Keene, 89.
25. Although there **are** subtextual layers in this poem involving feminine sensibilities, the characteristics and consequences of a Year of the Tiger, and an evocation of the new season in February and the poet's reaction to it. Incidentally, as their knowledge of both animals was secondhand, the medieval Japanese might be forgiven for believing that leopards were female tigers.
26. As with English Romanticism, bourgeois society motivated writers both to turn literature inward to the private vision while at the same time to broaden and popularize it. Prose was written (e.g. by Saikaku, 1642–93) in conscious repudiation of the ancient and revered courtly tales (most prominently *Genji Monogatari*, *Heiki Monnogatari*, and

Ise Monogatari) whose canonization had so long stifled the emergence of other prose styles. In drama, Chikamatsu (1653–1724) took the same route in escaping from under the long shadow of Zeami and revered Nó, by writing plays for puppet theatre (*bunraku*) and on contemporary subjects and common life (*sewamono* plays).

27. As ever in Japanese poetry, the allusions, wherein lies the power of normal *haikai*, speak only to the initiate into the religion of 'Japanese-ness': the native Japanese.

28. A *haikai* sequence opened with a *hokku*, the stanza to which the next poet in the linked poetry sequence added his two seven-syllable lines to complete the first *tanka*. From the beginning, *hokku* showed an internal unity and soon they began to stand on their own, their severe brevity congenial to that uniquely Japanese value of suggestiveness crossed with discipline. Collections entirely of *hokku* appeared with Bashó, and poems in this form, the *haikai no hokku*, eventually were called *haiku*. Literally, *haiku* is short for *haikai no ku*, meaning 'stanzas of *haikai*'. The Meiji-era critic and poet Masaoka Shiki (1868–1902) coined the term.

29. quoted in Earl Miner, *Japanese Linked Poetry* (Princeton NJ: Princeton UP, 1979), 111–12.

30. quoted in Miner, 15.

31. quoted in Odaka Toshio, *Zokuhen* (1956) 141, as quoted by Keene, 86. My only excuse for dependence on secondary sources (or tertiary, in this case) is the unavailability of some of these books in English translation and my inability to read the original in the Chinese characters, though I can the Japanese *kana* script.

32. quoted in Miner, 15.

33. Poem # 786 in *Sanka-shú*, adapted from the translation by LaFleur 161.

34. D. T. Suzuki, *Zen and Japanese Culture* (Princeton NJ: Princeton UP, 1959), 254.

35. This culture does not worship the closeted individual vision, nor fall prey to the dangerous Romantic illusion that private revelation is the route to universal understanding. Nor was Bashó's choice anything of pretense, for this would be betrayed in the poetry.

36. as quoted by Kenkó, Ton'a's greater contemporary, in his masterpiece, *Tsurezuregusa* ('Essays in Idleness', 1331) 7, translated by and quoted in Keene, 24.

37. *A History of Japanese Literature: Volume 2: The Years of Isolation*, trans. Don Sanderson (Tokyo: Kodansha, 1983), 96.

38. *The Monkey's Straw Raincoat: and other poetry of the Bashó school*, introduced and translated by Earl Miner and Hiroko Odagiri (Princeton NJ: Princeton UP, 1981), 313.

39. Janeira, 44.

40. Suzuki, 34. I will grant that this frog poem is referential in two ways: first by being a *haikai* change in breaking forcibly with a *renga* and earlier *haikai* tradition, second that it does have a classical reference. Yet, these are secondary, even irrelevant to the essence of this poem.
41. *Sie selbst sind die Lehre*, quoted in Blyth 250.
42. quoted in Suzuki, 13.
43. *Modern Painters*, 3, 268.
44. from *Sanzóshi* (pub. 1702–04), quoted in Kato, 102.
45. This fragment of linked verse comes from the thirty-six stanza *kasen* titled *Akuoke no no Maki* ('At the Tub of Ashes').

It All Happened Right Out of the Books: Romantic Imagination at Work in *The Adventures of Huckleberry Finn*

Manfred Malzahn

At a superficial glance, the attempt to locate Romantic elements any-where in Mark Twain's writing may look as promising as the search for delicate ice crystals among the flames of hell. Of course Romanticism features in *Huckleberry Finn*, but, as concise notes or any sophomore worth his salt will tell you, merely to be ridiculed by the great satirist, whose pen was ever heated in the aforementioned nether regions. Just remember the obvious symbolism of the wrecked steamboat 'Walter Scott'; Emmeline Grangerford's morbid verses which make the poetry of William McGonagall or even Emily Dickinson look remarkably sane; or Tom Sawyer's absurd efforts to act out what he reads in adventure stories. Non-fictional texts in the literary legacy of Samuel Langhorne Clemens provide plenty of evidence of his contempt for the likes of Scott, and of an even greater disdain for their American admirers and imitators of Romantic writing, most clearly epitomised by Tom as a reader and would-be practitioner.

This is all true enough, but it is not the whole truth, only an obvious stopping point for undergraduate inquiry. *The Adventures of Huckleberry Finn* is a book full of easily decoded signs, which nonetheless may take on a very different significance in any more mature reading. By a mature reading I mean one which takes into account the ironies and the several levels of meaning created through the narrative structure. On one such level of meaning, *Huckleberry Finn* can be interpreted as metatext, a discussion of literature within a piece of literature, or of Romanticism within a romance.

The title of the book does after all promise a tale of adventure; and that this tale may be described as a romance just as well as a novel has been very plausibly argued by Laurence B. Holland in his essay 'A "Raft of Trouble": Word and Deed in *Huckleberry Finn*'.[1] Holland is moreover one of the few critics who refuse to join in the general howl of complaint about the final part of the story, a noise produced by those who would love to see a resolution to the plot which leaves the dignity of Huck and Jim undiminished.[2] There is a considerable amount of irony in the fact that such people tend to applaud Twain as a realist or anti-Romantic, and then crab about his demontage of potential Romantic heroes.

And anyway, Twain is not the one who really does it. The romantic author within the final section of *Huckleberry Finn* is actually Tom Sawyer. Why does the omnipotent writer Clemens bring him back in and let him take over? Maybe this can be answered in one breath with the theological question why does God permit the existence of evil? Because without the devil or without Tom, there is no plot, and there is no end. In practical terms, the flight of Jim and Huck alone achieves as much as all the historic wanderings of the Israelites, namely, nothing palpable. What is needed to bring a conclusion to their episodic adventures is a radical change, and the last part of *Huckleberry Finn* is indeed the book's New Testament. Jim has to be crucified, Huck has to play Judas, and semi-omniscient Tom knows that all will be well, but still he has to make sure that everything happens as it is written.

So, just like Prospero directs the drama within Shakespeare's play, Tom comes in as the author of a romantic plot within a romance, staged with Caliban-Jim on props and groundwork, Ariel-Huck as production assistant, and various extras. The whole show is ultimately meant to glorify its maker, as Tom obliquely admits, but not until after his plan has been foiled by Clemens. In a story focusing on Huck, this intervention is clearly necessary, because Tom Sawyer does not possess any of Huck's fundamental humanity, and is consequently incapable of doing what Prospero does to show compassion by releasing the actors while they are still under his spell. The real writer of the book can thus not allow the internal author of this part to triumph completely, and Tom's mishap is in more than one sense of his own making. Huck's explanation of how Tom gets shot does not go down too well with the doctor, but there is actually a lot of truth in his bottom line:[3]

'He had a dream,' I says, 'and it shot him.'
'Singular dream,' he says.

This incident seems to me to be the fulfillment of a remark prefaced to the novel, and generally taken to be a tongue-in-cheek warning to the reader: 'persons attempting to find a plot in it will be shot' by order of the author. The narrator Huck is content with an episodic story, whose overall structure is governed by the chrono-logic of the journey with its largely accidental succession of various stages of events. On the last part of this, Tom attempts to superimpose a plot; and he does in fact meet with the punishment which is announced beforehand, and which appears to be not altogether undeserved.

When Tom finally orders Jim to be released for good, the reader has learned too much about him to give his righteous pose even the slightest credit. The sovereign and immutable disdain of human suffering which he has shown in his authorial role clearly makes Tom Sawyer a small-scale cousin of Satan in Twain's late work *The Mysterious Stranger*.[4] Both represent the hellish side of the split Romantic mind. To Satan as well as to Tom, people are merely part of a dream, and of no more consequence than laboratory rats, as objects of detached, clinical observation. In the later work, the protagonist is not checked by any intervention of a more humane spirit. The caustic vespertine fantasy of a Clemens who has become more and more one with his literary persona Twain allows Satan to conclude the tale with the ultimate truth or lie, the justification for any sovereign author or creator to do with his creatures as he wishes. What you took for real, the message says, was only the product of a superior imagination.

In *Huckleberry Finn*, there are two very similar revelations, to the effect that both Huck and Jim have long lost the reason for running away, Jim now being a free man, and Huck being a complete orphan. Samuel Clemens has apparently taken pity, and hence Mark Twain must intervene. He thus puts Tom Sawyer out of action, and once again raises Jim to the height of full humanity in the eyes of the reader before he is finally released, most probably to go looking for his family. Never mind the fact that this seems to have become singularly unimportant. Never mind either that one person needs to get injured, and two people killed in the process of finding a fictional resolution. The point is that they are not real to the authors of their harm. Tom himself would have 'waded neck-deep in blood'[5] if necessary, to make a genuine adventure out of an artificial situation. Why should Twain then not bump characters off with the same nonchalance, and insert a bullet in Tom's leg to put an end to Tom's capers? And it is all for a worthy cause. Even the good country folk now let themselves be persuaded that Jim 'is worth a thousand dollars – and kind treatment, too'.[6]

At least this is a twenty-five per cent increase on a previous estimate, and the doctor does shove in a humane angle on Clemens' behalf. But Jim is still a nigger to him as well as to the rest, and that rest includes Twain as well as Huck Finn. Like it or not, neither one has vanquished the morality of a racist society. Clemens has let Huck demonstrate the freedom of choice to act against its demands, but Twain must finally remind the reader that in spite of all that has happened, Huck is only a boy, and always more than likely to go along with changing circumstances. This is exactly what he does in the final section of the book, where Tom Sawyer is the boss.

Why are so many critics refusing to take that section seriously? Maybe because most academics are simply not critical enough of generally accepted views concerning great writers and books. This is what makes Victor A. Doyno assume that 'literary critics associated with English Departments' may be 'least likely to understand the ending'[7] of *Huckleberry Finn*. And consequently, I would add, most likely to misread the whole book. Have a look at the following statement, for instance:[8]

> Huck has rejected Tom's romanticising of experience; moreover, he has rejected it as part of the larger pattern of society's make-believe, typified by Sunday school. But if he cannot accept Tom's harmless fantasies about the A-rabs, how are we to believe that a year later Huck is capable of awe-struck submission to the far more extravagant fantasies with which Tom invests the mock rescue of Jim?

Both the contention and the question are indeed evidence of a complete failure to understand. If Huck has rejected anything, it has happened on a much smaller scale; he quite simply does not think in the same dimensions as social theorists or literary critics. Before such readers launch impressive interpretations, they should take the text, and that means the character of Huck, seriously. Huck is still no more than a boy.[9] Within the context of a work of fiction, his decision to go to hell rather than betray Jim does of course have larger implications. But what Huck himself has worked out is actually no more than a specific and emotional, rather than a general and logical solution to his personal dilemma: somehow he must help Jim, whatever the consequences. This, by the way, is also the exact reason why he goes along with almost every whim of Tom Sawyer at the end. He wants to set Jim free, and he does not dare look a gift horse in the mouth when Tom promises not only to keep mum, but even to lend active support. This is too good to be real – and indeed it is not. But Huck accepts it because to him, only one thing is really important at that moment: his loyalty to his companion Jim. If he crosses Tom at this critical stage, who knows but Tom Sawyer might go and blow the whole show sky-high?

Besides, we should not forget that although Huck knows that Tom is prone to telling lies, he is willing to believe a lot of Tom's statements until he has evidence to the contrary. After all, Tom has it all on written authority, and when he calls out his gang of robbers to attack a merchant caravan, Huck goes along as a matter of course. His one misgiving is not about Tom's information, but about something else which he knows for a fact, and which he evaluates realistically on the basis of Tom's fictitious data: the relative lack of strength in the assault force. Huck only writes the whole thing off as a lie after he has tried to conjure up a genie by rubbing a lamp and an iron ring. His attitude, in other words, combines a pragmatic-scientific approach with a basic belief in other people's superior knowledge. If one reads the book properly to the end, without any wishful thinking, the conclusion is bound to be that this approach does not change in any fundamental way, even if Huck may later occasionally curb Tom's wildest plans with an ironical remark. But even then, all Huck does is to suggest a more practical way of doing things by the book, 'if it ain't unregular and irrelegious'.[10]

In other words, Huck is a pragmatist, and hence basically a conformist who has to be hard pushed to make exceptions to whatever rule is valid. It does not really pay for any boy his age to be anything else than that. Yes, Huck once runs away from the Widow Douglas, but only to come back at the drop of a bait, and to get 'sort of used to the widow's ways',[11] as long as he can have some fun now and then. Yes, Huck also runs away from his father, but only after it is clear that he may get killed if he does not. For an archetypal fugitive, which is how Huck is perceived in run-of-the-mill criticism, his staying power is really quite extraordinary; and so is his chameleon-like agility in settling down to different roles played to different rules. Life in a miniature primitive society with Jim demands a kind of egalitarianism, and Huck acts accordingly. When real microcosmic feudalism invades the raft in the shape of the fake King and Duke, Huck of course complies with that new power structure, too. And when he joins a community on the shore, he tries his best to behave as is expected of him in whatever role he has assumed.

Huck may well try and set one particular nigger free, but he never questions the legitimacy as such of having nigger slaves. Yes, he will go to hell, but this is because of one instance where he puts personal loyalty above all other considerations, and not because he has subscribed to the view that all human beings of all races should be regarded as equal. But would such a step not really be too big to take for even the most exceptional kid in the given circumstances? Huck is, after all, not only the hero of a romance, but the protagonist of a novel, too, in the sense that he is and remains recognisably a product as well as an integral part of his surroundings.

His ability to adapt to any kind of setting or role makes Huck eligible as a picaro; but it is not his constant desire for change or adventure, but rather the force of circumstance, which actually makes him become one. Unlike Jim, Huck sees no concrete objective for a quest, nor even a vague abstract goal at the end of the road. The only substantial motive for his escape is the desire to get away from his potentially homicidal father. So forget the 'Ingean Territory'.[12] Huckleberry Finn is going nowhere far by himself. The only wilderness Huck can hack alone is one within earshot of the society he knows, and in this he seems to be very much his father's son. Pap Finn is a scavenger who drifts in and out of town, and Huck's initial 'sugar-hogshead'[13] dwelling is drift-wood of civilisation, conveniently close to the local store, and, above all, to fellow-humans. More than anything else, Huck needs a commu-nity, not only because of his desire to belong, but also as a supplier of unceasing action and distraction.

Jackson's Island is about the nearest Huck ever gets to any wild place in the course of the story. He copes pretty well in practical terms, but the loneliness disturbs him on the very first night already. He then acquires an unexpected companion in Jim, but still it does not take long until Huck finds the potential idyl 'slow and dull',[14] and promptly paddles off to the shore in female clothes, for no better reason than to generally catch up with local gossip. Huck could quite simply not have stayed content on the island. Contentment on the raft is only possible because it moves, and brings new encounters. Ultimately, what Huck needs is ever-renewed contact with the very crowd from which he is ostensibly running away.

As a Desert Island Dick, Huck is thus a genuine nine-day wonder, even if his departure is hastened by a threat to Jim. But the fact remains that Huck does not enjoy his sojourn on Jackson's Island overmuch. Perhaps a further reason for this is that he does not live the Robinson experience consciously, imaginatively. Neither Huck nor Tom Sawyer have apparently read the book yet, or Tom at least has not told Huck about it. But Clemens certainly knows it, and the fact that he does not allow Twain even to make Tom let Huck know it is significant. The episode can thus be read as an illustration of a fundamental Romantic tenet that reality is not really real until it is imagined.

There he is, Clemens the user of literary tradition, behind Twain the Scott-basher. It all happens right out of a book. While Twain makes the King and Duke perform a Shakespeare parody, Clemens stages a real-life Romeo-and-Juliet story as part of the Grangerford-Shepherdson feud.[15] Clemens likewise creates a Robinson-cum-Friday constellation with recognisable, if partly inverted roles like Crusoe. Huck is the one with the gun, but Jim has to persuade the hunter-collector to make a real home. In any case, we all know where we have read about such events before, and we are also likely to remember somebody on a dif-ferent island who shinned up a tree for safety. Robinson, however, did so for fear of wild animals, whereas Huck takes this precaution after stumbling upon the smouldering remains of a camp fire.

Of whom, then, is Huck so mortally afraid? The answer is really quite obvious, but textual evidence is not so easy to find. I would say that it exists in Chapter 4, where Clemens uses yet another motif from *Robinson Crusoe*. Huck's terror on discovering the embers on Jackson's Island is matched only by his panic at the discovery of his father's footprint. For the reader who is familiar with Defoe's novel, this parallel establishes a transtextual metaphor which casts Pap Finn in the role of a cannibal or ogre, while – a neat instance of dramatic irony – the campfire in Chapter 8 heralds a meeting with someone who is anything but a man-eater, in spite of belonging to a race frequently associated with cannibalism.[16]

Most of such metatextual communication, of course, goes on behind the narrator's back. At times, it may thus show us Huck's judgment as being yet unshaped or rather undeformed by authoritative texts; but in this instance, the gist seems to be that without tales from books, and hence to a large extent without Tom, the voracious reader of fiction, Huck seems unable to realise the Romantic potential of what he is experiencing. Tom, on the other hand, needs the co-operation of Huck and others in translating his literary experience into reality.

This process is indeed one of translation, which runs into predictable difficulties when the codes of fictional worlds differ from that of St. Petersburg, or the objects described in one world do not exist in the other. In such cases, Tom must improvise, and invent a meaning for 'ransom'[17] just as he manages to find substitute Missouri signifiers for 'A-rabs'.[18] Whether it all works depends on the willingness of others to accept make-believe without really trying to take it for real. And such is indeed the essential condition for fiction.

In Huck's mind, there seems to be no provision for the latter category. To him, statements are either the truth, 'stretchers',[19] or 'lies'.[20] But in spite of the gap in his categorisation of texts, he is an extremely clever writer, leading his readers along as he pleases. Consider the following two passages, one from Chapter 1 which describes the routine at the Widow Douglas's dinner table, and the other from Chapter 33, dealing with the Phelps's farm:[21]

> The widow rung a bell for supper, and you had to come to time. When you got to the table you couldn't go right to eating, but you had to wait for the widow to tuck down her head and grumble a little over the victuals, though there warn't really anything the matter with them.

> We had dinner out in that broad open passage betwixt the house and the kitchen... Uncle Silas he asked a pretty long blessing over it, but it was worth it; and it didn't cool it a bit, neither, the way I've seen them kind of interruptions do, lots of times.

Of course the second quote shows the changed perception of a more experienced Huck Finn, but it is this changed Huck who is also telling the story at the very beginning, and hence evokes a deliberate irony by exaggerating his erstwhile naivety.[22] This illustrates a major difference between the author-director Tom and the storyteller Huck. Tom can create fantastic plots on the basis of fiction which he has read, but he is incapable of either using or understanding irony, as is evident, for instance, from his total misreading of *Don Quixote*. Huck, on the other hand, has all the gifts of the raconteur, including a fine ear for ironic tones, but he apparently lacks those concepts which make a conscious creator of fictional texts as such. It is true that both boys are great liars, but whereas Tom lies for social prestige or for the heck of it, Huck's lies tend to arise from necessity. Huck can thus tell a story, whether true or false, but he can not really create a plot. And hence, neither Huckleberry Finn nor *Huckleberry Finn* could exist without an imaginative mind of the Tom Sawyer variety, however derivative its mechanisms might be.

It is hard to resist drawing a parallel to the Clemens/Twain dichotomy between the authorial person and persona, the grassroots frontiersman who has seen it all, and the polished gentleman who has read it all. In this context, I must identify the source of the phrase which I have borrowed for the title of this essay. It comes from a study by Robert E. Spiller, whose words 'it all happened right out of the books'[23] refer to Clemens' courtship of Olivia Langdon, the girl whom he first saw on a picture, and whom he then wooed with as many accoutrements as any romantic suitor – or indeed any Romantic author – could have thought up. In other words, Clemens himself was willing to translate romance into reality, and he knew the positive stimulus which romantic imagination can lend to life.

In Huckleberry Finn, such an imagination is actually at work, and quite independently from bookish sources. Some of Huck's best romantic prose is inspired by oral literature, or popular superstition. Folk tales and folk beliefs may be no less fantastic than the tales Tom reads, but as local lore they are at least immediately accessible to anyone with a natural sensibility, who can then use it to heighten his own perception of the real world around him. A good example of the possible result is the following passage:[24]

> I went up to my room with a piece of candle and put it on the table. Then I set down in a chair by the window and tried to think of something cheerful, but it warn't no use. I felt so lonesome I most wished I was dead. The stars was shining, and the leaves rustled in the woods ever so mournful; and I heard an owl, away off, who-whooing about somebody that was dead,

and a whippowill and a dog crying about somebody that was going to die; and the wind was trying to whisper something to me and I couldn't make out what it was, and so it made the cold shivers run over me. Then away out in the woods I heard the kind of a sound a ghost makes when it wants to tell about something that's on its mind and can't make itself understood, and so can't rest easy in its grave and has to go about that way every night grieving. I got so down-hearted and scared, I did wish I had some company.

The same profound sensation, or, talking in generative terms, the same deep structure which informed this syntactic sequence, could have been expressed in the form of a Romantic poem by, say, John Keats. And I myself would not really be willing to put too much money on the claim that Keats could have made a much better job of describing a simple but specific human emotion in relation to elements of human nature, non-human nature, and culture.

Many American versifiers of the mid-nineteenth century were certainly not making a better job of it, and the painful 'Ode to Stephen Dowling Bots, Dec'd' by Emmeline Grangerford, another Romantic author within Huck Finn's narrative, is actually not too different from the many real atrocities which were being passed off for poetry at that time. That Huck is in fact quite impressed with Emmeline Grangerford's poetical works, and unsuccessfully tries to produce some lines of his own to match, is once again important. Ostensibly exposing Huck's failure to discriminate between good and bad verse, Twain is laughing at those who teach others to think that conventional metre, rhyme, diction, or subject matter alone make poetry. Meanwhile, through the prose of the very same unsophisticated Huckleberry Finn, Clemens is expressing genuine poetic sentiments in the genuine plain language of men. Is he then really being a better Wordsworth than William himself? Think about that, and consider likewise Huck's description of daybreak on the Mississippi at the beginning of Chapter 19,[25] in comparison to Wordsworth's sonnet composed on Westminster Bridge. Meanwhile, I had better light out for the lavatory ahead of the rest, because the Coleridge buffs will catch me and sivilise me and I can't stand it. I been there before.

Notes

1. In Eric J. Sundquist (ed.), *American Realism. New Essays* (Baltimore, 1982), 66–81; cf. especially 75 ff.

2. A classic example is Leo Marx, who attacks two admittedly unconvincing attempts to make sense of the book as an organic whole in his essay 'Mr. Eliot, Mr. Trilling, and Huckleberry Finn', in Charles Feidelson, Paul Brodtkorb (eds.), *Interpretations of American Literature* (New York, 1959), 212–228. A more recent attempt to interpret the novel as a complete circular structure is found in Russell Reising, *The Unusable Past: Theory and the Study of American Literature* (New York, 1986), 151–62.

3. Mark Twain, *The Adventures of Huckleberry Finn: Edited with an Introduction by Peter Coveney* (Harmondsworth, 1985), 351.

4. Cf. Victor A. Doyno, *Writing Huck Finn: Mark Twain's Creative Process* (Philadelphia, 1991), 171. Doyno is maybe the most notable of the aforementioned exceptions among the critics; his detailed study certainly represents a much better-informed attempt to put the picture right than either Trilling's or Eliot's.

5. *The Adventures of Huckleberry Finn*, 365.

6. *ibid.*, 361.

7. op. cit., p. XV

8. Leo Marx, 'Mr. Eliot, Mr. Trilling, and Huckleberry Finn', 222.

9. The only critic I have found who gives appropriate emphasis to this fact is Janet Gabler-Hover, in *Truth in American Fiction: The Legacy of Rhetorical Idealism* (Athens, Georgia, 1990), 121–54.

10. *The Adventures of Huckleberry Finn*, 317.

11. *ibid.*, 65.

12. *ibid.*, 343.

13. *ibid.*, 49.

14. *ibid.*, 108.

15. Cf. Doyno, op. cit., 31.

16. It is maybe interesting to note that *Robinson Crusoe* is another book whose final part is more often than not regarded as somewhat less than essential, or even as detrimental to the whole. Such selective readings ultimately reduce works of art to selected highlights, in a way that somehow resembles Tom Sawyer's eclectic perception of literature. Maybe Tom is an early exponent, as well as a catalyst, of popular modern culture as we know it from condensed 'Hits on '45', or from abbreviated great novels in easily digestible anthologies. Most critics of *Huckleberry Finn* have so far been engaged in a similar operation, that is, the pruning down of a complex and complete structure to something altogether less ambiguous and confusing.

17. *The Adventures of Huckleberry Finn*, 57 f.

18. *ibid.*, 62.

19. *ibid.*, 49.

20. *ibid.*, 64.

21. *ibid.*, 49 f., 300.

22. This, incidentally, is a common feature in 18th and 19th century slave narrative; cf. e.g. Paul Edwards, David Dabydeen (eds.) *Black Writers in Britain 1760–1890* (Edinburgh, 1991).

23. *The Cycle of American Literature: An Essay in Historical Criticism* (New York, 1955), 116.

24. *The Adventures of Huckleberry Finn*, 51.

25. *ibid.*, 100.

'Welcome, oh mine own rugged Scotland!': Gender and Landscape in Scottish Fiction*

Glenda Norquay

The title of this essay, 'Welcome, oh mine own rugged Scotland' is taken from a journal entry by the early nineteenth-century novelist, Mary Brunton, in which she expresses her emotions on the return to her native country after a holiday in England.[1] Embracing the landscape as her own, she is at the same time constructing it in what might be seen as a masculine characteristic – its ruggedness. For her the Scottish landscape is simultaneously 'mine own' yet also presented in terms of difference. It is both her own and 'other'. Mary Brunton was one of several female Scottish novelists and travel writers who wrote with passion about the landscape of Scotland, and in particular about the mountainous and beautiful Scottish highlands in the late eighteenth and early nineteenth centuries. In their detailed yet romanticised descriptions of that geographical but also mythic terrain, these women were precursors of Sir Walter Scott, who gave the rugged Scottish landscape its symbolic significance throughout Europe, building on a particularly female tradition in his writing.

What I want to do in this paper is to explore that embrace of sameness and articulation of difference found in Mary Brunton's words and to examine the relationships between gender and landscape established in a range of fictional texts from the nineteenth and twentieth centuries, looking in particular at the topography of the Scottish highlands and the construction of that landscape in gendered terms. I am interested in the positioning of characters against or within that 'gendered' highland landscape and, through a consideration of this in a range of texts, want to raise some wider questions about the ways in which a sense of place and the symbolic function ascribed to the highland landscape might relate to 'Scottishness' and the construction of a sense of national identity. Does a gendered landscape in fact offer different paradigms of national identity for men and women?

The romanticisation of the Scottish highlands began after the defeat of the Jacobites in 1746 and was enhanced by the fashion for picturesque tours of the highlands in the 1760s. Its most popular literary articulation came at the time in Sir Walter Scott's poem *The Lady of the Lake* (1811) but Scott's first novel, *Waverley* (1814) is also a key text in examining representations of the highland landscape. In this novel we can see the way in which a sense of Scottish identity is explicitly linked both to femininity and to the contours of the highland landscape. In *Waverley* the young Englishman, Edward Waverley, politically uncommitted but with a vivid imagination, journeys north and in the Scottish highlands becomes involved in a series of adventures which lead him to take the Jacobite side in the rebellion of 1745. His allegiance to the Jacobite cause is partly brought about through the friendships he forms with the young highland chieftain Fergus MacIvor and his beautiful sister Flora. Although his youthful enthusiasm later gives way to disillusionment with the cause, his romantic imagination is initially engaged both by the beauties of the highland landscape and by the lovely Flora. From the start, the landscape of the highlands offers an explicitly feminine lure for the young man. Journeying north through bogs, woods and hills he emerges to rest in a countryside of seductive qualities:

> . . . issuing from the woods he found himself on the banks of a large river where his conductor gave him to understand they must sit down for a little while. The moon, which now began to rise, showed obscurely the expanse of water which spread before them and the shapeless and indistinct forms of mountains with which it seemed to be surrounded. The cool, and yet mild, air of the summer night, refreshed Waverley after his rapid and toilsome walk, and the perfume which it wafted from the birch trees, bathed in the evening dew, was exquisitely fragrant.
>
> He had time now to give himself up to the full romance of his situation. Here he sate on the banks of an unknown lake, under the guidance of a wild native, whose language was unknown to him.[2]

Within this moonlight scene of a mysteriously liquid beauty, of obscure yet protectively surrounding shapes, and in a world outside language, the construction of the landscape in feminine terms is obvious. Waverley is drawn towards it as if to a woman, seduced by its scents, and enveloped in its romance. He also appears released from the pressures of the social world into one in which the imagination can have free play. From his first encounter, the Scottish highlands represent a pre-social world for the hero.

Other critics have, of course, noted the feminisation of Scott's landscapes. Perhaps the most interesting analysis on the construction of the highlands in feminised terms has come from the work of Peter Womack. In his book, *Improvement and Romance: Constructing the Myth of the Highlands,* he suggests that in the eighteenth and nineteenth centuries the highlands are represented as a pre-lapsarian world in which nature flourished both in the uncultivated landscape and in the innocence of its people.[3] In the work of women novelists and travel writers before Scott, he argues, we can see specific moral values attached to a highland education. In this sense, we can view the highlands as being a kind of 'nursery annexe' of British society, where virtues are inculcated that might then reinvigorate the British state beyond. Taking this model further, through the use of a psychoanalytic discourse, he points out that we might, in fact, understand this world – which is occupied by the very old or very young and in which Gaelic is spoken – as occupying a feminine space in which Gaelic becomes the language of the Imaginary and English the paternal tongue of the Symbolic order. This reading draws on Lacan's distinction between the pre-social maternal space occupied by the child and the Symbolic, as the order of socialisation governed by the Law of the Father and entered with the acquisition of language. And, Womack, points out, the purest articulation of that highland identity comes in Scott from a woman, Flora MacIvor. Furthermore, within travel writing of the time the discourse of 'Caledonia' allows the highlands, by a process of synecdoche, to become representative of Scotland as a whole, According to his reading then the highlands, which become representative of a mythical Scottishness, are constructed in terms of the feminine; and in his use of terms such as the Imaginary, and the phrase 'nursery annexe' it would appear that this feminine space is, by implication, a maternal landscape.

We can see this feminising of the landscape and the association of that female space with national identity in a famous scene at the heart of *Waverley* in which the hero is led by Flora's handmaid through the craggy landscape to discover Flora herself playing the harp against a background of rocks and waterfall:

> In a spot, about a quarter of a mile from the castle, two brooks which formed a little river had their junction. The larger of the two came down the long bare valley, which apparently extended without any change or elevation of character, as far as the hills which formed its boundary permitted the eye to reach. But the other stream which had its source among the mountains on the left hand of the strath, seemed to issue from a very narrow and dark opening betwixt two large rocks. The streams were very different also in character. The larger was

placid and even sullen in its course, wheeling in deep eddies,
or sleeping in dark blue pools; but the motions of the lesser
brook were rapid and furious, issuing from between precipices
like a maniac from confinement, all foam and uproar.

It was up the course of this last stream that Waverley, like
a knight of romance, was conducted by the fair damsel his
silent guide.[4]

We can, without too much imagination, discern the female aspects of
this scene, even in the bodily contours created by the topography, with
its two streams, two orifices. Waverley is led further into this scene by
his guide, and the landscape becomes wilder:

The rocks assumed a thousand peculiar and varied forms. In
one place, a crag of huge size presented its gigantic bulk, as if
to forbid the passenger's further progress; and it was not until
he approached its very base, that Waverley discerned the sudden and acute turn by which the pathway wheeled its course
around this formidable obstacle. In another spot the projecting
rocks from the opposite sides of the chasm had approached so
near to each other that two pine-trees laid across and covered
with turf, formed a rustic bridge at the height of at least one
hundred and fifty feet. It had no ledges and was barely three
feet in breadth.

While gazing at this pass of peril which crossed, like a single black line, the small portion of blue sky not intercepted by
the projecting rocks on either side, it was with a sensation of
horror that Waverley beheld Flora and her attendant appear,
like inhabitants of another region, propped as it were, in mid
air, upon this trembling structure.[5]

The feminine within this landscape, which is still presented very much
in terms of its otherness, is now also seen as distant, inaccessible,
dizzyingly separate: for Waverley it occupies a dimension which he
cannot enter. Journeying on, under this bridge, he arrives in front of
a waterfall which cascades into a 'romantic reservoir'. Here the scene
reaches its climax:

Here, like one of those lovely forms which decorate the
landscapes of Poussin, Waverley found Flora gazing on the
waterfall. Two paces further back stood Cathleen, holding a
small Scottish harp . . . The sun now stooping in the west, gave
a rich and varied tint to all the objects which surrounded
Waverley, and seemed to add more than human brilliancy to

the expressive darkness of Flora's eye, exalted the richness and purity of her complexion, and enhanced the dignity and grace of her beautiful form. Edward thought he had never, even in his wildest dreams, imagined a figure of such exquisite and interesting loveliness. The wild beauty of the retreat, bursting upon him as if by magic, augmented the mingled feeling of delight and awe with which he approached her, like a fair enchantress of Boiardo or Ariosto, by whose nod the scenery around seemed to have been created, an Eden in a wilderness.[6]

Flora then goes on to offer an English version of the long Gaelic ballad Waverley had heard earlier that day.

In this scene we can see a movement which symbolises larger trajectories within the text. Waverley traverses a feminine and inaccessible landscape in which Flora is embedded. She is an almost static element within its other beauties. With the scenery behind her and the harp playing she offers a fusion of the picturesque terrain, feminine beauty, and Scottish culture. Here the contours of the female body are mapped on to the landscape, and a Scottish identity overlayers the whole. Within the context of the novel this particular juxtaposition is particularly significant because Flora is a lost love object for Waverley: she rejects him because her first allegiance is to the Jacobite cause. And the cause itself is lost so an independent Scottish nation is also, in a sense, abandoned: it becomes another lost love object. For Waverley who, at the end of the novel, goes back to his English inheritance, a suitably domesticated wife and a more stable and lawful existence, the Scottish highlands remain the lost realm of imagination and romance.

Again it is not difficult to read this in psychoanalytic terms. The highlands are indeed a pre-symbolic landscape which Waverley must cross, but emerge from, if he is to take up his place in the symbolic order. A rather crude Freudian reading of this might see Waverley as symbolically moving from an affiliation with the maternal (landscape) and undergoing a process of separation from it and a transition into the social world of patriarchal authority in which he takes his place. Freud wrote: 'A boy's mother is the first object of his love, and she remains so too during the formation of his Oedipus complex and, in essence, all through his life.'[7] The maternal landscape reproduces/images that role. Or, to understand this in Lacan's reworking of Freud's Oedipus complex through threat of castration the Law demands sacrifice of the boy's corporeal closeness to and pleasure in the mother. In exchange the boy is offered the name of the Father, a position like his fathers and a place within the symbolic order as a phallic speaking subject.[8] The lost landscape becomes the (m)other land and Waverley moves from being a rebel, outside the law and outside English in this Gaelic world into a position where he becomes a representative of the law himself: estate owner, husband. He can only attain this place in the Symbolic order by leaving the highlands behind; his 'adult' identity is predicated upon his difference and movement away from that maternal space. And in marrying Rose Bradwardine he effectively makes the transition into adult sexuality by finding a replacement for the lost realm represented by Flora. The lost maternal dimension remains an ideal perhaps but one that is quite clearly unattainable. (Flora herself goes into a nunnery which effectively seals her off as a sexual possibility for Waverley.)

So, the idea of the Scottish highlands as representative of a lost maternal landscape, necessarily put behind in the masculine entry into the world of adult sexuality, of language and law seems to work quite neatly. In Scott's novel at least, national identity appears predicated upon a sense of loss and can be understood as constructed in terms of the lost landscape of the highlands. Moving on from Scott to other examples of Scottish fiction set in the highlands, we can discern similar patterns in which this mapping of maternity onto the landscape and its resulting elevation into a symbol of national identity takes place.

In Robert Louis Stevenson's novel *Kidnapped* (1886), set in the aftermath of the Jacobite rebellion, another famous traverse of the landscape is described. In this novel, the stolid, lowland David Balfour (who is also the narrator), and the fiery and unpredictable Jacobite supporter, Alan Breck, are forced to flee across the highlands, hiding from the law, until they reach Edinburgh. There David can, like Waverley, lay claim to his inheritance and leave the world of romance and rebellion behind. One of the most visually memorable scenes in the novel is that in which David and his companion are forced into hiding from the English soldiers (the redcoats) and take refuge on a high rock in the midst of the highland landscape; in fact, it was 'two rocks, being both somewhat hollow on the top, and sloping one to the other, made a kind of dish or saucer, where as many as three of four might have lain hidden . . . a little peaty earth had drifted in between the top of the two rocks, and some bracken grew there, to be a bed to me'.[9] Within this earthy cradle, protected by the two haunches of rock – again, easily seen as a mothering terrain – the two men wait. When day breaks and the sun rises their position becomes increasingly uncomfortable, but they are unable to do anything because they can hear the English soldiers moving down below. On their rock, without water, they get hotter and hotter in their vulnerability; in their exposure to the sun's rays, in their thirst, they appear as new born infants, thrust from the maternal haunches, exposed to the light of the day, desperate for sustenance. And it is from this exposed position that David first hears the language of authority – the voices of the redcoats:

It was in this way that I first heard the right English speech;
one fellow as he went by actually clapping his hands upon
the sunny face of the rock on which we lay, and plucking it
off again with an oath. 'I tell you its 'ot', says he; and I was
amazed at the clipping tones and the odd sing-song voice in
which he spoke and no less at the strange trick of dropping
out the letter 'h'.[10]

Here, it would seem, was David's first encounter with the language of
the law.

Unlike Flora the two men are not embedded within the landscape.
Rather than being part of its contours they are expelled from it. Moreover, they do eventually move away from their discomfort which makes
this scene a turning point in the novel. It is from here that David begins his literal and metaphoric journey back into the lowlands and his
place in the Symbolic order. Once again it is only in a movement away
from the lost maternal landscape of the Scottish highlands that entry
into the social can be achieved. But, as with Waverley, his association
with that other world retains a positive symbolic power in terms of a
national romance, and his adult identity is predicated upon loss of the
primary love object.

This fusion of the highlands with both a maternal space and the
motherland, is even more evident in the work of Neil Gunn. His
novel *Highland River*, published in 1937, offers a moving account of
a childhood in the far north of Scotland, which focuses on the young
boy Kenn and contextualises the purity of his early years by comparison with his experiences in the First World War. Gunn's story makes
the connections between the land and the maternal more explicit by
presenting Kenn's mother as the embodiment of all that is special
about his early years. As the narrative comments, his mother grows
in mythical significance for the boy until in later years he sees her as
'the mother that abides from everlasting to everlasting'.[11] Even in his
youth, however, she is, for him, associated with the qualities of the
land:

> Her eyes, grey and wide spaced are lifted towards the trees
> of the plantation. Her straight dark hair is parted smoothly
> midway over her pale smooth forehead . . . Her heavy body is
> neither unshapely nor billowing but is deep bosomed and solid,
> and stands with quiet poise.
>
> So vividly does Kenn become aware of her presence that he
> finds himself looking where she is looking as though he might
> glimpse the things she sees. But the trees are quiet, save for the
> odd notes of birds, little twists of song, like twists of crystal
> water in sunlight. There is no sunlight, however. Beyond the

trees the sky is grey, with the greyness not of wet clouds, but of smoke, of distant promise. There is a soft warmth descending from it and penetrating the earth so that life stirs there in its sleep.[12]

Through a process of metonymy the warmth of his mother's body and that of the earth becomes associated, as does the greyness of her eyes and that of the sky, the penetration of her gaze and the penetration of the air and earth. The mother, moreover, is seen to possess a special kind of pre-linguistic communication with the land; a vision that Kenn cannot share. He can, however, gain strength from his sense of that vision. His mother becomes for him someone: 'So quiet and contemplative and abiding . . . that from the shelter of her skirts one may brave God, and all the unknown and terrifying things.'[13] Not only is Kenn emboldened to go forward and out into the world, by his mother's particularly passive strength but he also attributes to her a significance beyond the temporal: 'All the history of her people is writ on her face. The grey seas are stilled in her eyes; danger and fear are asleep in her brows; want's bony fingers grow warm at her breast; quietly against the quiet trees the struggle of the day lies folded in her hands.'[14] Made more explicitly metaphorical here, the mother becomes the land; both are somehow outside language, outside the temporal and the social. From this otherness Kenn is excluded but he is also strengthened by it, both in memory and in his movement away from it, in all his subsequent experiences.

This specific association of the atemporal dimension of the landscape with the feminine is also evident in *A Scots Quair* (1932–4). For various reasons, Lewis Grassic Gibbon's trilogy about life in the north-east of Scotland offers a rather more complex representation of the maternal and the national. The landscape of the Mearns, that part of the north-east in which the novel is set, carries different cultural associations from the mountainous and rugged highlands and does not occupy the same symbolic place in the national imagination. The trilogy, focusing on the character of Chris Guthrie, has moreover been seen as exceptional in its explorations of female identity. And here, although Chris does run up into the hills at every major crisis in her life, there is no traversing of the landscape, no moving into a world outside Scotland. Nevertheless the *Quair* still maintains a linkage of the land, the maternal, and Scottish identity. Rather than emerging in specific scenes, this can be traced in a movement across the trilogy as a whole.

The first novel, *Sunset Song*, begins with the young Chris Guthrie growing up on a farm in the north-east, very much part of the rhythms of that world and of the peasant farming community. In this section of the trilogy she marries and has a son, although her husband, also from the land, is killed in the First World War. In the sequel, *Cloud Howe* we see her married to a minister, the Reverend Robert Colquhoun, and living in a small town, the weaving community of Seggett. *Grey Granite* closes the trilogy with, as the title suggests, Chris living in a city, similar to Aberdeen. In this final novel the focus is as much, if not more, on Chris's son, Ewan, and his involvement in radical labour politics. In the trilogy then we can trace a movement away from the land, which of course reflects the historical patterns of the times and the decline of the rural community, but which takes the embodiment of its feminine – Chris Guthrie – with it. In both its plot and narrative voice the whole text is characterised by a sense of loss, of severance from the land.

In a parallel to this movement, Chris, who in the first novel is a lively and energetic character, within whose consciousness the reader is very much placed, gradually moves beyond the scope of the narrative and has a far less significant role in its plot. The trilogy ends with Ewan leading a labour march, going south and away from Scotland. At the end of the novel he is shown making lists, checking off marching equipment, noting down addresses, routes, and speakers: in other words, he is engaging with the social and material, moving out into the world. His role is that of activator, in a wider sphere of action, 'forgetting them both, finishing his lists while she laid the supper'.[15] His mother, in contrast, is increasingly peripheral. The trilogy closes with her retreating to a hillside, where she appears to lose both voice and consciousness, blending into the landscape itself in a world where time itself seems not to matter. The last paragraphs of the novel read:

> Over the Hill of Fare, new-timbered, a little belt of rain was falling, a thin screen that blinded the going of the light; behind, as she turned, she saw Skene Loch glimmer and glow a burnished minute; then the rain caught it and swept it from sight and a little wind soughed up the Barmekin. And now behind wind and rain came the darkness.
>
> Light had sprung up far in the hills, in little touns for a sunset minute while the folk tirred and went off to their beds, miles away, thin peeks in the summer dark.
>
> Time she went home herself.
>
> But she still sat on as one by one the lights went out and the rain came beating the stones about her, and falling all that night while she still sat there, presently feeling no longer the touch of the rain or hearing the sound of the lapwings going by.[16]

So our final view is of Chris being assimilated into the land itself, while her son moves outwards in a politics designed to change the world.

This fusion of the feminine and the landscape carries political as well as personal connotations. Although it is often quoted out of context, the remark made by Chris's second husband, 'Chris Caledonia, I married a nation!' cannot be ignored. While it may be reductive to see this as summing up the trilogy, the comment does indicate one model used to structure a sense of national identify. More than the other writers mentioned, Gibbon appears aware of the over-easy linking of femininity and the land. The cry of Chris's husband is as much an indictment of his short-sighted romanticism as it is a limiting analysis of her character. But it offers, nevertheless, a key to the workings of this romanticising structure, one which Gibbon could see elsewhere in Scottish literature and one which appears all too attractive to the Scottish imagination. The land becomes the woman, and the woman the nation.

In each of the texts I've considered we can see the ways in which the landscape might occupy the space and role of the maternal. This then becomes the location of a lost and ideal Scottishness. Within such an account the maternal landscape of the highlands does indeed appear to function as a kind of Imaginary. Using this Lacanian model we could argue that the acquisition of adult identity and entry into the symbol order is mirrored by the process whereby entry into the British world of power is achieved through separation with the (m)otherland. Adult social identity is predicated upon this separation, which also allows the lost object to remain symbolically significant.

There are, however, problems with this reading which relate to debates within psychoanalysis itself. If we are to see these texts, all by male writers, as operating along the Freudian or Lacanian lines suggested, whereby acquisition of identity in the symbolic order, the social world of language and law, is predicated upon a movement away from the maternal, then we have to take on board a central criticism of Freud and his model of sexuality. That is, while this structure might appear convincing in relation to the boy child, is it so appropriate to the girl? And if, in the movement across and away from the highland landscape, we can see a masculine fantasy at work in the association of a lost landscape with a lost mother and with an idealised Scottishness, what happens when women writers explore this setting? Moreover, is it possible for women to construct their sense of a national identity in such terms? These are the questions I want to explore in the second half of this essay.

Within psychoanalytic accounts of gender identity the acquisition of femininity has been much debated. Freud in his 1933 essay on 'Femininity' himself presented it as a problem, although in terms guaranteed to enrage feminists: 'Throughout history people have knocked their heads against the riddle of the nature of femininity . . . Nor will you have escaped worrying over this problem – those of you who are men; to those of you who are women this will not apply – you are yourselves the problem.'[17] Freud suggested that entry into adult sexuality is a more fraught and precarious process for the girl who has two tasks before her to make the transition from clitoral to vaginal sexuality, and to replace the mother with the father as the love object. He also argues that the girl child's attachment to the mother who was the primary love object can, and often does, end in hate.

Jacques Lacan's reworking of this idea is more complex but equally negative: the boy child is positioned with reference to the father, given a name and an authorised speaking position, becomes an 'I'. Because the feminine is an object not a subject, the girl's position within the symbolic order must be marginal and tenuous; when she says 'I' she never speaks as herself but in a form of masquerade. Within the Symbolic order, Lacan suggests, the mother is denigrated because her powerlessness within patriarchy is perceived.[18] So, we can see again that the posited relationship between the girl child and the maternal is problematic and potentially negative.

Both Freud and Lacan's accounts have of course been challenged or reworked, in particular by French feminists who still adhere to psychoanalytic practices but who read the gendering of identity rather differently. Julia Kristeva, who has written much about the pre-imaginary space of the maternal chora stresses that the (phallic) 'Mother' is the consequence of a masculine fantasy of maternity rather than a woman's lived experience of it. The semiotic – equivalent in Kristeva to Lacan's Imaginary – is a feminine and maternally struc- tured space, but although the semiotic is feminine in relation to the symbolic it has no special relationship to women. The maternal body, during gestation and as a chora in infancy is conceived of as a space, a channel which is retrospectively fantasised as if it were inhabited by a subject. It is therefore a maternity which women can never inhabit and which cannot be spoken – especially not by mothers. Maternity therefore is a process without a subject, which has been culturally constructed to instill 'the subjectless biological program into the very body of a symbolising subject, this event called motherhood'.[19] She describes motherhood within the context of Western Christianity as a 'the fantasy that is nurtured by the adult, man or woman, as a lost territory'.[20]

Approaching these issues rather differently, Luce Irigaray in her work has suggested that the patriarchal symbolic order leaves no space or form of representation for women's autonomy. In the idea of the phallic mother it effaces women's earliest formative relationship, leaving them without a pre-history and without a positive identificatory role model. The boy is confronted with the male sex – as represented in himself – and the (m)other. There is no representative of the 'female' sex as such. But why, she questions, should the girl child necessarily be constrained in this way? For the girl under patriarchy there is no woman with which to identify: she has no representation. Irigaray writes: 'As for us, the daughters, if our relationship with our mothers is a relationship with need, with no possible identity, and if we enter into desire by becoming objects of the desire of/for the father, what do we know about our identities and our desires? Nothing.'[21]

These are complex theoretical positions from a variety of perspectives, but what emerges from the different account is a general agreement that the girl child's relation to the maternal is less clear cut than that of the boy's, and that entry into the symbolic order, predicated upon the lost mother, cannot be read in quite the same way. For the girl, in Freudian terms, the maternal is that which she might come to hate; in a Lacanian reading, the mother is a figure of perceived powerlessness. With Kristeva for both men and women the mother is lost territory, but not in herself a subject, and therefore is hardly a positive image for the girl; and in Irigaray's work the mother is a loss to the girl in systems of representation: mothers cannot be women to them. It would therefore appear that the neat elision of Scotland's highlands into a maternal landscape (a primary love object) and into the symbol of a lost national identity is not so simple a model if the subjectivity is female.

This becomes apparent in the work of women writers who focus on the same kind of material as Scott, Stevenson, Gunn and Gibbon, but who do so through female subjectivities. A short piece from Mrs Ann Grant indicates the nature of the problem. Grant's *Letters from the Mountains, being the real correspondence of a Lady between the years 1773 and 1807*, a series of reminiscences of highland life, did much to increase the appetite for tours of the highlands and to foreground its romance. In many ways her writing appears to confirm Womack's reading of the highlands as a 'nursery annexe' and a pre-lapsarian world. She reflects on the grandeur of the scenery, the way in which the highlanders handle poverty with dignity, and works very much within the aesthetics of the picturesque. The following words in a letter to her friend Mrs McIntosh in 1794 sound a rather different note:

> The paths that lead from nature and simplicity, towards elegance and false refinement in manners, and artificial modes of living do not indeed intend to happiness but they slope with our inclinations and wind with our caprices . . . These paths can never be retrodden. When tired of the idle and frivolous

battle, and the vain empty pursuits, that fill up fashionable
life . . . we now retrace our first and purest ideas of happiness;
the rural ease that dwells in the pastoral valley; the soothing
quiet and artless innocence of the cottage; the solemn gloom
of the forest . . . and the sublime solitude of the mountains
from whose elevation we wish to look down on low pursuits
and give a kind of repose to the wearied mind . . . Estranged
from nature, enervated by luxury, and softened by false delicacy, we set about the experiment; we find the cottage quiet
indeed, but smoky, confined and deficient in a thousand things
on which we are become too dependent. The narrow bounds
imprison us, the low roof crushes, and the scanty light which
struggles in through the little casement, bewilders us. The
inhabitants we find innocent, hospitable and willing to please;
but we are shocked with their vulgar language, disgusted with
their uncouth manners and tired with the sameness to which
their narrow circle of ideas confines their conversation . . . The
forest walls are damp and intricate and its gloom melancholy
and oppressive . . . In vain we climb the mountains in search of
more extended prospects and more exalted serenity; fatigue
follows and chagrin overtakes us; the wind pierces and the cold
numbs us . . . and we hasten back, weary and unsatisfied, from
scenes that expand the soul and tranquilise the spirit of the
faithful lover of nature who has never admitted in her bosom
artificial joys, or wandered in the vain search of happiness not
meant for this threshold of existence.[22]

Two things are striking in the passage: firstly the element of cynicism
about the ways in which those who have left the simple pleasures of
life for the sophisticated social world romanticise nature in general and
the highland landscape in particular. Grant mocks this by pointing out
some of the realities that might be encountered on such a supposedly
'spiritual' quest. Secondly there is a very poignant and rather contradictory longing for that lost world expressed in terms of exclusion:
'these paths can never be retrodden'; we are 'estranged from nature'
and their pleasures are 'not meant for this threshold of existence'. This
language of exclusion, of estrangement, of barriers to any return to
the landscape combines the sense that reunification with the maternal
landscape might not be possible, with an awareness that it might not
even by wholly desirable. Or, at least, there is an indication that desire
for this lost object of love is based upon an illusory construction of
that landscape.

This sense of no return, of no possible enfolding in the maternal
bosom of the highlands, becomes an issue in a range of women's texts

which use the highland landscape, including the two novels written by Mary Brunton. Brunton was a contemporary both of Sir Walter Scott and of Jane Austen. Her first novel *Self-Control* was published in 1811 and, although she once wrote that she would sooner exhibit as a rope-dancer than be considered a literary woman, she was serious and passionate about her work.[23] *Self-Control* opens in a highland setting, and her second novel, *Discipline* ends in one. She was however unfortunate in publishing the latter just after the appearance of *Waverley*. As she wrote to a friend at the end of 1814: 'What a competitor for poor little me! The worst of all is that I have ventured unconsciously on Scott's own ground by carrying my heroine to the highlands.'[24] She was, of course, justified in her fears that her own work would be eclipsed. Brunton, however, was not above expressing a certain shrewd cynicism about the subject matter as a letter written to her brother in 1815 reveals: 'As for the highlands, you know, they are quite the rage. All the novel-reading misses have seen them and admired them in the verdure and sunshine of July. Now, what novel-reading miss ever had common sense enough to doubt, that what is pleasing to the eye should be desirable in possession; or that what charms for an evening, should delight for ever?'[25] Like Anne Grant she mocks the romanticisation of the landscape by those with little knowledge of its substance. Both women share a sense of unease about the symbolic significance attributed to the highlands, although both were contributors to that myth.

In Brunton's novels the highland landscape functions rather differently from the romantic terrain found in Scott's work. In this respect, there are two aspects of *Self-Control* worth note: the way in which the central female character is positioned in relation to the landscape, and secondly, the values that are associated with or ascribed to the Scottish highlands and their function in the novel as a whole.

The novel begins in the highlands, with a heroine, Laura Montreville, who has enjoyed all the benefits of a rural Scottish childhood. Through a long series of adventures she moves to London, then to Canada, finally returns to Scotland and then steps into marriage with the hero De Courcy, owner of a large estate in England. Although the highland landscape itself is important only at the start of the novel, it plays an important part in the opening scene which depicts the attempted seduction of Laura by the rakish Colonel Hargrave, who remains the villain and threat to Laura's happiness and moral purity throughout. Walking alone one fine evening through the highland glen, she meets the Colonel. Inspired by the romantic setting, she listens with 'silent rapture to the glowing language of her lover' until it becomes apparent that the offer he is making is not an entirely honourable one. Struck with horror, she faints away and, while Hargrave seeks some water to revive her, she makes her escape across that wild terrain they had just traversed together.

> Terror gave her strength to proceed. Every path in her native wood was familiar to her: she darted through them with what speed she could command; and, reckless of all danger but that from which she fled, she leapt from the projecting rocks, or gradually descended from the more fearful declivities, by clinging to the trees which burst from the fissures; till, exhausted with fatigue, she reached the valley and entered the garden that surrounded her home. Here, supported no longer by the sense of danger, her spirits utterly failed her; and she threw herself on the ground without a wish but to die.[26]

Coming right at the start of the novel, this scene has considerable impact, as does its parallel scene at the end of the three volumes when Laura, having been abducted to Canada by the now desperate Colonel only escapes from him by shooting down Niagara Falls in an Indian canoe. What is remarkable about these scenes is the vigour with which the female figure traverses the contours of the landscape; rather than being a static embodiment of its feminine nature, she is crossing it – and with speed. (This energetic movement becomes even more remarkable when we think this novel was produced at about the same time as Jane Austen's *Emma* in which the heroine can hardly move outside her little town of Highbury on a gentle country walk without being subject to attacks from disreputable elements such as gypsies.) At both the beginning and end of *Self-Control* wilderness landscapes become terrains of precarious sexuality. In both scenes Laura is fleeing from threats to her purity. And, unlikely as it may sound, this violent movement, this fleeing across the landscape, rather than standing picturesquely or serenely against it, is a feature common to several of the texts by women writers who use a highland setting. And in their novels it is consistently related to sexuality.

So far, then, we can question whether there is any 'feminine' embodied in the highland landscape in *Self-Control*. (Laura, after all, barely stands still long enough to become assimilated into it.) With the feminine dimension apparently removed as a symbolic embodiment of its characteristics, what else does the highland terrain embody? In some ways, *Self-Control* does substantiate the idea of the highlands providing a set of moral values which are then exported to strengthen Britain as a whole. Laura, we are told, has gained from her childhood environment 'an active mind, a strong sense of duty, and the habit of meeting and of overcoming adverse circumstances'. And yet, if we are to see these qualities as gendered in any way they are more likely associated with the rugged and masculine than any feminine characteristics. Even the qualities symbolised by 'Scottishness' are, apart from Laura, more generally associated with the masculine in the text. Laura's father is the product of a Scots upbringing and values it as a result whereas her dead mother is thoroughly English and is described as 'showy'; her manner, we are told 'had the glare rather than the polish of high life'. When Laura moves to London and has to earn a living and withstand the attentions of Colonel Hargrave it is her 'masculine' strengths that stand her in good stead.

This pattern is almost reversed in Brunton's second novel, *Discipline* (1814) where the spoilt heroine Ellen makes the movement north from London, where she suffers a series of character-building misfortunes, until at last she finds happiness in the highlands. Part of that happiness is when she discovers that the stolid Mr Maitland, whom she initially thought the most boring and morally constrained man in the world, is in fact the dashing highland chieftain Henry Graham. Once in the highlands she can appreciate all his qualities and romance ends in marriage. Again the highlands seem to retain certain moral qualities but also to occupy a space in which sexual desire can be expressed. The plot, however, would suggest that entry into this sexual terrain becomes acceptable through the acquisition of a husband. As *Self-Control* has shown, to be in that landscape alone can be dangerous.

A similar pattern appears Susan Ferrier's novel *Marriage* published in 1818. Here too there is a linking of a highland upbringing, moral worth, an inadequate mother, and sexual happiness in a highland context. In Ferrier's novel the weak and selfish Englishwoman, Lady Juliana makes a foolish marriage to the handsome but penniless Henry Douglas, son of a highland Laird. Short of funds, they are forced to seek refuge with her husband's family where Juliana is horrified by the rough ways of the highlands. After the birth of twin daughters they return to London, leaving Mary, the weaker of the daughters to be brought up in the highlands by relatives. Much of the novel follows her adventures when she later seeks out her family in London. Like Laura, she is armed with her highland virtues, and is horrified at the ways of life she encounters in the south. She is particularly upset by the behaviour of her mother who exhibits little in the way of maternal feelings. So excited is Mary at the prospect of meeting her mother that she faints on the first encounter, much to Lady Juliana's disgust:

> . . . no sooner was the nature of her daughter's insensibility ascertained than all her former hostility increased . . . as Mary at length slowly unclosing her eyes, stretched out her hands and faintly articulated 'My mother!'

'Mother! What a hideous vulgar appellation!' thought the
fashionable parent to herself; and instead of answering her
daughter's appeal, she hastily proposed that she should be
conveyed to her own apartment.[27]

Only after she has found a husband is Mary able to return to the
highlands and to the woman who had brought her up as a mother.
On this occasion, the embrace is warm: 'Oh, there are moments in
life keen, blissful, never to be forgotten! and such was the moment to
Mary when the carriage stopped and she again heard the melody of
that voice familiar from infancy – and looked on the face known with
her being – and was pressed to that heart where glowed a parent's
love.'[28] This embrace by the maternal – by the surrogate mother and
the mothering landscape – can only be permitted, it seems, when the
girl is secure within the order of heterosexuality, her identity acquired.
As with *Discipline* the 'maternal' space can only be safely re-entered
when accompanied by a husband – once a social identity of 'normal'
adult sexuality has been acquired.

The structure of *Marriage* can also be compared with that of a novel
written later in the nineteenth century. Margaret Oliphant's *Kirsteen,*
published in 1888 but opening in 1814, the year that *Waverley* was
written, again details a highland childhood, although this time one
of repression. Kirsteen's father cares little for his daughters, valuing
only his sons and their lost inheritance as the Douglas family. He re-
ceives little opposition from Kirsteen's mother who is both physically
and emotionally weak. Secretly plighting her troth to a friend of her
brothers, off to fight in India, Kirsteen has to resist her father's attempts
to marry her to someone else by running away to London. There, again
it seems strengthened by her childhood virtues, she makes her way in
the world as a mantua maker. Even on learning of the death of her lover
she does not return to her family, making only two brief trips back to
Scotland – one to see her lover's mother, another on the death of her
own mother. Although when in London Kirsteen is shown as feeling
the occasional longing for her homeland, the process of idealisation is
quite consciously interrogated:

That she should be seized with a yearning now and then for
the sound of the linn, for the silence of the hills, for the whole-
some smell of the peats in the clear blue highland air, was as
natural as that she should hear that wail for Kirsteen in the
midst of her dreams. These longings gradually built up in her
mind an ideal picture of the beauty and perfection of nature as
embodied in her own glen, such as is a stay and refreshment to
many a heart in the midst of alien life – to many a heart which
perhaps in presence of that glen not idealised would be uncon-

scious of any beauty in nature . . . Go back! Oh no, she would
not if she could go back, and she could not if she would.[29]

There is a telling finality to these last lines. Although the landscape
functions in her imagination in the same way as her mother's cries
draw her in her dreams, there is a clear sense that no return is ever
possible, and that even the beauty of the glen is to an extent built
upon a fantasy. Again we can hear echoes of that sense of exclusion,
of the problematising of return, encountered in Ann Grant and Mary
Brunton.

In this novel too, the highland landscape becomes associated with
threats to virginity. It is Kirsteen's younger sister, Jeanie, left alone
in the family home with little guidance from her stern father, who
encounters the highland landscape in terms of a dangerous sexuality.
She pleads with Kirsteen to take her back, feeling unable to resist
the advances of a local landowner, Lord John, who has attempted
to seduce her. Matters come to a head when the couple meet in a
another secluded and romantic setting above a waterfall. But when
the seduction is underway Jeanie is saved by her father who, pay-
ing uncharacteristic attention to his daughter, comes up behind the
couple, seizes Lord John by the neck, and throws him to his death
over the waterfall. Again passion and precariousness, specifically associated with sexuality, threaten a woman alone in that landscape.
Jeanie is finally saved and continues to live in the highlands with
her new husband. Kirsteen, however, never goes back. Her return, it
appears, is impossible because she never fully settles into adult and
domesticated sexuality: her would-be husband is dead in India. When
she returns to take up her independent life in London we are told:
'It had been but a temporary dwelling place before, to be replaced
by a true home, perhaps in her own highlands, perhaps, – what did
it matter? – or in the incomprehensible Indian world, when he came
back. Now he would never come back; and Kirsteen recognised that
this was her established place.'[30] Alone, her condition must always
be one of estrangement from the motherland. Interestingly, however,
she does offer her father the money to buy some of the ancient land
that had been lost to the family, although it is her brother who in-
herits the property, not fully aware of his sister's contribution. In this
sense Kirsteen occupies a masculine role, not only earning her own
living but also providing financial support. This is a role, however,
that cannot be accommodated within the territory of the highlands.
As she never marries but ends the novel as a respectable old lady living in Edinburgh, her clearly unmaternal role would seem to suggest
that her place within the social order is blurred in terms of the gender
demarcations.

Nor is this pattern, whereby landscape is associated with a problematic and potentially threatening sexuality and constructed in terms
of estrangement, confined to the nineteenth century. In finishing this
brief survey I want to discuss two novels by twentieth century Scottish
women writers *Open the Door!* by Catherine Carswell (1918) and *The
White Bird Passes* (1958) by Jessie Kesson.

Carswell's story about a young woman, Joanna Bannerman, who
grows up in Glasgow, makes a disastrous marriage to an Italian and
has an equally unfortunate affair with a married man in London, before coming to appreciate the love of Lawrence Urquhart, a Scot who
has pursued her with a dogged devotion throughout, repeats several of
the features found in the earlier texts. Again we have an inadequate –
if much loved – mother in Julia Bannerman, driven to distraction by
her involvement in various evangelical causes. We find departure from
Scotland into a sexually 'normative' if unhappy marriage, when Joanna
falls in love with an Italian. It is, however, on holiday in the highlands
as a young girl that she first encounters a sexual dimension to her
existence. Roaming around the hills, communing with nature, flinging
herself upon the ground and embracing the earth, she meets a young
local boy, who tells her how bonny she is and says: 'If ye'll come up
yonder on the moors wi' me, Joanna . . . I'll show ye what lads is for.'[31]
When she returns to these childhood haunts at the close of the novel,
seeking a resolution to her tempestuous existence, she spies Lawrence
Urquhart, at some distance from her across the moors, on a walking
holiday and apparently unaware of her presence. In an extraordinary
scene, a reversal of Laura's flight in *Self-Control*, she is shown chasing
him across the landscape to impart her newly understood love for him:

> She plunged down the hill, not zig-zagging now, but jump-
> ing and stumbling straight forward, sometimes falling on her
> hands and knees. The braid of her skirt was torn into fes-
> toons and her knees trembled shockingly. It was even worse
> going downhill than up. But she went on and on across the
> amber-coloured dip which was full of quivering air . . . Again
> she had lost sight of him and the knowledge that as she was
> crawling up the next slippery hill, he was going pell-mell
> downwards, nearly killed her. She uttered his name now in
> gasping, voiceless breaths though she knew it was worse than
> useless . . . With the tears pouring down her scarlet cheeks,
> and all her features convulsed like a frantic lost child's,
> she got somehow over the brow of the hill and looked for
> him.[32]

While this scene may initially appear very different from Brunton's,
both Laura in *Self-Control* and Joanna in *Open the Door!* are fl-

eeing from sexual danger, the former escaping from seduction and dishonour, the latter running from the previously unsatisfactory and humiliating sexual relationships she had been involved in. In each scene the contours of the highland landscape itself determine the runner's routes, unpredictable in their shapes and features. And in the later novel, Joanna herself is likened to a lost child pursuing her mother. But, it seems, it is only through gaining Lawrence that Joanna can be reunited with the lost comfort of her highland childhood.

Finally I want to consider Jessie Kesson's novel, *The White Bird Passes*. Set in Inverness and Aberdeenshire this is partly an exploration of urban life and the experiences of Janie, whose mother, a prostitute, is also an outcast. The novel follows her life in the streets, then her time in an orphanage in the country, visited only once by her mother who is dying of syphilis. Although when in the children's home Janie finds the presence of the rural environment and the surrounding hills comforting they are presented as an illusory protection:

> Long ago Janie had thought that if she ran very fast and hidden, along the side of Leuchar's wood, she could catch up on the Cairngorms. Rush right into their foothills and take them by surprise before they had time to hide behind their mists again . . . But no matter how fast she ran nor how hidden her race was, the Cairngorms were ever swifter, ever more wary, and she had never caught up with them.[33]

Again the writing is characterised by a sense of exclusion and isolation from the landscape. Again the novel ends with a movement away from the land, as Janie is about to leave the home and move into a world of adult sexuality, hinted at by the sudden attention she is being given by the men around her. Before that movement away however, the text pauses, as Janie stands outside at dusk and the laughter of the men who had been teasing her recedes:

> Their laughter had belched upwards...But Janie had stood holding on to it. Holding on to her awareness of the possession of her body. She had been aware of it before . . . a mild awareness. But grown men were beginning to acknowledge it now. There was something cruel and fierce in their knowing.
>
> The Cairngorms had begun to close in and were pressing down upon the howe . . . Silence had circled all the landscape, and held it trembling prisoner. A peesie had cried through the silence, weeping its grief across the stubble field. Some long long grief that had found an echo in Janie herself. Her pain be-

came submerged in the peesie's cry. Herself and the landscape
had stood in some ache, waiting for release . . . the aloneness of
the night was beyond the bearing of the land itself. It caught
you, the land did, if you walked it at night. Held you hostage.
Clamped and small within its own immensity, and cast all the
burden of its own aloneness upon you.[34]

While, in its image of a figure engulfed by the immensity of the land
at the onset of nightfall, this scene appears to mirror the ending of *A
Scots Quair*, the construction of the land itself and its relationship to
the focalising female consciousness are very different. Janie is not becoming at one with the land; rather it calls to an ache, an emptiness
in her. And rather than finding comfort in it, she is made even more
aware of her own isolation. Significantly this sense of exclusion is again
linked with an emergent sexuality which propels her away from the
lost mother and away from the land, but offers nothing in its place.

These texts obviously work within very different contexts, and it
would be foolish to push the connections between writers of such different backgrounds, from different historical periods and each with
her own particular interests, too far. What I am suggesting, however,
is that all of them are, in one way or another, negotiating the relationship between women and mothers and between women and the
Scottish landscape. In these explorations of the feminine, positioned
within maternal and national identities, certain shared characteristics
emerge.

Firstly, all the texts by women engage with problem mothers as
characters. Whether weak, inadequate or shallow these mothers offer
unsatisfactory relationships to their daughters, although in several instances there may be a strong bond of love portrayed between them.
Nevertheless there is always some lack – whether social, moral, or even
physical – associated with these mother figures. In these texts, then, the
'maternal' is not in itself a necessarily positive symbol; in every case it
is characterised by feelings of ambivalence and associated with a sense
of loss. In none of these novels do we find that easy movement from
the maternal to the land, noted in Neil Gunn's *Highland River*.

Secondly, while the maternal as a symbol of stability and endurance
is mapped on to equally enduring landscape in the works of Scott,
Stevenson, Gunn and Gibbon, the highland countryside in the work
of these women writers appears less durable and much more disruptive. The instability of the terrain itself is indicated in its unpredictable
contours, especially treacherous for those running women. One aspect
of this disruptive quality is the way in which the rugged landscape
appears to inculcate masculine values of strength and independence in
the female characters, destabilising gender categories. But even more

disruptive are the ways in which the landscapes become sites of sexual danger, where sexuality is aroused in often threatening ways. Such landscapes can only be safely viewed, or can only be contained, it seems, by the domesticating presence of 'a husband'. Re-entry to the lost landscape is only possible through a secure position within the social (Symbolic) order; otherwise, that return to the 'Imaginary' is too problematic, too threatening.

Lastly, the highland landscape is symbolically structured in images of exclusion; it is formed out of barriers, boundaries, and is located on thresholds. While there may be a longing to reintegrate with that lost landscape there is a recognition that such a reunification would be neither possible nor comfortable. In none of these texts, in other words, is the highland landscape shown to retain its reassuring symbolic significance for the characters, or for the readers. Rather than serving as the symbol of a lost ideal, of a pre-lapsarian world, the landscape of the highlands, with its mountains, glens, lochs and waterfalls, appears to operate as a geographic terrain of instability and a space of psychic disruption.

Patterns emerging in these novels by Scottish women writers suggest that we need to question the appropriateness of the model of a maternal landscape which works so well with the fiction of Scott, Stevenson, Gunn and Gibbon. In their fiction the highland landscape does appear to be symbolically structured as a maternal space. In their crossing of and departure from that site the male characters move towards and into the Symbolic order: a social order of Englishness, inheritance, and the law of the father. If the highlands themselves stand for a synecdochal representation of Scotland, then Scottishness, and national identity, becomes associated with that maternal space, which remains as the lost realm upon which identity is predicated. Scottishness, if a fantasy, nevertheless operates within a recognisable framework of subjectivity. In contrast, the women's texts offer a rather different paradigm of subjectivity and of national identity. A rhetoric of a lost (m)otherland provides women with a less secure space within the social order. It appears to represent both sameness and difference, becoming a threshold that can never be recrossed and functioning as a site of instability.

In conclusion, the idea of the maternal landscape as represented in the work of Scott, Stevenson, Gunn and Gibbon, would seem to offer a male fantasy of the mother and of the motherland. For a critic like Womack to impose that model of feminine space upon all writing which created the myth of the highlands is in itself, perhaps, a form of masculine critical fantasy. As an alternative to this, just as the girl's relationship to the mother and her entry into the symbolic order has been problematised by recent rereadings of psychoanalysis, so the female relationship to the maternal landscape needs to be acknowledged as more complex. In the texts by women there is no easy sliding from love of the landscape, to love of (m)otherland, to the identification with a lost Scottishness.

If we take gender into account in rethinking the models in which that romanticised space of the Scottish highlands has been constructed, then I think we also need to reconsider the myths in which issues of national identity are formulated. When the only paradigm for understanding the relationship to our native land is that of a motherland, what does this offer Scottish women? How can women in any context of national identity understand their position? To quote again the words of Luce Irigaray: 'As for us, the daughters, if our relationship with our mothers is a relationship with need, with no possible identity, what do we know about our identities and our desires? Nothing.'[35] Until we question these models and myths of identity, Scotland, in all its ruggedness, can never fully be 'mine own'.

* A version of this essay appeared in the conference proceedings, *La Europa (Culturel) de Los Pueblos Voz Y Forma*, ed. F. Eguiluz *et al* (Vittoria: Universidad de Pais Vasco, 1994).

Notes

1. Journal entry of 1815, included in *Emmeline with some other pieces, to which is prefixed a memoir of her life, including some extracts from her correspondence*, edited by her husband, Alexander Brunton (Edinburgh: Constable & Co, London; Dent, 1819).
2. *Waverley*, Scott (Edinburgh, 1814; London, Dent: 1969), 156. All pages references are to the 1969 edition.
3. *Improvement and Romance: Constructing the Myth of the Highlands*, Womack (London: Macmillan, 1989), chs. 1, 6, and 8.
4. *Waverley*, 189.
5. *ibid.*, 190.
6. *ibid.*, 191.
7. 'Femininity' (1933), *New Introductory Lectures on Psycho-analysis*, Freud (Harmondsworth: Penguin, 1964; 1973). All page references are to the 1973 edition.
8. *Ecrits*, Lacan (London: Tavistock Publications, 1977).
9. *Kidnapped*, Stevenson (1886; London: Tusitala Edition, *Works*, Vol VI, 1924), 138–9. All page references are to the 1924 edition.
10. *ibid.*, 141.
11. *Highland River*, Gunn (1937; London: Arrow Books, 1975), 98. All page references are to the 1975 edition.

12. *ibid.*, 100.
13. *ibid.*, 101.
14. *ibid.*, 101.
15. *A Scots Quair*, Gibbon (1932–4; London: Pan, 1982), 217.
16. *ibid.*, 220.
17. 'Femininity', Freud, *op. cit.*, 146.
18. Lacan, *op. cit.*
19. 'Motherhood according to Giovanni Bellini', first published in *Peinture* (December, 1975), no. 10–11, in *Desire in Language a semiotic approach to literature and art*, Kristeva (Oxford: Blackwell, 1982), 242.
20. 'Stabat Mater', Kristeva in *The Kristeva Reader*, ed T. Moi (Oxford: Blackwell, 1986), 161.
21. 'Women-Mothers, the Silent Substratum of the Social Order', Irigaray, (tr. D. Macey), in *The Irigaray Reader*, ed. M. Whiteford (Oxford: Blackwell, 1991), 52.
22. Letter to Mrs McIntosh, Glasgow, *Letters from the Mountains, being the real correspondence of a lady between the years 1773 and 1807*, Grant (London: Longman, Hurst, Rees and Orme, 1807), Vol. III, 8–10.
23. Letter to Mrs Izett, 30 August 1810: 'To be pointed at – to be suspected of literary airs – to be shunned, as literary women are, by the more unpretending of my own sex; and abhorred, as literary women are, by the pretending of the other! – My dear, I would sooner exhibit as a rope-dancer.' in *Discipline. to which is prefixed a memoir of the life and writings of the author, including extracts from her correspondence* (London: Richard Bentley, 1837), 16.
24. *ibid.*, Letter to Mrs Craigie, 10 December 1814, 38.
25. *ibid.*, Letter to her brother, 21 April, 1815.
26. *Self-Control*, Brunton (1811; London: Pandora Press, 1986), 10.
27. *Marriage*, Ferrier (1818; Oxford: O. U. P., 1971), 223.
28. *Marriage*, *op. cit.*, 466.
29. *Kirsteen*, Oliphant (1888; London: Dent, 1984), 177–8. All page references are to the 1984 edition.
30. *Kirsteen*, *op. cit.*, 240.
31. *Open the Door!*, Carswell (1920; London: Virago, 1986), 37. All page references are to the 1986 edition.
32. *Open the Door!*, *op. cit.*, 395–6.
33. *The White Bird Passes*, Kesson (1958; London: Virago, 1987), 121. All pages references are to the 1987 edition.
34. *The White Bird Passes*, *op. cit.*, 156–7.
35. Irigaray, *op. cit.*

The Wilderness of the Self: Identity and Otherness in the Fiction of Carol Shields

Faith Pullin

In a recent interview with Carol Shields,[1] the interviewer asked 'What were you trying to accomplish in *The Stone Diaries*? It seems to be the autobiography of a woman who wasn't there'. Shields answered:

> I was interested in the notion of autobiography and, in particular, the idea of women's life stories. A lot of women are erased from their lives, sometimes as a result of their own actions and attitudes, but mostly for societal reasons. The saddest thing about women like Daisy Goodwill is that they didn't know what was owed them. They didn't have the words to say "I Want". Ninety-nine percent of the women of Daisy's generation never claimed their own lives.

Although *The Stone Diaries* presents itself as the autobiography of Daisy Goodwill Flett, other lives are also foregrounded and the categories of reality and fiction are constantly disrupted. Shields says that she wanted to have other voices filtering in and out, representing fantasies of what other people imagined about Daisy. She also wanted to include legend along with facts. The birth scene, for example. 'Daisy wouldn't remember her own birth, but doubtless she heard stories about it, remarkable as it was.'

Is *The Stone Diaries* meant to represent Daisy's 'real' life? To fill in the gaps that the people around her failed to recognise? Shields says that when she read back over her manuscript, she saw that Daisy had somehow leaped over her experiences with childbirth, sexual initiation, and education. 'But that's how life stories are. It's as though you end up your life with a boxful of snapshots. They may not be the best ones, but they're the ones you have.' Shields' formal experimentation in this novel encompasses the use of actual photographs, thereby further interrogating the distinction between fiction and autobiography. 'I'm always checking the image against the text. I found the photo of the Ladies Rhythm and Movement Club at a small country museum in Manitoba.' The photos of Daisy's grandchildren are actually of her own children. Shields here seems to be characteristically subversive, involving her own life in her fiction, questioning the concept of reality itself.

Daisy's 'erased' life is redeemed in the novel by friendship with other women – lifelong groups of friends whom Shields considers forerunners of consciousness-raising groups – 'early feminist cells' as she puts it. Erasure is apparent not real. Shields' subversiveness illuminates every aspect of *The Stone Diaries*.

The text relies heavily on coincidence and synchronicity: 'I like to collect stories of other people's coincidences because I suspect that that's how the universe really works. For a while I was worried because *The Stone Diaries* didn't seem to have a plot. And then I read an interview with Patrick White in which he says, "I never worry about plot. I worry about life going on toward death"'.

The first chapter of *The Stone Diaries* is the only one narrated entirely in the first person. The narrative 'I' returns at a later stage. So, the question arises 'Who is telling Daisy's story?' There are many discrepancies between Daisy's version of her life and the book's documentation. For example, Daisy describes her mother as 'extraordinarily obese' and taller than her husband but a photo reveals that Mercy Goodwill is actually shorter than Cuyler and not particularly fat. In many respects, Daisy seems not to understand her own experience; Shields constantly indicates that life and the self are intrinsically unknowable.

In addition to Daisy's own version, 'Life is an endless recruiting of witnesses'[2] and these unreliable narrators confuse the issue with their own versions of Daisy's life. In Chapter 7, 'SORROW', a number of characters offer explanations for Daisy's depression; no interpretation is valorised. No one really knows Daisy, nor does the reader know her at the book's end. Related to this radical destabilising of categories of knowledge and meaning is Shields' use of memory as itself a defamiliarising tool. When Cuyler Goodwill dies, he is unable to remember his wife's name, although he had built a tower in her honour. In the same way, it is impossible to decipher how much of Daisy's diary is created, or recreated.

Daisy herself is excessively reticent. She never refers to the death of her first husband – *that* story remains untold. This female reticence is bound up with Shields' use of sexual reversal. In her study of the work of Susanna Moodie, Shields comments on the fact that Moodie's 'women figures tend to be strong, moral and aggressive, while the males, almost without exception, are weak, easily corrupted and malleable'[3]. In an example of inter-textuality, Shields' own treatment of gender and sexuality is itself oppositional. From the passionate Cuyler Goodwill to Barker Flett who is fascinated by Daisy when she is still a child, the male characters in *The Stone Diaries* are erotically enthralled by women and fulfilled in their relationships with them. In contrast, the women appear bewildered by, or at best tolerant of, male sexual desire. To some extent, then, *The Stone Diaries* subverts not only conventional narrative structures but also traditional sex roles suggesting that women gain their pleasure elsewhere, even that men are irrelevant.

There is considerable irony implicit in the fact that Mercy Goodwill is unaware of her own pregnancy and Daisy herself experiences a catastrophically chaste honeymoon. The female characters in this novel seem to experience sex, pregnancy and childbirth at one remove; female roles are treated ambiguously. *The Stone Diaries* does not allow its readers to make facile judgements about any aspect of its protagonist's experience.

As Coral Ann Howells has pointed out[4], there are close parallels between the historical situation of women and of Canada as a nation. The case of Carol Shields is even more complex in that she is an American who has chosen to live and work in Canada; and has also spent time in England, at the University of Exeter and in Manchester. She also lives for part of every year in France.

As Coral Howells indicates, the crucial question concerning nationality and inheritance is 'What does being a subject mean?':

> If it means self-awareness, then it involves taking into account inconsistencies and contradictory impulses inside the self, so that the search for boundaries which self-definition implies would highlight multiple differences within and blur those very boundaries through which the self is constituted. If on the other hand being a subject refers to a political category, then self-definition is something imposed from outside by a superior power in a colonial situation and therefore reductive of inner diversity.[5]

Howells goes on to suggest that:

> the colonial mentality and Canada's recent emergence from it have close affinities with women's gendered perceptions of themselves . . . it might also be argued that women's stories could provide models for the story of Canada's national identity . . . women's stories about procedures for self-discovery which are as yet incomplete may be seen to parallel the contemporary Canadian situation. If the basic condition of

twentieth-century women writers can be said to be that of unbelonging, contemporary Commonwealth women writers have a problematic sense of cultural identity.[6]

It follows from this that 'none of them has an exclusive preoccupation with the traditions of a single country, gender or genre'.

Margaret Atwood definitively articulates this sense of dislocation felt by Canadian writers in the afterword to her edition of the *Journals of Susannah Moodie* (1970):

> We are all immigrants to this place even if we were born here: the country is too big for anyone to inhabit completely, and in the parts unknown to us we move in fear, exiles and invaders. This country is something that must be chosen – it is so easy to leave – and if we choose it we are still choosing a violent duality.

The psychic situation in the case of Carol Shields would seem to be triadic rather than dualistic since she participates in three traditions, English and American as well as Canadian. Her fiction questions all stereotypes and consistently challenges conventional value judgements.

To return to *The Stone Diaries*, the problem Carol Shields addresses here is the significance of the life of an ordinary, unremarkable Canadian women, who was born in 1905, died in 1985 and whose last (unspoken) words were 'I am not at peace'. The questions Shields raises are how closely do our versions of our lives correspond to objective facts? Can facts be said to exist at all in the context of something as changeable and arbitrary as a life? To what extent do 'our stories' really belong to us, considering the tendency that other people have to intrude in them, interpret them, and claim them? Shields' basic conceit in *The Stone Diaries* is to disguise her fiction as a 'real' biography, complete with period photographs and a family tree. But beneath the spurious documentation and banal rural and suburban settings, are fantastic incidents comparable to the inventiveness of Gabriel Garcia Marquez. An enormously fat woman dies in childbirth without ever realizing she was pregnant; a man from Orkney returns to the island he had left decades before, severing all his ties and eventually living on till the age of 115, his one claim to fame being the ability to recite the whole of *Jane Eyre*; a young husband falls to his death as the result of his wife's sneeze and his wife never mentions the grotesque ending to her marriage. The protagonist of the novel experiences her life without ever fully occupying it.[7]

As Daisy herself admits in her preliminary narrative: 'The recounting of a life is a cheat . . . even our own stories are obscenely distorted' [p. 28] and again: 'History indeed! As though this paltry slice of time deserves such a name. Accident, not history, has called us together' [p. 39]: 'Her autobiography, if such a thing were imaginable, would, be, if such a thing were ever to be written, an assemblage of dark voids and unbridgable gaps' [p. 75–6]. In these ways Carol Shields points up the incomprehensibility of experience in and of itself. Only Daisy's father, having finished a carving, comes near to 'the fever of transcendence' [p. 65]. But when the work is finished the artist has to move on to something else: 'How does a poet know when a poem is ended? Because it lies flat, taut; nothing can be added or subtracted' [p. 71]. *The Stone Diaries* is full of travel, psychological and physical, inner and outer:

> Cuyler Goodwill travelled in his long life from one incarnation to the next. In his twenties he was a captive of Eros, in his thirties he belonged to God, and, still later, to Art. Now, in his fifties, he champions Commerce. [pp. 91–2]

As Goodwill travels to America from Canada, Magnus Flett is undertaking a reverse migration from Manitoba 'home' to the Orkney Islands. Goodwill's horizons are expanded: 'Canada with its forests and lakes and large airy spaces lies now on the other side of the moon, as does the meagerness of its short, chilly history' [p. 93]. In the translation from artist to businessman his sensibility will coarsen and he will grow out of touch with his craft. Goodwill figures in different, contradictory stories but he appears to be in control of them, whereas, as Daisy points out, in 1939 anyway, women were smothered and silenced by their stories. But story does not contain the whole truth. Daisy, by the age of 31, has a 'tragic' history – 'a mother dead of childbirth, and then a ghastly second chapter, a husband killed on his honeymoon'. But Daisy's version is:

> Her poor heart must be broken, people say, but it isn't true. Her heart was merely squeezed and wrung dry for a time, like an old rag. [p. 122]

Daisy lives outside her story as well as inside it. The narrator warns us that:

> She is not always reliable when it comes to the details of her life; much of what she has to say is speculative, exaggerated, wildly unlikely . . . Furthermore, she imposes the voice of the future on the events of the past, causing all manner of wavy

distortion. She takes great jumps in time, leaving out important matters . . . Sometimes she looks at things close up and sometimes from a distance, and she does insist on showing herself in a sunny light, hardly ever giving us a glimpse of those dark premonitions we all experience. [pp. 148–9]

In fact, Daisy's garden, like Cuyler Goodwill's tower, is more meaningful, more satisfying and more inclusive than personal relationships are capable of being:

> This garden of Mrs Flett's is lush, grand and intimate – English in its charm, French in its orderliness, Japanese in its economy – but there is something, too, in the sinuous path, the curved beds, the grinning garden dwarf carved from Indiana limestone and the sudden sculptured wall of *Syringa vulgaris* that is full of grave intelligence and even, you might say, a kind of wit. [p. 195]

Creativity of this calibre is a release from the pressure to perform the female role that Daisy feels even on her death-bed:

> She's kept so busy during her hospital stay being an old sweetie-pie, a fighter, a real lady, a non-complainer, brave about the urinary infections that beset her, stoic on the telephone with her children, taking an interest in young Jubilee's love affairs, going coquettish with Mr. Latterby, and being endlessly, valiantly protective of Reverend Rick's sensibilities [p. 322–3]

The real questions that Alice wants to ask – 'Have you found fulfillment . . . Has it been worth it? . . . Has it been enough, your life, I mean?' [p. 326] – are not asked, cannot be asked. In death Daisy becomes an artifact, comparing herself to the stone bishops and saints she has observed in Kirkwall cathedral. The narrator's description carries overtones of poems by Emily Dickinson and Sylvia Plath:

> With polite bemusement she lingers over each detail of her frozen state . . . the folds of her dress, so primitive and stiff, are softened by a decorative edge, a calcium border of seashells of the kind sometimes seen on the edges of birthday cakes. A stone scroll dips gracefully across her slippered feet, the date worn away, illegible, and a stone pillow props up her head,

the rigid frizz combed smooth at last. Her hands with their gentled knuckles curve inward at her sides, greatly simplified, the fingers melded together, ringless, unmarked by age, but gesturing . . . toward the large, hushed, immutable territory that stands beyond her hearing. From out of her impassive face the eyes stare icy as marbles, wide open but seeing nothing, nothing, that is, but the deep, shared common distress of men and women, and how little they are allowed, finally, to say. [p. 359]

In *Mary Swann* (1987), Carol Shields had earlier considered the nature of art and its confrontational position vis-à-vis the world of experience. The central mystery in a novel of detection and suspense is 'how did she do it?':

Where in those bleak Ontario acres, that littered farmyard, did she find the sparks that converted emblematic substance into rolling poetry? [p. 31]

This sense of bleakness and lack of nourishment in the environment (contrasted implicitly with the relative richness, natural and cultural of Emily Dickinson's New England) resonates both with W. H. New's concept of the 'exile syndrome'[8] and with Coral Ann Howells' suggestion that just as 'wilderness' is part of Canada's cultural myth about itself, so too is the sense of 'home' being partially unknown and full of unmapped possibilities.[9]

In a further elaboration of this idea that contemporary women's fictions can be read as analogues of Canadian dilemmas about identity in general, it could be said to be the case that women are always exiles, even on 'home' territory because of their marginalised status in relation to centres of power. Carol Shields is also an insistent questioner of cultural and literary authority and constructs a female identity which is multiple, changing and responsible to the unexplored territories of Canadian place and space.

Mary Swann, Shields' fictional poet, is the subject of a Symposium at which a paper on her work is presented by Sarah Maloney, a feminist writer and teacher 'who's having second thoughts about the direction of feminist writing in America':

Some days Virginia Woolf is the only person in the universe I want to talk to; but she's dead, of course, and wouldn't like me anyway. Too flip. And Mary Swann, also dead. Exceedingly dead. [p. 11]

Mary Swann has been shot by her husband and her body dismembered. The violence of her death is paralleled by the Dickinsonian intensity of her poems; she made the quotidian meaningful:

> A morning and an afternoon and
> Night's queer knuckled hand
> Hold me separate and whole
> Stitching tight my daily soul [p. 21]

Among many other things, *Mary Swann* is a satire on the academic world of literary scholarship, presenting, for example, Mary Swann's biographer as a thief and her first publisher, as, in effect, a co-producer of her poems – defaced soon after he received them and 'restored' by him and his wife. Since Mary Swann is brutally murdered as soon as she has relinquished her poems, there can be no check on their authenticity. Consequently, Carol Shields raises alarming questions about scholarship, accuracy and the very existence of 'text'.

As in her other novels, Shields makes playful use of different literary modes and discourses in telling the 'story' of Mary Swann; her narrative technique ranges from the pseudo-documentary *A Saturday Night in Nadeau*:

> In Nadeau, Ontario, as in other towns and villages on the continent of North America, and indeed around the world, there is a social structure that determines more or less how people will spend their disposable time. A social historian would be seem suited for certain people, while others seem inappropriate, even unthinkable. [pp. 139–40]

to the symposium itself which is presented as a film script. Some of Shields' best comic writing is in the letters written to and from Frederic Cruzzi, retired newspaper editor of Grenoble, Casablanca, Manchester, and Kingston, Ontario. The novel ranges widely over the geography of North America, setting rural Ontario against California and Chicago.

Everything is brought into question in this complex work for, unlike Rose Hindmarch's satisfying espionage stories, life does not provide answers to mysteries. Art itself is elusive though Mary Swann's biographer, Morton Jimroy, believes that 'the best and worst of human experiences were frozen inside these wondrous little toys called poems. Poetry was the prism that refracted all of life' [p. 86].

The narrator of *Small Ceremonies* (1976) is also a biographer and in a disarming gesture towards inter-textuality is working on Susanna

Moodie about whom Carol Shields has herself written a book of criticism called *Voices and Vision* (1977). According to Judith Gill, protagonist of *Small Ceremonies*, her subject has 'a pleasing schizoid side . . . she could never make up her mind what she was or where she stood' [p. 6]. Carol Shields characteristically invokes the mysterious nature of the human personality and the impossibility of definition – who is the real Susanna Moodie?

> She presents a stout and rubbery persona, that of a gener-
> ous, humorous woman who feeds on anecdotes and random
> philosophical devotions, sucking what she can out of daily
> events, the whole of her life glazed over with a neat edge-to-
> edge surface. It is the cracks in the surface I look for; for if
> her reticence is attractive, it also makes her a difficult subject
> to possess. But who, after all, could sustain such a portrait
> over so many pages without leaving a few chinks in the var-
> nish? Already I've found, with even the most casual sleuthing,
> small passages in her novels and backwoods recollections of
> unconscious self-betrayal, isolated words and phrases, almost
> lost in the lyrical brushwork. I am gluing them together . . . into
> a delicate design which may just possibly be the real Susanna.
> [p. 7]

Judith Gill asserts that the 'task of the biographer is to enlarge on avail-able data' [p. 35]. Throughout *Small Ceremonies*, Carol Shields makes postmodern play with categories of truth and reality. Judith Gill, her fictional biographer, is working on a real person and perceives herself as an unscrupulous voyeuse:

> It is a real life, a matter of record, sewn together like a leather
> glove with all the years joining, no worse than some and better
> than many. A private life, completed, deserving decent bur-
> ial, deserving the sweet black eclipse, but I am setting out to
> exhume her, searching, prying into the small seams, counting
> stitches, adding, subtracting, keeping score, invading an area
> of existence where I've no real rights . . . but I keep poking away.
> [p. 34]

And when Judith pokes into John Spalding's writer's diary, she is more moved by its awful candour than by his inept fiction:

> I read the notebook to the end although the terrible open qual-
> ity of its confessions brought me close to weeping. Silly, silly,
> silly little man. Paranoiac, inept, ridiculous. But he reached me

through those disjointed bleeding notes as he hadn't in all his seven novels. [p. 39]

And yet, in the end, Shields comes back to one of the dilemmas that inform all her own writing – the ineluctable nature of human character – 'so much of a man's life is lived inside his own head, that it is impossible to encompass a personality' [p. 53]. Although Carol Shields attributes this remark to Leon Edel, it is a neat summary of one of her most characteristic themes.

Small Ceremonies also provides Shields with many opportunities for discussing the different genres of fiction and biography as well as making satirical thrusts at features of the literary life like the television interview, the launch party, the creative writing class. But her main focus is the issue of plagiarism and as usual she points out that it is not as simple as it might seem.

In the Renaissance, Judith Gill recalls, creativity was a shared enterprise, but is taking over 'an underlying plot structure' acceptable practice in the late twentieth century? Her agonising transmutes into farce when the writer Furlong Eberhardt steals her own stolen novel for his *Craven Images*. She confronts him at an English Department party in the language of 1940s comic books – 'you feelthy schwine'. Furlong's complete denial that he stole her main idea stuns Judith:

> Writers don't steal ideas. They abstract them from wherever they can . . . One uses what one can find. One takes an idea and brings to it his own individual touch. His own quality. Enhances it. Develops it. Do you know there are only seven distinct plots in all of literature? [p. 131]

Judith suffers similar confusion when her husband's bizarre pictorial representation of *Paradise Lost* is received with acclaim.

In this novel, nothing is what it seems: Furlong Eberhardt, Canadian prairie novelist, the man who embodies the ethos of the nation, is revealed to be an American! [p.154] His guilt is concerned not with writerly but with national, plagiarism. The concluding joke in this paradoxical novel is John Spalding's plagiarism from real life. His novel *Alien Interlude* concerns Judith's family's sabbatical year at an English University in an English city.

But at this point Judith has realized 'how facts are transmuted as they travel through a series of hands'; by the time this story reaches print 'the least dram of truth will be drained away'.

In the companion text, *The Box Garden*, (1977) Judith's sister is represented as having a contrasting response to their deprived parental situation, writing bitter poems rather than balanced, objective biography. While Judith mocks the concept of 'Canadianness' in the manufactured persona of Furlong Eberhardt, Charleen attends to the idea of wilderness adduced by Margaret Atwood as intimately bound up with survival and victimhood. Taking the train from Vancouver to Toronto, Charleen had 'forgotten about the thousand miles of bush between Winnipeg and Toronto . . . nothing but curved glass separating us from turquoise lakes, whorled trees, the torn, reddened sky, and, here and there, clumps of Indian cabins' [p. 61].

Poetry was a survival mechanism for Charleen; 'poetry became the means by which I saved my life . . . my survival was hooked into my quirky, accidental ability to put words into agreeable arrangements' [p. 152].

Like all Shields' texts, *The Box Garden* is a playful many-layered narrative, postmodern in its use of a variety of genres, subversive linguistic play and parodic humour. Inter-textual references to thrillers, detective stories, murder and kidnap often add a melodramatic quality to a fiction that is intimately concerned with the strangeness of life. Carol Shields, like her protagonist Judith Gill, 'doesn't believe there is such a thing as an ordinary person' [p. 100]. In particular, she makes effective use of the Irigarayan masquerade – the ways in which women 'perform' femininity in a male-dominated society:

> His wife Polly is about fifty too, a woman both stout and shy. Sadly, she is the victim of academic fiction, for she is never free of her role as faculty wife. [p. 126]

Like other postmodern writers, Shields constantly advertises the fictionality of her texts, giving virtuoso renderings of many different styles and modes.

However, in spite of the fact that she makes Furlong Eberhardt say that 'writers are no more than scavengers and assemblers of lies' [*Small Ceremonies* p. 144], her novels are the reverse of negative. In fact, a reading of the Shields *oeuvre* brings to mind that line from Philip Larkin's 'An Arundel Tomb': 'What will survive of us is love'.

Notes

1. Penguin USA Books (Web Construction by HuskyLabs July 13 1995).
2. *The Stone Diaries* (London: Fourth Estate, 1993), 36.
3. *Susanna Moodie: Voices and Vision* (Ottawa: Borealis, 1977), 34.
4. *Private and Fictional Worlds* (London: Methuen, 1987), 2.
5. *ibid.*, 3.

6. *ibid.*, 3, 19.
7. Resumé from Penguin USA Books.
8. *History of Canadian Literature* (London: Macmillan, 1989).
9. 'No Transcendental Image: Canadianness in Contemporary Women's Fictions in English', *British Journal of Canadian Studies vol 6 no 1* (1991), 113.

The Demon of the Stream:
Looking at Waterfalls

Peter Womack

1

It is, indeed, a fearful place. The torrent, swollen by the melting snow, plunges into a tremendous abyss, from which the
spray rolls up like the smoke from a burning house. The shaft
into which the river hurls itself is an immense chasm, lined by
glistening, coal-black rock, and narrowing into a creaming,
boiling pit of incalculable depth, which brims over and shoots
the stream onward over its jagged lip. The long sweep of green
water roaring for ever down, and the thick flickering curtain
of spray hissing for ever upward, turn a man giddy with their
constant whirl and clamour. We stood near the edge peering
down at the gleam of the breaking water far below us against
the black rocks, and listening to the half-human shout which
came booming up with the spray out of the abyss.[1]

Sherlock Holmes stands on the path with his arms folded, gazing mo-
tionlessly down at the scene of incessant agitation; for Dr Watson, and
for the readers of the *Strand Magazine* in 1893, it is their last glimpse
of the great detective. What is he looking at? He is a phenomenon
of London, devoid of all feeling for the natural or the picturesque,
exclusively devoted to the labyrinthine passages of a man-made environment. What could possibly have engaged his attention in this
banality of sublime landscape, the Reichenbach Fall?
   The language of the description itself gives us the beginnings of an
answer. The fall is full of human motifs. The river is a sentient being,
plunging and hurling itself into the gorge, which is first like a burning
house, then something like a coal-mine (oddly recalling the apocalyptic
torrent which destroyed the mine in Zola's *Germinal*, eight years before), and then, by association, something like an industrial process –
creaming, boiling, shooting its material onward. Amid this overheated

interplay of metaphors, it's no surprise when the counterpointed roaring and hissing resolve themselves into a half-human shout. There is someone in there. At the same time, the atmosphere is heavy with theology: the decor is oppressively black and white, and the process is eternal, the water falling, and the spray rising up, for ever. Listening serenely to the inarticulate cry which rises from the boiling pit, Holmes is like an angel gazing down upon hell.

His situation, then, is not so new to him as it seems – and later it appears that he feels this, for his farewell note to Watson is written in as firm and clear a hand 'as though it had been written in his study' (479). That study, in the first-floor apartment on Baker Street where almost every story begins and ends, is also a vantage-point above an inferno, from which Holmes maintains surveillance over the abyss of criminal London. In this story, 'The Final Problem', he has finally penetrated the veil (471), the 'thick flickering curtain' which shrouds the demiurge of the abyss, Professor Moriarty; and now he is contemplating his final descent. Reichenbach is the smoky, mechanised city in essential form, purified of its incidental details in order to become the sympathetic scene of the last battle between crime and the law.

But this ultimate location is also, of course, the site of a complicated deception. The reason Dr Watson departs, leaving Holmes brooding over the torrent, is that he has been summoned to the sickbed of an Englishwoman at the nearby hotel; it transpires, not only that the message was a ruse of Moriarty's to detach Holmes from his companion, but also that Holmes perceived the subterfuge and allowed Watson to be deceived in order to bring about the final encounter. So the eventual wrestling match on the brink of the chasm is wholly artificial. Holmes could have avoided it, and Moriarty could have engineered it without danger to himself (for example by bringing a gun), but both antagonists co-operate with the author to bring their contest to an appropriately elemental climax. Aesthetic *choice* is wearing the costume of tragic necessity, and the most important feature of the costume is the waterfall itself. Turned giddy by its constant whirl and clamour, the reader doesn't notice that he has been taken for a ride.

But then, unlike Dr Watson, the reader *wanted* to be taken for a ride – and this opens up a further layer of subterfuge. The Reichenbach Fall was a beauty spot, already known to English tourists for over a century.[2] It was part of a holiday: one stayed at the hotel, viewed the waterfall, experienced its terror and wrote about it in one's journal. Dr Watson's description, indeed, with its clumsy notation of impressiveness, reads appropriately like an average specimen of such touristic writing. So when, earlier that afternoon, Holmes and Watson leave the hotel with 'strict injunctions . . . on no account to pass the falls of Reichenbach . . . without making a small detour to see them' (478), the injunctions are bizarrely double-voiced; this is the imperative mood of both Baedeker and Destiny; the waterfall must not be omitted, both because it is *unmissable* (like a hit show) and because it is *inescapable* (like death).

The relationship between the two voices is an intricate one. The tourist's terror is a sort of pretence, a feeling exactly like the enjoyable fear aroused by a frightening story. To be frightened in this sense is a kind of entertainment; and it is in order to be entertained that, according to this story, the narrator, as a tourist, takes the small detour to the waterfall. His voluntarily indulged-in fear is then, ironically, transmuted into the coercively real fear which accompanies his realization that the desperate arch-criminal has struck. But then, clearly, the real function of the entire story – arch-criminal, detective, waterfall and all – is precisely entertainment: the ordinary reader's attitude to the fury of Moriarty is the same as the ordinary tourist's attitude to the fury of the torrent. A small falsification marks the site of the substitution. In reality, visitors to the Upper Fall of Reichenbach in 1893 didn't simply wander up that lonely and perilous path, but paid 50 centimes for admission to a specially constructed viewing-hut.[3] Sherlock Holmes dies, not in the real place which includes the hut, but in the spectacular and exclusive space which is viewed *from* the hut. In other words the waterfall, for the reader as for the tourist, is a piece of illusionist theatre the auditorium is designed to disappear from view.

There is a third subterfuge, however, no less revealing. As everyone knows, it turned out later that Sherlock Holmes had not perished at Reichenbach after all, but had faked his own death in order to throw his enemies off the scent. The story was apparently written with no thought of this sequel, but it lent itself to the necessary re-interpretation with astonishing readiness. The two essential features of the case, so to speak, were that the narrator had been decoyed away so that the final struggle was unobserved and had to be deduced from the footprints on the soil of the path, and that the 'dreadful cauldron' at the foot of the waterfall made it impossible to recover the bodies. Thus, with no witness and no corpse, there was very little hard evidence to prevent Holmes's resurrection from attaining that minimum plausibility which the reader of detective stories requires.

Conceivably, this convenient arrangement is the mark of a half-conscious escape-clause in the author's mind. But if we ignore this possibility, and choose to read 'The Final Problem' as if it really were final – as it *was* for the first ten years of its life in print – the crucial details convey no premonition of evasion. They simply have another meaning, which is that Sherlock Holmes is a mythic hero whose death, like that of Moses or Oedipus, is removed from the sight of men. He doesn't die like us; he becomes one with the violent forces which he has mastered through the profundity of his vision and the splendour of his mind; that is, the sublimity which the waterfall denotes is ultimately his. It's not so surprising, on this view, that he subsequently returns from the abyss alive.

Reichenbach, then, is a double sign. On the one hand, it is the massively tangible manifestation of the absolute – of finality, eschatology, heroic transcendence. On the other hand, it is a trick – the device by which the author wipes out the traces of a sleight of hand. This odd combination of sublimity and deception is not simply an effect of Conan Doyle's narrative cunning. Rather, the story reflects and exploits a doubleness which was already part of the character of waterfalls in general. Natural as it undeniably is, the torrent is somehow also show business.

2

The injunction to visit a waterfall is a well-established statute of picturesque tourism. It is still in force: waterfalls today, much like those in the Bernese Oberland in the 1890s, are marked by brochures, signposts, railed paths – the apparatus of access. The story of this institution, in Britain at least, would perhaps begin in the 1760s. At that point, the Lake District, the Scottish Highlands, and the Alps entered the culture as picturesque objects, soon promoted by an endless procession of published 'Tours';[4] the cult of Ossian disseminated a language for the celebration of mists, rocks and streams;[5] Burke's essay on the sublime simultaneously offered a theoretical language for the same appreciation;[6] the first topographical paintings of Niagara appeared in London;[7] William Gilpin began his long and influential series of picturesque tours, to which waterfalls made a conspicuous contribution.[8] Individually, of course, people will have been deriving pleasure from looking at waterfalls for centuries. But the institution is not reducible: to that it adds the socially produced fact that a waterfall – whether or not I happen to wish to see it myself – is something to see. In 1772 the travel-writer Thomas Pennant could speak of a waterfall having been recently 'discovered' two miles from Blair Atholl in the Perthshire Highlands.[9] He regards the discovery as evidence that Scots are at last becoming aware of the beauties of their country; and certainly the choice of word marks a moment of transition. Atholl was a fairly well populated part of Scotland; hundreds of people will have been familiar with this waterfall all their lives. What was 'discovered' was not the river itself, but a new object of attention, of representation, of deliberately sought-out experience; if that had not existed before, it was not for want of the water, but of want of the framework needed to form its falling into a spectacle.

Samuel Johnson in the Scottish Highlands the following autumn documents this framework with a clarity all the more forceful for coming from a traveller notoriously immune to the pleasures of what was already being called the 'romantic' in scenery. He and Boswell made their small detour to visit the fall of Foyers, but found it, after a dry summer, 'divested of its dignity and terror':

> and we were left to exercise our thoughts, by endeavouring to conceive the effect of a thousand streams poured from the mountains into one channel, struggling for expansion in a narrow passage, exasperated by rocks rising in their way, and at last discharging all their violence of waters by a sudden fall through the horrid chasm.[10]

Johnson is so secure in his grasp of 'the pleasure expected from the fall of Fiers' that it isn't necessary for him to have seen it in order to describe it. Instead of direct experience, he has two rhetorical figures: personification (the streams struggle, are exasperated, discharge their violence), and narrative (the waterfall is rendered as an intelligible series of events, whose phased move from the mountains to the chasm is controlled by markers of time such as 'at last' and 'sudden'). The combined effect of these inventions is to make the waterfall into a drama – that is, a spectacle with characters, a story, and a catastrophe. Knowing the text of the play, Johnson is only mildly disappointed at missing the performance.

This theatricalization can be traced concretely in the career of another Highland waterfall, the one on the Bran near Dunkeld where the Duke of Atholl laid out a pleasure-ground in the late 1750s. The fall itself was exhaustively described by William Gilpin in 1776:

> The two rocky cheeks of the river almost uniting compress the stream into a very narrow compass, and the channel, which descends abruptly, taking also a sudden turn, the water suffers more than common violence from the double resistance it receives from compression and obliquity. Its efforts to disengage itself, have in a course of ages undermined, disjointed and fractured the rock in a thousand different forms, and have filled the whole channel of the descent with fragments of uncommon magnitude . . . Down this abrupt channel the whole stream in foaming violence forcing its way, through the peculiar and happy situation of the fragments, which oppose its

course, forms one of the grandest, and most beautiful cascades we had ever seen . . . The whole scene, and its accompaniments, are not only grand, but picturesquely beautiful in the highest degree. The *composition* is perfect; but yet the parts are so intricate, so various, and so complicated, that I never found any piece of nature less obvious to imitation.[11]

The negotiation here between nature and art is extremely delicate. It is part of the waterfall's appeal to Gilpin that it is natural elsewhere: in his account of Dunkeld he deplores some *artificial* cascades as 'puerilities' which deform the natural grandeur of the landscape (I, 114). But at the same time, his appreciation of it is expressed in the terms of art, not only because he is writing to guide the taste and technique of landscape painters, but also because he conceives of Nature herself as a kind of artist: her 'pieces' are 'compositions', her textures 'finishing', and so on. The description takes the form of a sort of analytic narrative which tries to explain how the rocks and the water have come to be disposed in the happy arrangement which the visitor sees: Nature has been at work, as it were, creating this picturesque object. Even before they are transferred on to canvas and framed literally, these 'scenes' are framed *in situ* by the way they are being looked at.

For this kind of visual sensibility, waterfalls are particularly rewarding because their 'grandeur' is so firmly contained like a picture, and unlike the other counters of sublime scenery, such as mountains or oceans, a waterfall can be seen whole from a single viewpoint, and is so arranged that it's reasonably clear where the waterfall stops and something else starts. Elsewhere in his Highland book, Gilpin discusses the difficulty of painting landscapes which are characterized by vastness: the size which is essential to their impact is impossible to reproduce, so the artist has to resort to a subtle falsification to obtain the *impression* of size (I, 146–8). Waterfalls, delightfully, perform this trick for you as Johnson's description also makes clear, they concentrate nature's largeness into a narrow compass which is at once intense and convenient.

This achievement has a paradoxical effect. As a natural phenomenon which is already, in Gilpin's phrase, a 'piece of workmanship', the waterfall is a special instance of nature coming to meet the human artist half way. This is, so to speak, a technical advantage, but also something else: a source of philosophic pleasure because, like comparable effects such as natural arches or caves that resemble churches, it prompts the idea of design in the universe. In that sense it addresses a broadly Enlightenment appetite for signs of natural order.[12] But then the content of this particular design is, as Gilpin neatly puts it, 'violence, opposition, and every species of agitation' (I,125): it affirms the presence of a creator, but the affirmation contains an anarchic violence. Thus the waterfall combines harmony and horror in exceptional, gratifying tension: the horror saves the harmony from insipidity and makes it affective; the harmony circumscribes the horror and, by confining it to a purely aesthetic sphere, disarms it.

The noble owner of the waterfall on the Bran was less delicate about this than Gilpin. Visitors after 1758 found the rock overlooking the fall surmounted by a little neoclassical building called the Hermitage, from which the rushing waters could be viewed through panes of red and green glass.[13] Gilpin was severe on this idea – 'tricks below the dignity of scenes like these' (I, 123) – but at least one contemporary visitor was so affected by the illusion of 'sheets of liquid fire rolling down the rock like the lava of Mount Etna' that she was obliged to leave the viewing-room.[14] In 1783 the coloured glass was replaced by a more elaborate arrangement, when the building was transformed, according to the currently fashionable Scottish imagery, into the Hall of Ossian. The effect is described by Dorothy Wordsworth:

> We were . . . conducted into a small apartment, where the gardener desired us to look at a painting of the figure of Ossian, which, while he was telling the story of the young artist who performed the work, disappeared, parting in the middle, flying asunder as if by the touch of magic, and lo! we are at the entrance of a splendid room, which was almost dizzy and alive with waterfalls, that tumbled in all directions – the great cascade, which was opposite to the window that faced us, being reflected in innumerable mirrors upon the ceiling and against the walls.[15]

Like its predecessor, this *coup de theatre* provoked mixed reactions: in 1798, an influential tourist writer named Mrs Murray thought that the mirrors 'magnify and multiply every object they reflect, and thereby increase the delight', but in 1803 the Wordsworths reacted by bursting out laughing.[16]

The building, and its trick decor, had the effect of exaggerating both sides of the opposition we saw in Gilpin. On the one hand, it was a form of amplification, seeking to make natural grandeur and agitation yet grander and more agitated. But on the other, it neutralized the qualities it was ostensibly magnifying, by subordinating the torrent so conspicuously to human ingenuity and pleasure. In the dazzling confusion described by Dorothy Wordsworth, it must have seemed possible that there wasn't really a waterfall there at all, but that it was all done by mirrors. Her brother later retaliated with a poem denouncing the device in the wounded tones of a devotee of nature who has been implicated in an act of sacrilege;[17] but its rhetoric is almost embarrassingly shrill and insecure, because the taste which built the shrine to the waterfall and the taste which sympathizes with its affronted deity are not as dissimilar as the latter wishes to insist. Both celebrate the impressive inhuman otherness of the spectacle in terms which actually appropriate it to a myth; both make the waterfall speak for them; in both, because of this unacknowledged ventriloquism, the language of the response is whimsical and posed. Both even give the spirit of the waters the same name that of the faked Gaelic bard Ossian. The confusion of reactions in the Wordsworths, as well as the diversity of reactions from the different visitors, suggest that reading the sign is not quite so straightforward as Johnson makes it seem. The problem is not that the Duke's touristic stunts are false to the semiotic of the waterfall, but that they are not entirely false to it. Even without them, the waterfall is a case of nature itself making a scene, and so entering upon the ambiguities of theatricality.

3

This is of course a scandalous paradox for Wordsworth; as the Bartholomew Fair sequence of *The Prelude*[18] makes clear, it is in a sense the whole point of his 'Nature' that it is not theatrical; he is accordingly ill at ease in the auditorium at Dunkeld. How about the happy spectators? They have their voice in Sir Walter Scott. The interface of literature and scenic tourism, which makes Wordsworth so uncomfortable and which provides the decor for the apotheosis of Sherlock Holmes, is Scott's special home. In 1810 he virtually founded the tourist industry in the Perthshire Highlands by writing *The Lady of the Lake*,[19] and four years later he returned to the same scenes for his first novel, *Waverley*. It features an extraordinary set piece which is worth exploring in some detail.

To understand how it works, it's necessary to be detained a little over its place in the plot. The year is 1745. Edward Waverley, a naively romantic young army officer, has been staying with family connections on the fringes of the Highlands, and out of curiosity has undertaken an expedition into the mountains where he is entertained by the local clan chief Fergus MacIvor and his sister Flora. For Waverley, the excursion is no more than a fairly adventurous holiday, but there is a serious agenda of which he is unaware. The MacIvors are committed Jacobites who know the Young Pretender has already landed; they also realize that the coming insurrection will succeed only if it attracts significant support in England as well as Scotland. Waverley's family are traditional High Tories, so he is a potentially valuable contact, whose clueless tendency to fall in love – with the scenery, with the exoticism of Highland culture, with the beautiful Flora – it is therefore wise to encourage. The charm offensive begins with a feast at which the clan bard sings a stirring Gaelic song which Waverley can't understand, but which he can see from people's reactions contains allusions to himself. He asks Flora what the song was about, and she promises to perform a translation for him if he will meet her at a short distance from the castle. She goes to the rendezvous first, and then he is conducted there by one of her attendants:

> In a spot, about a quarter of a mile from the castle, two brooks, which formed a little river, had their junction . . . The larger was placid, and even sullen in its course, wheeling in deep eddies, or sleeping in dark blue pools; but the motions of the lesser brook were rapid and furious, issuing from between precipices, like a maniac from his confinement, all foam and uproar.
>
> It was up the course of this last stream that Waverley, like a knight of romance, was conducted by the fair Highland damsel, his silent guide.[20]

Rounding a bend in the path, he sees Flora crossing a narrow and perilous bridge high above the stream; on approaching nearer, he finds that it crosses at the point of a romantic waterfall, surrounded by heather and crags, and also by trees which Flora has had planted 'so cautiously, that they added to the grace, without diminishing the romantic wildness of the scene' (224). Beside the fall, touched by the light of the setting sun, Flora stands 'like one of those lovely forms which decorate the landscapes of Poussin', with an attendant who carries a Celtic harp. To its accompaniment, blended with the sound of the waterfall, Flora sings her translation, which turns out to be a call to arms on behalf of the Stuart claimant.

Unravelling the semiotics of this bizarre sequence involves separating out at least three levels. At one level, which it's misleading to ignore, it is pulp fiction. The waterfall is mechanically adjusted to be on the exact borderline between the beautiful and the sublime, the point being that this combination encodes the double impression Flora is to make on Waverley and on the reader: the beautiful signifies her attractiveness, the sublimity signifies her dangerousness, the union of the two constitutes the sexual allure by which the narrative holds the reader's

attention, and the displacement of the allure on to the innocent pleasures of scenery enables the reader to surrender to it without anxiety.
The capacity of waterfalls to evoke and sanitise sexual reverie is obvious from most of the descriptions I have quoted; it is perhaps the
most banal form of the sign's duplicity, and is certainly being deployed
fairly blatantly here.[21]

On the second level, however, it is being made clear that this seductive effect is deliberate. Flora is not after all presented as a natural
denizen of the Highland stream. On the contrary, she and her brother
have both been educated at the exiled court in France, and their social and verbal style is that of the drawing-rooms of Paris or London.
Their relation to the natural simplicities of their environment is sophisticated, even ironic. For example, Fergus teases Flora about her
waterfall:

> A simple and unsublimed taste now, like my own, would prefer
> a jet d'eau at Versailles to this cascade with all its accom-
> paniments of rock and roar; but this is Flora's Parnassus . . .
> (230)

The wit here is very complicated. It picks up the historical fact that, as
we have seen, a taste for wild waterfalls, which was a touristic cliché
by 1814, was positively *avant garde* in 1745: Fergus claims, playfully,
to be a simple, straightforward fellow who likes artificial cascades, implicitly atrributing Flora's preference for the wild kind to her extreme
refinement. This typically self-parodying tone casts a shadow over the
whole of the McIvors' relationship with the primitive society they rule;
it seems that they are not simply wearing the national dress, but getting themselves up in it as if for a masquerade, or a conspiracy; they
are not the folk but the folklorists.

Thus the staginess of the waterfall scene is itself part of the story.
The reference to Poussin is not vague hyperbole: it points out quite
sharply that the apparition of Flora by the stream is composed, like
a painting, with regard to its picturesque effect, by Flora herself;
and that the arrangement whereby Waverley comes upon it without
warning, giving it the character of a *coup de théâtre*, is the artificial plotting, not of the novelist, but of one of his characters. The
waterfall Waverley sees, like the native song he hears, is already a
translation.

Thirdly, the set-up is clearly designed to be read as political allegory. The large placid brook with its dark blue pools is Hanoverian
England, the smaller but more furious and attractive mountain stream
is Jacobite Scotland. Waverley could choose between them, but, in
thrall to his Highland damsel, he is conducted into the dangers of
the latter without noticing that he has passed the decisive moment.

This dimension of the imagery makes the subsequent romantic *mise-en-scène* into a political seduction enchanted by its emotional appeal, Waverley is diverted from the regular course of duty into the rocky paths of enthusiasm. The Unionist teleology of the novel as a whole is firmly implied by the terms of the allegory distinct as they are, the two streams flow into a single river; and even before that, the wilder one is marked with signs – the perilous bridge, the sunset light – that its attraction is the elegiac beauty of a lost cause. The Hanoverian stream, inferior in imaginative vitality, is nevertheless objectively dominant: one visits the waterfall and dreams by its side, but the 'placid, even sullen' mainstream is where one actually lives. The over-written picturesqueness of the waterfall is the accent of political bad faith, a compensatory idealisation of wildness projected out of a tame and prudential compromise.

The betrayed value is not in essence Jacobitism, or even Scottish nationalism. Comparison with some of the Waverley Novels' other strategic waterfalls helps to refocus the image. In *Old Mortality* the hero, Morton, is led to the Black Linn of Linklater in order to hold his last meeting with the Covenanting leader Burley, who is in hiding in a cave on the far side of another perilous bridge, refusing to accept the betrayal of the Saints by the settlement of 1688. Approaching the waterfall, which in this case is unambiguously and melodramatically sublime,

> Morton listened . . . and out of the very abyss into which the brook fell, and amidst the tumultuary sounds of the cataract, thought he could distinguish shouts, screams, and even articulate words, as if the tortured demon of the stream had been mingling his complaints with the roar of his broken waters.[22]

The tortured demon turns out to be the defeated fanatic, distractedly wrestling with imaginary adversaries. Like the Jacobites of Waverley, he represents a heroic fidelity to an ancient and idiomatically Scottish cause which is absolutely incompatible with the good order and civilised society of the Scottish present. The rhetorical funtion of the waterfall, then, is to naturalize these subversive elements of the past – that is, to monumentalize them by surrounding them with scenic grandeur, and at the same time to excise them from the available political discourse by merging them with the inchoate roar of the torrent. Ideologically, the waterfall is a device for the depoliticisation of residual oppositional voices.

The other climactic waterfall appears on a domestic rather than a national stage, but the meaning of the spectacle is similar. It is the one at the end of *The Heart of Midlothian* which is visited by Effie, the pious heroine's sexually guilty sister. Led by her enthusiasm for natural beauty 'to penetrate into its utmost recesses',[23] she gets stuck on the rock face opposite the fall, endangered both by her precarious situation and by the dizzying effect of the water's violence. She is eventually rescued by a savage young bandit who is, unknown to either of them, her own illegitimate son. Here the connotations of the waterfall are heavily sexual as they are not in *Old Mortality*: the 'fallen' woman is re-enacting her original error. But the structure of feeling is closely parallel: the dark, wild legacy of the past is reproduced as the demon of the stream, whose violence, at once picturesque and frightening, troubles but is prevented from disrupting the enlightened accommodations of the happy ending. In every case the waterfall stands for a historical and erotic vitality which, excluded as a real narrative possibility, is thus preserved as an object of aesthetic appreciation. In short, a Scott waterfall typically marks the site of a narrative sublimation, safeguarding the essential respectability of his fiction. The sleight of hand in this case is repression.

4

But the waterfall is not only mirror images, textual refractions. Beyond the glass there is a real thing. What qualifies it for its curious cultural role? What do the generations of spectators actually see?

Looking at a waterfall is mysterious because it is at once an object and not an object. Certainly it is a material, located thing: it can be marked on a map, named, recognized, revisited. But its substance is only water, which constantly flows through it and turns into something else; its objective existence is a sort of optical illusion; it is not its material that makes it what it is, but its movement. Yet this defining movement is compatible with fixity: the fall has a shape. This can be experienced by looking at the waterfall from a distance and then approaching it. If you start from far enough away, the movement is invisible; you see only the tall white shape on the hillside. The nearer you go, the more the sense of a shape is undermined by the awareness of the amorphous falling water until, at very close quarters, there is no shape at all, only movement. When these impressions are in balance, you see a paradox a vertical structure entirely composed of something which is falling. To put it schematically, it is a thing which is also an event.

This is the paradox which is realised with extraordinary violence in the famous apocalyptic moment in the Simplon Pass in Book VI of

The Prelude. Despite its familiarity, it is worth quoting again in order to notice how much, how literally, it is a description of waterfalls:

> The immeasurable height
> Of woods decaying, never to be decayed,
> The stationary blasts of waterfalls,
> And in the narrow rent at every turn
> Winds thwarting winds, bewildered and forlorn
> The torrents shooting from the clear blue sky,
> The rocks that muttered close upon our ears,
> Black drizzling crags that spake by the way-side
> As if a voice were in them, the sick sight
> And giddy prospect of the raving stream,
> The unfettered clouds and region of the Heavens,
> Tumult and peace, the darkness and the light
> Were all like workings of one mind . . . (624–636)

The enormous subject of the sentence, miming the traveller's struggle to comprehend everything, takes the form of a list of things seen and heard it seems, designedly, to be an impossibly fragmented pile-up of impressions. But in fact, it keeps repeating the image of falling water – the waterfalls, the torrents, the drizzling crags, the raving stream. And the other images group themselves round the paradox of the waterfall: the woods decaying and never decayed, and the winds which thwart one another, are like the 'stationary blast', which falls forever and therefore never falls. The description is full of violent, extravagantly personified motion, but the motion is not change: the Simplon is always like this. It's this unmanageable combination of movement and stasis, time and timelessness, which pushes the scenic description to the very verge of transcendence, so that the elements of the landscape become 'The types and symbols of Eternity' (639).

My account here makes no attempt to amount to a full 'reading' of the Simplon sequence, but it does serve to show, at the opposite end of Wordsworth's range from the petulant Dunkeld poem, the scope of the waterfall as a signifier. It is a question, to continue with the language of *The Prelude*, of the 'Wisdom and Spirit of the Universe':

> Thou Soul that art the eternity of thought,
> That givest to forms and images a breath
> And everlasting motion. (I, 401–4)

Ostensibly, externally, the forms of the world are what they are in a Lockean epistemology: inert things, finished, bearing the marks of creation only as the trace of their origin. To resist that closure is the project which informs the poetic language of *The Prelude* in its endless oscillation between natural description and philosophical reflection, and in its repeated series of shifting, strategically imprecise abstractions, the writing reaches, again and again, for a presence within objects which is itself not object-like, but which creates, works, breathes, ministers. In this sense the poem's dominant mode is invocation: it is designed to raise the spirit that informs the world's matter. The waterfall then acquires the value of a special place where that inner dynamism breaks through the surface – where, all but impossibly, the omnipresent life of things appears as a thing itself.[24] A waterfall *looks like* what the whole physical world invisibly *is*.

Putting it in that way places the image in the territory of Romantic Platonism, and it isn't hard to confirm the pertinence of that context. Shelley under Mont Blanc, for example, sees a dizzying pattern of translucent surfaces:

> Thine earthly rainbows stretched across the sweep
> Of the etherial waterfall, whose veil
> Robes some unsculptured image . . .
> Thy caverns echoing to the Arve's commotion,
> A loud, lone sound no other sound can tame;
> Thou art pervaded with that ceaseless motion,
> Thou art the path of that unresting sound.[25]

Every sense impression here is secondary – the rainbows and the echoes emanate from the waterfall; the waterfall robes (that is, conceals and manifests) the unmade image within or behind it; and the Arve itself is an emanation of the glacier above. The phenomena tremble at their proximity to their noumenal source; Shelley's waterfall is a paradigm of nature because it is an agitated veil. One condition of this excited consciousness is the simple fact that the waterfall goes on for ever unlike organic life, the life of the river which 'Over its rocks ceaselessly bursts and raves' (line 11) is unshadowed by death. Raptly, the poet watches nature *being eternal*. We can see how specifically Romantic this pleasure is by turning abruptly from Wordsworth or Shelley in the Alps to Vaughan's poem 'The Waterfall', written in the middle of the seventeenth century. Vaughan's waterfall is an allegory of death and resurrection: the waters plunge into a chasm but then 'Rise to a longer course more bright and brave'.[26] The visible scene is not so much described as textualized through a dazzling series of biblical allusions to light and water, and in the end, having carried the mind to a meditative grasp of the its 'invisible estate', it is discarded. The pleasure of visiting the place is the pleasure of hearing the creation speak in this specific and doctrinal way of the Creator's mercy. Thus the waterfall is an opening into eternal truth in a way, but for Vaughan, the waterfall is a divine signature upon nature, which the poem reads; in Shelley, it is a natural display of divinity, which the poet experiences. The waterfall's medium of signification, so to speak, has changed, from script to theatre.

This Romantic theophany is inseparable from the idea of power. Most of the various descriptions I have quoted so far attach the sublimity of the spectacle, in classic Burkean fashion, to the impression of irresistible force: the water insists on its passage through a narrow gap in the rock, raging against the obstacles which vainly stand in its way. Shelley registers this theme the most clearly; the ravine is the

> awful scene,
> Where Power in likeness of the Arve comes down
> From the ice gulphs that gird his secret throne,
> Bursting through these dark mountains like the flame
> Of lightning through the tempest. (15–19)

In a characteristic idealist inversion, what one sees is not a waterfall which prompts the idea of power, but power itself in the likeness of a waterfall. This revelation of the direct presence of an immaterial principle is also dramatised by the extraordinary synaesthetic freedom of the writing; the permanent relation of the stream to the mountains turns into the momentary relation of the lightning to the storm, and the sight and sound of the Arve cross over and merge in the higher idea of motion. Although the diction here is particular to Shelley's own habit of passionate abstraction, it is picking up something central to the general possibilities of the sign: the way that the waterfall, by giving off energy in so many different forms, outruns the merely visual closure of the picturesque. It throws off spray, rainbows, noises; it shakes and shapes the rocks over which it falls; it even creates its own breeze.[27] The fact that the waterfall's power appears in several sensible forms means that it isn't identified with any one of them, and so comes into view as a principle informing them all.

At this historical point – the turn of the nineteenth century – the idea that falling water is essentially a form of power was of course not confined to poets. For at least the last quarter of the eighteenth century, water was the principal energy source of the industrial revolution. In the 1780s, 'there is scarce a stream that will turn a wheel through the north of England that has not a cotton mill upon it',[28] and water was not only powering spinning mills, for cotton and wool, but also grinding corn, making paper, and working the bellows in blast furnaces. Although steam was usable for these purposes from 1781, the technology of water power continued to be developed and widely used well into the nineteenth century, as engineers devised increasingly sophisticated ways of transmitting the ceaseless motion through water wheels to a widening range of machinery. For the mills which were transforming the social and economic structure of Britain in these years, power literally did come down in likeness of the Wharfe, the Ribble, the Carron. In abstracting the power from the visible phenomena, Shelley is operating in a fashion characteristic of his age; the mental move is similar to what is happening when the expression 'horse power' ceases to denote physical horses and becomes instead a way of expressing the capacity of a water wheel or a steam engine. To think power as something other than its material embodiments is a poetic idealization, but also a technical necessity.

The same mode of thought can be seen in one of Coleridge's metaphysical improvisations, in a letter from Germany in 1799:

> What if the vital force which I sent from my arm into the stone, as I flung it in the air & skimm'd it upon the water – what if even that did not perish! – It was *life* – ! it was a particle of *Being* – ! it was *Power* ! – *& how could* it perish – ? *Life, Power, Being* ! – organization may & probably *is*, their *effect* ; their *cause* it *cannot* be! – I have indulged very curious fancies concerning that force, that *swarm* of motive Powers which I sent out of my body into that Stone; & which, one by one, left the untractable or already possessed Mass, and – ...[29]

The context is the news of the death of Coleridge's baby son: it is at an extreme of emotional yearning, as well as an extreme of speculative physics, that the flung stone becomes a momentary part of an everlasting circulation of power. In search of a consolatory intimation of immortality, Coleridge turns away from organic growth because it includes the idea of death, and contemplates inorganic motion. This conception of nature could be described as industrial in character, as opposed to agrarian: it locates nature's life, not in its visible processes, but in its invisible power.

The waterfall, at once momentary, everlasting and powerful, is a privileged emblem for this industrial imagination. The apocalyptic energies which Scott presses firmly into the theatrical frame of the picturesque appear in the work of the more revolutionary poets as symbols of an unmediated life-source. But then in that move, too, there is an unacknowledged tension, as if the waterfall is somehow being asked to do too much. Time and again, the natural revelation needs to be discreetly supplemented by a kind of magical presence:

the half-human shout heard by Dr Watson echoes not only Scott's anthropomorphic demons of the stream, but also the disturbing speaking rocks in *The Prelude*, and the daemonic voices of the ravine in Shelley. It is a fanciful resolution of the operative contradiction of the entire cult that the essence of the waterfall must be visible and invisible at the same time. A visual spectacle with a mysterious half human voice is a means of having it both ways. In the popular fictions, the vocal supplement is provided by the plot: the presence is that of Moriarty or Burley. In the more elusively realized world of Romantic invocation, we can hear that the voice is ultimately the poet's own.

At their different points of greatest intensity, all three of these poets – Wordsworth, Coleridge, Shelley – find a located symbol of the 'universal spirit' in a kind of waterfall. But in each of these strikingly comparable and philosophically crucial moments, the waterfall is subtly augmented and supernaturalised. For Wordsworth, it is the rift in the cloud in the Snowdon sequence in *The Prelude* – 'A fixed, abysmal, gloomy, breathing-place' from which:

> Mounted the roar of waters, torrents, streams
> Innumerable, roaring with one voice. (XIV, 58–60)

More explicitly magical, there is the chasm in *Kubla Khan* from which:

> with ceaseless turmoil seething,
> As if this earth in fast thick pants were breathing,
> A mighty fountain momently was forced.[30]

And one of the poetic progeny of that breathing fountain is clearly the entrance to the realm of Demogorgon in *Prometheus Unbound*, another clouded abyss which, amid the 'howl of cataracts', flings up 'the maddening wine of life'.[31]

All these imaginary places take over the picture of a waterfall's plunge into the abyss and partly invert its movement in order to make it a rift in the visible surface of life which then appears as the source of an absolute, chthonic power. But although the touristic thrill of the cataract serves to substantiate and focus the symbol, the fabulous inversion, the elaboration and mystification of the waterfall, is a measure of its own falling short of the transcendence attributed to it. Just like the Duke of Atholl with his mirrors, or the Reichenbach Hotel with its Bengal lights,[32] the poets have to supplement the natural phenomenon with a special illumination in order to get it to spell out the revelation for which they look to it. The real demons are invisible after all; they have to be worked up into visibility by the active, intervening voice of the poet. This is the underlying reason why waterfalls are theatrical – they are naturalisations of an elaborate human composition, and although their meanings look as if they are spontaneously thrown off by the impetuous meeting of water and rock, that fine effect is always a little dependent on the spectator's willingness to be deceived. The literary imagination, no less than the mechanical imagination, is *utilising* the waterfall's power, and this utilisation must be kept out of sight, like stage machinery, if the sublime unity of the image is not to be spoiled.

Notes

1. Arthur Conan Doyle, 'The Adventure of the Final Problem' in *The Complete Sherlock Holmes* (London: Secker & Warburg, 1981), 469–80 (478).
2. See Andrew Wilton, *Turner and the Sublime* (London: British Museum Publications, 1981), 123, in a note on Turner's magnificent watercolour of the Upper Fall.
3. Karl Baedeker, *Switzerland* (15th edition, London, 1893), 170–1.
4. For the Lake District, Peter Bicknell, *The Picturesque Scenery of the Lake District 1752–1855* (Winchester St Paul's Bibliographies, 1990); for the Scottish Highlands, Peter Womack, *Improvement and Romance: Constructing the Myth of the Highlands* (Basingstoke: Macmillan Press, 1989), ch.4.
5. The poems of Ossian, by James Macpherson, appeared between 1760 and 1763, and began to permeate the perception of mountainous scenery almost at once: see for example, I. S. Ross, 'A Bluestocking Over the Border: Mrs Elizabeth Montagu's Aesthetic Adventures in Scotland, 1766', *Huntington Library Quarterly*, 28 (1965), 213–33.
6. Edmund Burke, *A Philosophical Enquiry into the Origin of our Ideas of the Sublime and Beautiful* appeared in 1757, with an expanded second edition in 1759.
7. Elizabeth McKinsey, *Niagara Falls: Icon of the American Sublime* (Cambridge: Cambridge University Press, 1985), 19–21.
8. Gilpin's books appeared in the 1780s and 90s, but his theorising dates back to the 1740s, and his actual journeys were mostly made in the 1770s. See John Butt, *The Oxford History of English Literature: The Mid-Eighteenth Century*, edited and completed by Geoffrey Carnall (Oxford: Oxford University Press, 1979), 259–60.
9. Thomas Pennant, *A Tour in Scotland and Voyage to the Hebrides, MDCCLXXII*, 2 vols (second edition, London, 1776), II, 59–60.
10. Samuel Johnson, *Johnson's Journey to the Western Islands of Scotland and Boswell's Journal of a Tour to the Hebrides with Samuel Johnson*

LL.D., edited by R.W. Chapman (Oxford: Oxford University Press, 1930), 29.

11. William Gilpin, *Observations, Relative Chiefly to Picturesque Beauty, Made in the Year 1776 on Several Parts of Great-Britain Particularly the High-lands of Scotland*, 2 vols (London, 1789), I, 121–2.

12. 'We take delight in . . . any thing that hath such a variety or regularity as may seem the effect of design in what we call the works of chance.' Joseph Addison, *Spectator* No. 414 (1712), quoted in Wilton, *Turner and the Sublime*, 31.

13. The story of the building is told in Tim Buxbaum, *Scottish Garden Buildings* (Edinburgh: Mainstream Publishing, 1989), pp.150–1.

14. [Mary Anne Hanway], *A Journey to the Highlands of Scotland* (London, 1776), 105–6.

15. Dorothy Wordsworth, *Recollections of a Tour Made in Scotland A.D. 1803*, edited by J.C. Shairp (Edinburgh, 1874), 210.

16. Mrs S. Murray, *A Companion and Useful Guide to the Beauties of Scotland*, 2 vols. (London, 1799–1803), I, 198–9.

17. William Wordsworth, 'Effusion in the Pleasure-Ground on the Banks of the Bran, near Dunkeld', *Poetical Works* (Oxford: Oxford University Press, 1936), 238. Subsequent references to Wordsworth poems are to this edition.

18. *The Prelude*, VII, 675–771.

19. Womack, *Improvement and Romance*, 155–6.

20. Walter Scott, *The Waverley Novels*, 48 vols. (Edinburgh, 1902–3), i, 221–2.

21. One example will do. In T. J. Horsley Curties, *The Scottish Legend, or the Isle of Saint Clothair*, 4 vols (London, 1802), the heroine is abducted by the villain's retainers and led across 'an almost impassable and trackless chain of desert wolds, whose rude uncivilized rocky steeps admitted through their opening fissures the rushing torrents, pouring with tremendous velocity, their foaming waters down immeasurable heights, and burying themselves amid the frightful untrodden chasms of the deep, the bottom of which could never be found, and seemed to exclude the light of the sun, whose cheering rays had never pierced so deep since that chaotic deluge sent by an offended Creator, had overwhelmed the guilty lands' (III, 175). The heroine is in danger of being raped, and the impossibility of saying so produces both the waterfalls and the adjectival overkill.

22. Walter Scott, *Waverley Novels*, xi, 313.

23. Walter Scott, *Waverley Novels*, xiii, 395.

24. Compare James Bruce on the Nile in about 1770, to whom it seemed that 'one element had broken loose from, and become superior to, all laws of subordination; that the fountains of the great deep were again extraordinarily opened, and the destruction of a world was once more

begun by the agency of water'. (Quoted in Butt, *The Mid-Eighteenth Century*, 263).

25. 'Mont Blanc', 11. 25–33, in *Shelley's Poetry and Prose* (New York: W.W. Norton, 1977), 89–93.

26. Henry Vaughan, 'The Waterfall', *Works*, ed. L.C. Martin (2nd edn., Oxford: Oxford University Press, 1957), 537.

27. Noted in S.T. Coleridge, 'This Lime-Tree Bower My Prison', ll. 13–16, *Poetical Works* (Oxford: Oxford University Press, 1912), 178.

28. Quoted in Eric Pawson, *The Early Industrial Revolution* (London: Batsford, 1979), 82.

29. *The Collected Letters of Samuel Taylor Coleridge*, ed. E.L. Griggs, 2 fols. (Oxford: Oxford University Press, 1956), I, 479.

30. 'Kubla Khan', 11. 17–19.

31. Prometheus Unbound, II, iii. ll.1–36.

32. Bengal lights were a kind of blue floodlight used during the tourist season to illuminate several of the falls around Meiringen, including Reichenbach: see Baedeker, *Switzerland*, 170ff.

List of Contributors

Angus Calder was Reader in Cultural Studies at the Open University of Scotland and is now a freelance writer in Edinburgh. His latest book, *Revolving Culture: Notes from the Scottish Republic,* contains a tribute to Paul Edwards.

Geoffrey Carnall, for many years a colleague of Paul Edwards in Edinburgh, has published a good deal on eighteenth- and nineteenth-century topics, but is now writing the life of an English friend of Gandhi. He was delighted to learn that Paul Edwards himself, at the age of five, saw Gandhi in Birmingham.

Jon Curt came to Edinburgh in 1981 where he immediately became one of Paul Edwards keenest students. He graduated in 1985 and stayed on, under Paul ssupervision, to write a Ph.D. thesis on Byron, though this was never presented. Formerly a lecturer in North Africa, he is now a primary school teacher at George Heriot sin Edinburgh.

Ian Duffield is Senior Lecturer in History at the University of Edinburgh and was 1994-6 President of the British Australian Studies Association. He worked closely with Paul Edwards for many years, on the History of Africans in Britain. Some results of that collaboration appeared after Edwards' death. Thus Edwards contributed to J. S. Gundara and I. Duffield (eds), *Essays on the History of Blacks in Britain* (Aldershot: Avebury, 1992). Both Edwards and Duffield contributed to D. Killingray (ed.), *Africans in Britain* (Ilford: Frank Cass, 1994). Duffield's most recent major publication is I. Duffield & J. Bradley (eds.), *Representing Convicts* (London: Cassell Academic/Leicester University Press, 1997).

Wilson Harris's novels have been called one of the major fictional achievements in English in this century. Generally set in his native Guyana, his fiction observes humanity cast against symbolic and impressionistic landscapes. His seminal *Guyana Quartet* appeared between 1960 and 1963. His most recent work, *Jonestown,* was published by Faber in 1996.

Christopher Heywood studied English at Stellenbosch and at Oxford, and has been Professor of English at the University of Ife, Nigeria. He was Senior Lecturer at Sheffield University and Professor of English at Seto College, Kobe Women's University, Japan. He is currently writing on the Brontes and slavery, and on South African literature.

Paul Hullah completed his Ph.D. (*The Poetry of Christina Rossetti*) at Edinburgh University under Paul Edwards' tireless, gentle supervision. Currently Lecturer in English at Okayama University, Japan, he has published several literary texts for University students and co-edited, with Y. Muroya, an international, authorised edition of *Poems by Iris Murdoch* (UEP: Japan, 1997). A collection of his own poetry, *And Here's What You Could Have Won*, was published in 1997 by Dionysia Press.

Douglas Kenning lectures at Fukuoka Jo Gakuin College, Japan: 'Paul Edwards was both mentor and fellow traveller in my long journey toward a Ph.D. on Romantic Poetry. He guided me to my first academic post, teaching Shakespeare and Henry James to the Arabs, and my second, teaching Shakespeare and Henry Miller to the Japanese. The echoes of his voice are what lure me into the wry irreverences in Japanese poetry'.

Manfred Malzahn joined the German Department at Edinburgh University in 1985. From his room opposite Paul Edwards' office, he went on to teach in Tunisia, Algeria and Malawi. He is now Professor of English and German at Chung Cheng University, Taiwan, and has written extensively but not exclusively on Scottish literature.

Glenda Norquay took her M.A. and Ph.D. at Edinburgh University, from which time she has vivid recollections of Paul Edward's readings of Wordsworth's 'Lucy' poems. Currently Senior Lecturer at Liverpool John Moore's University, she has published widely on Scottish fiction and women's suffrage writing.

Faith Pullin has taught at Edinburgh University for many years and ran courses on West African and Commonwealth literature with Paul Edwards as well as co-supervising research students with him. Her research interests are in feminist and postcolonial theory, and in women's writing of the nineteenth and twentieth centuries. She has forthcoming books on *Women Modernist Writers* and *The Literature* *of the American South* and has published widely on British, American and African literature.

Peter Womack's Edinburgh University Ph.D. thesis eventually became *Improvement and Romance: Constructing the Myth of the Highlands* (1989). Since then, he has been teaching at the University of East Anglia and mostly writing about theatre. *English Drama: A Cultural History* (with Simon Shepherd) appeared in 1996.